HOW TO START A RETIREMENT BUSINESS

The 21st Century ENTREPRENEUR

HOW TO START A RETIREMENT BUSINESS

JACQUELINE K. POWERS

A Third Millennium Press Book

AVON BOOKS NEW YORK

VISIT OUR WEBSITE AT
http://AvonBooks.com

THE 21ST CENTURY ENTREPRENEUR: HOW TO START A RETIREMENT BUSINESS is an original publication of Avon Books. This work has never before appeared in book form.

AVON BOOKS
A division of
The Hearst Corporation
1350 Avenue of the Americas
New York, New York 10019

Library of Congress Cataloging in Publication Data:

Powers, Jacqueline K.
   How to start a retirement business / by Jacqueline K. Powers.
      p.   cm.—(The 21st century entrepreneur)
   "A Third Millennium Press book."
   Includes index.
   1. New business enterprises—Finance.   2. Retirement income.   I. Title.   II. Series.
HG4027.6.P68   1996   96-22183
658'.041—DC20   CIP

First Avon Books Trade Printing: December 1996

AVON TRADEMARK REG. U.S. PAT. OFF. AND IN OTHER COUNTRIES, MARCA REGISTRADA, HECHO EN U.S.A.

Printed in the U.S.A.

OPM   10 9 8 7 6 5 4 3 2 1

Acknowledgments

This book has been both a pleasure and a test for everyone involved. My heartfelt thanks to all of you, but especially to my children, Jenneka and Alex, who somehow understood that their mother has a life of the mind and of the world that nourishes her and does not diminish them.

Thanks, too, to my husband, Mike, whose humor renewed me when my energy and patience flagged.

And finally, many, many thanks to Mark Levine for the opportunity, the frequent inspiration, and the on-the-money advice.

❦❦CONTENTS❦❦

HOW TO START A RETIREMENT BUSINESS

I.

IF YOUR
RETIREMENT BUBBLE
HAS BURST

❦1❦

WHOSE IDEA WAS THIS ANYWAY?

You're approaching the age at which most people retire, and you've got a queasy feeling in the pit of your stomach. Or you're already retired but feel ill contemplating the rest of your life. Whichever is the case, one thing's for certain: Somewhere along the line you were sold a seductive vision of floating through your golden years in a gilded retirement bubble. But now you're fifty-five, sixty-five, or seventy-five. You're feeling tired and depressed. Face it, you're more than a little bored.

You don't need a dose of megavitamin-and-mushroom therapy. If you just don't have the old get-up-and-go, chances are it's because you don't have anything to get up and go to. You're suffering from what I call repressed pre- or postretirement syndrome, or RPRS. Your retirement bubble has burst, and suddenly you're wondering what to do with the rest of your life.

You're not alone. Legions of people are depressed and miserable about the idea of a traditional retirement. Some simple numbers tell the story. A 1990 study by the Commonwealth Fund, a New York–based philanthropic organization, found that almost 2 million retired Americans aged fifty to sixty-four were interested in returning to work. According to another study, almost a third of male retirees reject retirement and return to work, mostly in the first year after they retire.

Since 1955, the American Association of Retired Persons (AARP) reports, the number of workers aged forty-five and older has risen from 25 million to almost 34 million. And these older workers no longer are rushing to retire at earlier and earlier ages. From 1945 to 1982, the age at which men received

3

their first retirement checks steadily dropped. Since 1982, however, it has remained steady at 63.7 years.

Polls by the AARP and the National Council on Aging have found that the closer workers get to retirement age, the more they want to continue working. Another poll found that most people want to continue working after age sixty-five even if they have enough money to live well for the rest of their lives. More than 90 percent say the reason is they just like working. The idea of spending those golden years floating idly on Golden Pond is a washout.

WHAT'S CAUSING THIS MASS ATTACK OF RPRS?

Retirement's a washout for scores of Americans for two main reasons:

- It isn't working out financially.
- It isn't working out emotionally.

Some people find they can't maintain the kind of lifestyle they want on a combination of Social Security benefits, pension payments, and savings. They need more money.

Others need to be more active. They discover they get bored quickly in traditional retirement because they need and want the challenge of work. They need to be active and productive in the marketplace, which they still consider to be the hub of society.

Or they hear the siren call of long-ignored creativity and the lure of a whole new career. Their interests have grown and shifted over the years, and now they find they can indulge those new interests. Perhaps even turn them to profit in a second or third career. Why not? Their retirement world is theirs to do with as they will.

HOW DID WE GET INTO THIS MESS?

I'll explain the seeds of the retirement nightmare in detail in chapter 2, but for now let's just say you were sold a bill of goods. Like millions of people before you, you bought the American dream as packaged by Madison Avenue for political and business convenience. That meant following a rigid sequential path through life from nursery to school, then to work, and finally to the long-sought reward: easy retirement. But the concept of retirement isn't a natural part of the life cycle of any animal, including humans. And despite the slick propaganda we've all come to believe as gospel, it isn't a right granted to every U.S. citizen at birth.

Retirement actually was created in the depths of the Great Depression by the Social Security Act of 1935 as a means of curing wholesale unemployment. It worked for a time. Forcing older workers—those over age sixty-five—to retire opened up scores of jobs for younger ones.

But financially the retirement dream isn't going to work for you like it did for your parents. The Social Security system today is ailing, if not quite expired. If inflation, increased longevity, and the gray wave of baby boomer retirements don't kill it off, it will have to be resuscitated and given a much different form. Private pension plans are going broke and being dismantled. And boomers aren't saving like their parents did, so they won't have fat bank accounts to fall back on.

TODAY'S POTENTIAL RETIREE FACES A FINANCIAL PIT

Let's take a look at this financial pit. Despite living in a two-career household, you haven't saved all that much. You needed nice vacations over the years to recuperate from those stressful dual careers. Not luxurious, maybe, but nice. You put three kids through college, are helping maintain one parent in a decent nursing home, and are still paying off a second mortgage and a car loan for your youngest son, who just can't seem to find a job.

The price of everything keeps increasing, employers have steadily cut back on pension contributions, and Social Security is doomed. Not only that—if you're lucky you'll live a lot longer than your own parents did. If you're not all that lucky, you'll live a lot longer but in deteriorating health, with expensive medical bills.

Not a pretty picture, and bound to get worse. Who can actually afford to retire? Or retire and maintain a decent life? You may not be reduced to eating cat food, but I'm sure you'd like something more exciting than McDonald's when you dine out in the next century. Face it, more of us will need to continue working one way or another into our golden years.

BESIDES MONEY, YOU MAY NEED AN EMOTIONAL BOOSTER SHOT

Emotionally, you're going to need more than traditional retirement can offer. Through advances in medicine, nutrition, and technology, people today are healthier and living decades longer than they did sixty years ago. They don't want to stop being active and productive in this new, more mature prime of life. They're just not ready for someone to pull their productivity plug.

Think about it. All your life you've been a Type A person— a hyperactive, overachieving workaholic. You've achieved financial security and career status by putting in killer days and working weekends, moving ever upward on at least one career ladder, maybe more. You've also managed the lives of a nuclear family, done freelance work in your "spare" time, run marathons, practiced a martial art, cooked gourmet vegetarian meals, and dabbled in holistic herbal healing.

Suddenly the years pile up, a magic date and age arrive, and you're supposed to retire and live a Type ZZZZ lifestyle. Wait a minute, you think, I'm not ready for the rocking chair yet.

Neither are a lot of others. While some older adults genuinely look forward to retirement and find they really do enjoy it, many are finding that it just isn't enough. After three months of no work and all play they've taken enough naps for three lifetimes and have earned their black belts in shopping and ceramics. They're just plain bored and may be bordering on depression. They need more intellectual, emotional, and physical stimulation than they can find in a life without meaningful work. Or they still have career dreams to realize.

RESEARCH SHOWS PRODUCTIVITY IS KEY TO HEALTH AND HAPPINESS

Recent research has shown a definite correlation between work and good mental and physical health in older people. Older adults who continue working at jobs that aren't beyond their physical abilities stay healthier longer. And physical limitations are being stretched further than ever before. Anyone around the country who has seen more and more men and women in their fifties, sixties, and even seventies and eighties competing in marathons can attest to that. These runners aren't supermen and superwomen, they've just stayed active and fit. And their high level of activity has promoted their enhanced level of fitness and performance.

Phyllis Moen, a professor of life course studies at Cornell University, has done extensive research on longevity, aging, and productivity. She believes her research shows that "social integration, defined by the number of roles occupied, promotes well-being, health and longevity. Being socially connected—whether through employment, volunteer work, religious activities or neighboring—is positively linked to mental and physical health and may well have greater impact on health than other roles.

"I see paid work and unpaid volunteer work as particularly integrative in that they provide culturally sanctioned ways of participating in the broader community as well as access to various components of society. To the degree that social integration promotes health and well-being, post retirement participation in paid jobs may extend the third stage of healthy aging, reducing demands on the health care system and enhancing quality of life."

Researchers at Yale University and the University of Michigan also have linked active aging and productivity. Based on a study of the productive activities of men and women aged seventy to seventy-nine, they found that active aging adults do a third more housework, twice as much yard work, three times more paid work, and four times as much volunteer work compared with more sedentary aging persons.

Not only do activity and productivity promote health, research also has shown that age isn't a reliable predictor of mental and physical abilities. In fact, when a correlation exists, research shows that performance tends to improve with age in many areas. While some older adults may proceed more cautiously and deliberately in their actions, they often make fewer errors and have fewer job-related accidents.

While the stereotype of the befuddled, unproductive older adult still persists, it is now widely accepted that in the absence of specific neurological diseases, simple aging does not cause any impairment in mental faculties until the mid-seventies, on average. And then, the only decrease in mental capacity that can be attributed directly to aging is some short-term memory loss.

Clearly, creativity, that mysterious unknown factor that transforms mere work into art, doesn't fade with age. Pablo Picasso continued to be a prolific painter almost until the day he died, producing great works into his eighties. Cervantes' *Don Quixote* was completed when he was sixty-eight. Martha Graham, the mother of modern dance, continued choreographing and teaching into her seventies. The list could go on and on. There's painter Norman Rockwell, country singer and songwriter Willie Nelson, and writer Vladimir Nabokov.

For many of the world's most creative geniuses, their mental faculties and creative powers fermented like fine wine over the years, producing richer, headier works as they aged.

OKAY, SO YOU'RE NOT PICASSO

You may not be Picasso or Martha Graham, but you may have untapped creative potential, buried all these years under a mountain of weighty domestic obligations, career responsibilities, and bills. Creativity still struggling for expression. Did you have a flair for design and love to sew? Maybe it's time to open a small, one-of-a-kind costume shop. Or did you love relaxing on weekends with embroidery floss, canvas, and needle? Maybe you can open a needlework supply shop and sell some of your own creations as well. Or perhaps you're devoted to exotic beer and are dying to dabble in your own microbrewery. Chances are, if you get any good at it, a local café will be more than happy to carry your special brew.

Whatever your long-suppressed interest or skill, it's time to dust it off and reexamine it in the light of your newfound freedom to work when and how you will, for the sheer pleasure and spare change of it. Be self-indulgent with your interests—you've earned the right.

SO WHAT'S THE CURE FOR RPRS?

The good news is there's a cure for RPRS: entrepreneurship. Better yet, today is the best time in the world for you to become an entrepreneur. In chapter 3 I'll explain more about why the best solution to your need for more money and more activity is starting a business. But for now, keep these points in mind:

YOUR AGE HASN'T IMPAIRED YOUR BRAIN, YOUR PHYSICAL CONDITION, OR YOUR PRODUCTIVITY

In fact, you're wiser, more skilled, and more efficient than you were twenty years ago. But it's going to be tough to get employers to see that. The notion that older people are less productive is a myth—but still a widely held one.

YOU'RE GOING TO WANT FLEXIBILITY

You want to reenter the workforce, but you want to do it on your own terms so you can still enjoy a rewarding, semiretired lifestyle. You may want to work only part of the year or only part-time. You may want to work only weekdays or perhaps only two days a week. Whatever your particular desires, it's going to be hard to find an employer willing to plan his or her business schedule around your needs.

DON'T FORGET THAT CREATIVITY WE TALKED ABOUT A FEW PARAGRAPHS AGO

That's going to be hard to express in a McJob. Slinging burgers or running a car wash probably isn't what you had in mind when you started dreaming about a fulfilling new career.

YOU DON'T NEED A POSTGRADUATE DEGREE TO BE A SUCCESSFUL ENTREPRENEUR

Entrepreneurs come with all kinds of educational backgrounds. According to a recent survey, 3 percent of entrepreneurs who own small businesses have some high school education, 24 percent graduated high school, 23 percent have some college, 38 percent have a college degree, and 12 percent have some postgraduate study.

If you've never quite had the nerve to do it before, now is the perfect time to start your own business, custom-tailored to your own "semiretired" specifications.

JUST LOOK AT WHAT HAPPENED TO ALEXANDER FAULKER

Alexander Faulker retired six years ago, at age sixty-five, a moderate millionaire. That is, he had earned a moderate number of millions—2.9, to be exact. He started with nothing, second son of a Polish immigrant who came to America believing the streets were paved with gold, only to die poor in a Polish ghetto in Newark, New Jersey.

Alexander did better than his father. He started as a construction worker, paid his way through night school, and parlayed his architect's salary into a nice nest egg with the help of a lucky investment portfolio. He worked hard, and by age sixty-five he and his wife, Marie, decided they had earned the right to relax and enjoy their money and each other.

Their plan? To spend a few months each winter in Florida and play golf daily year-round. There was a small retirement party, then they hit the road for the first of their winter retirement sojourns in Florida. "Retirement is going to be heaven," they exclaimed.

Six months later, heaven had metamorphosed into hell. Alexander, who for years had walked three miles each morning with Marie before going to work, was not only too tired to walk, he was too tired to get out of the recliner in front of the TV. He napped mid-morning and mid-afternoon, and then fell asleep on the sofa after dinner. Marie had to wake him to get him to go upstairs to bed at night. His only interest was food, which he consumed nonstop when he wasn't sleeping. He gained thirty pounds.

Alexander wasn't sick. He was depressed. To cure his depression, his daughter bought him paints and canvas, one son bought him a bread maker, and the other son bought him a mini–beer brewery kit. They tried everything but a pottery wheel, knowing ceramic ashtrays were not his thing. He ignored the toys, kept sleeping, and gained even more weight. Marie was distraught. This wasn't the retirement dream she had long dreamt; this was a nightmare, and her depressed husband was driving her crazy.

One day his old boss called and asked if Alexander would mind coming in one afternoon to do the payroll. It seemed the boss, who used to rely on Alexander for such tasks, had totally botched the payroll records. That was the start of Alexander's "recovery."

"I realized I wanted and needed to work," says Alexander, who soon made an arrangement to work four to six hours a week doing the payroll and other office paperwork in return for a small salary that wouldn't jeopardize his Social Security benefits. "And," he adds, "the extra money helped buy some luxuries I might have thought twice about otherwise. After all, I have a bit of money saved up, but who knows how long Marie and I will live and what kind of care we might need down the road."

From there, Alexander's new retirement career mushroomed. He now has his own home-based consulting business, doing payroll and other office accounting and paperwork for several small firms in town, and works ten to twenty hours a week. The work earns him extra income, but more important, it brings him a feeling of self-esteem, of "connectedness" to the outside world.

"Some retirement," Marie now says with a big grin. "He's the only retiree I know who can't take a long weekend because he has to get the payroll out Friday afternoon." But Marie's happy. Now she has her husband back—the vital, energetic, take-charge man she married. Okay, he's older and still has a few of those extra pounds from his sofa days, but once again he can't wait to leap out of bed in the morning. He even set up that minibrewery his son gave him, and they're getting ready to sample the first batch of Big Al's Best Brew.

IT'S TIME TO REALLY KILL OFF THAT RETIREMENT MYTH

On the doorstep to retirement, Alexander thought he had died and gone to heaven, and that heaven would be rest, relaxation, and endless rounds of par golf. Then, after a few months, he thought he simply had died, or perhaps been buried alive. It took a chance call from his old boss with a plea for him to return to the world of work to make Alexander realize that it wasn't him that was dying. Instead, for Alexander—and for many others who have worked hard all their lives and loved it, loved the challenge and the sheer energy of it—it was their illusions of retirement that were dying.

Okay, so you're not as lucky as Alexander. Your phone hasn't been ringing off the hook with people begging to be your first client. You're going to have to be proactive. And the first step in that process is to finally put the retirement myth totally to rest, once and for all, by understanding where it came from.

⟨⟨ 2 ⟩⟩

HOW DID WE GET INTO THIS BIND?

Let's say for a minute you *don't* get queasy at the thought of retirement. You buy the gilded American retirement dream lock, stock, and barrel. You're practically salivating at the thought of your not-too-distant sixty-fifth birthday, followed by a life of well-earned leisure. It's your right, after all, you say firmly. You worked hard all your adult life and earned your retirement just like all those hardworking Americans before you. By god, you're going to enjoy it. Right? Think again.

You've been sold a bill of goods. You're going to be in trouble trying to live that dream, and you won't be alone. Almost two thirds of Americans believe a decent retirement is their right. And even more—almost three quarters—see it as a basic part of the American dream.

But the retirement bubble that's been floated since World War II is about to burst, and if you've been floating along on it, dreaming of sailing blithely into a well-cushioned retirement life on the links, get ready for a sharp jolt. Retirement as we know it simply will not exist in the future.

America's biggest generation ever—the 76 million baby boomers born between 1946 and 1964, who represent fully one third of our total population—are beginning to turn gray. And as they hit retirement age, this gray wave threatens to capsize an already shaky Social Security ship, and with it your dream of a secure, work-free retirement. There are more folks getting ready to line up with their hands out at one time than ever before in history. And those already receiving benefits are living longer than previous generations. That means they'll be collecting Social Security benefits longer, too.

13

In 1940, when the first Social Security checks were mailed, around 50 percent of American men and 60 percent of American women could hope to blow out sixty-five candles on their birthday cakes. After that, men could expect to live thirteen more years and women fifteen. By 1990, more than 70 percent of men and almost 85 percent of women could qualify for senior citizen discounts, and those are percentages of a much larger population. Beyond age sixty-five, men are now living, on average, an additional fifteen years, and women twenty. And many experts predict that *average* life spans will soon be in the high eighties and low nineties.

Don't forget that, following the baby boom, there was a baby bust from 1965 through 1975. That means there will be fewer and fewer workers paying taxes to support more and more retirees. Social Security is going to go bust. Those collecting or about to collect benefits may be the only ones with their heads still stuck in the sand. A recent poll showed that more people under the age of thirty-five believe in UFOs than in the idea that Social Security will pay them benefits when they retire. They may be out in left field on the UFOs, but they're on the right track on Social Security.

At the same time, company pension plans are on the way out. And where they will continue to exist, they are almost certain to be stingier than those current retirees collect. Over the past decade the trend has been shifting away from paying specific amounts based on salary and years of service toward worker contributions matched by employers, like 401(k) plans. These matching plans don't guarantee anything and are vulnerable to sharp decreases in the instruments in which they are invested. Under these plans, if workers don't save, they lose out. Some may end up with no pension at all.

RETIREMENT ISN'T A BASIC HUMAN RIGHT

Despite the general assumption, retirement is not a basic right of all Americans. The idea that we work for a period of our adult years and then retire was a plot hatched by business leaders and politicians to serve their own ends.

Retirement as we know it didn't exist before the age of industrialization. Before the Civil War, America was an agrarian society. Older people continued working as they aged, helping with the farm work and housework, caring for the younger generations as they arrived, and passing on their skills and knowledge. They shouldered less of the heavy work as they aged, but they continued to work at whatever tasks they could manage. It took all members of the family, even the youngest and oldest, to survive and thrive when you had to produce just about everything you consumed, used, and wore.

With the end of the war came the industrial revolution and an even more profound revolution in the way people lived and worked—and the way in which they thought about the two.

As members of an agrarian society—as farmers or small shopkeepers—people found that their lives and work were one and the same, not separate as they are today. People's homes actually were their workplaces. Work was not a distant place they traveled to, separated from the rest of their life. And the work they performed was intertwined throughout the day and night with the other tasks of their lives, including those related to their family.

That all changed with industrialization. As people moved into cities and into factories, their work lives and family lives became separated by both physical and psychological distance. No longer did a person live an integrated life in which home and work were one and the same and over which he or she had relative control. With the move to the assembly line, the worker lost that integrated life, lost hours of contact each day with family, and lost control over his or her environment—especially the work environment. For many, work became a drudgery from which release came only after a seemingly endless day.

This was the beginning of the end of the work ethic that had driven Americans from the time of the Puritans. This was the fallow field from which the concept of retirement grew.

DON'T GET IN THE WAY OF PROGRESS

At the birth of the twentieth century the United States was poised for progress, for the transition from a self-absorbed, isolationist nation to a world power. Anything that wasn't perceived as essential to that march toward progress was pushed out of the way. Older Americans quickly were perceived as standing in the pathway to progress and eventually were steamrollered out of the way. The sugar-coated solution to this public relations problem was called retirement.

With industrialization also came advances in safety, medicine, and nutrition. The U.S. population began to live longer and to age. But in many ways working on an assembly line in a dank, dark factory for an absentee employer was harder than working on the family farm. It was a more demanding, less forgiving work environment. Factories were built on the regenerative energy, strength, and ambition of young people. They ate up the youth of the nation and then spit them back out when they aged and were no longer able to keep up with the ever-increasing speed of the assembly lines.

The elderly began to be perceived as having nothing left to offer. They weren't wanted in jobs that demanded youth and strength, and there were no other jobs. They were considered part of the old world order rather than the new. They were accused of being resistant to change, to new ideas. They were as obsolete as their rusty farm equipment. The words *youth* and *progress* began to be linked irrevocably in the nation's collective consciousness. Society began its worship of youth, and the elderly became a problem to solve.

So did unemployment. The population was growing, remember. People were living longer. Industry was creating new jobs, but the numbers of people migrating from bare-sustenance farms and small towns to snatch their share of wealth from the new industrial revolution swamped the cities and factories. In 1887, a report by the Massachusetts Bureau of Labor Statistics coined the word *unemployment*, presenting it for the first time as an issue separate from poverty. Almost inevitably, the idea of forcing older workers out of their jobs to alleviate unemployment took root and bloomed among businesspeople and politicians.

At the same time, the union movement also was new. Only about 10 percent of American workers were unionized, and they were busy fighting for the right to strike. Labor leaders recognized an opportunity when they saw it and seized on the idea of retirement as a way in which older, nonunion workers could be replaced by younger union members. The only problem facing all those pushing for retirement was how to finance it.

FINALLY, A TAXING SOLUTION

Enter private pension plans and Social Security. The first pension plan was created by American Express in 1875; the second followed in 1900, created by the Pattern Makers League of North America. The unspoken but clear goal of these plans was to get older workers out of their jobs earlier. By 1910, when the Taft administration began touting pensions in its push for industrial efficiency, the idea was taking hold. Between 1910 and 1920 the number of private pension plans grew each year, and changes in tax laws began to make such plans more attractive to businesses.

Despite all this, by 1932 less than 15 percent of American workers were covered by a pension plan. And few of those plans covered dependents. Retirement had been hailed as a perfect solution by progress-hungry American leaders, but it still wasn't embraced by the average worker, who didn't yet see a way to make it work.

The Great Depression marked the turning point. By 1933, 13 million Americans, a quarter of the labor force, were without work. Families lost their savings and their homes. Many people were starving. These armies of the angry unemployed, camped in U.S. cities, were a powder keg ready to be ignited at any time. Something radical had to be done to forestall civil war between the have-nots and the haves.

A whole new deal was needed. And that's just what President Franklin D. Roosevelt provided. In 1935, Roosevelt and his New Dealers introduced the Social Security Act, paving the way for the social and financial acceptance of retirement as part of the American dream. Roosevelt's pay-as-you-go plan was beautiful in its simplicity: It would provide instant benefits for those of retirement age by taxing those who were still working.

At the time there were few retirees compared with the total number of workers, so no one would have to pay very much.

And in settling on sixty-five as the magical retirement age they risked little. When the Social Security Act was passed, the average American died at age sixty-three. Clearly, most people wouldn't live to collect benefits, and those who did would not cash in for long.

But the American retirement dream was still just that—a distant dream. The benefits provided in the first decade or two of Social Security provided a meager existence, at best. It certainly wasn't something to look forward to. Golden Pond was still a muddy puddle, and it would take another world war, politically astute increases in benefits, and some slick megamarketing to sell the retirement dream wholesale.

THE PLOT THICKENS, AND WE GET THE HARD SELL

Government, labor, and business all knew they were on the right track in trying to solve the unemployment problem with retirement. And Social Security and private pension plans certainly helped make the idea more palatable. But the reality still didn't resemble the dream. Life in retirement, unless you already were among the wealthy elite, still looked grim.

But following World War II, politicians used the Social Security program for their own ends, and gained brownie points by improving it. First they extended Social Security coverage—to husbands of working women in the private sector and then to members of the armed forces, the self-employed, farmworkers, and some government employees. Then cost-of-living adjustments were added so benefits could keep pace with inflation.

Suddenly, between private pension plans and Social Security, retirement began to look like an okay deal for the tired worker. And when the financial services industry executives sat up and took notice, they realized they could make money on retirement, too. So business, labor, government, and the insurance and financial services industries began promoting retirement hard.

They told workers they had earned the right to a leisurely, well-cushioned retirement right along with their weekly paycheck. They convinced masses of Americans that retirement was a basic American right. And then they wrote stories and placed advertisements showing scores of happy, fulfilled retirees living out their golden years in a state of bliss.

After the penny-pinching, tension-filled war years, people were ready to indulge themselves again as full-time consumers with leisure to spare. They liked the very idea of relaxing. Life itself was getting easier as industry shifted from war production to producing consumer goods for a nation that wanted to play again, and play happily into a pleasant retirement. And for almost half a century, that's what many did. Or appeared to do.

According to a poll cited by *American Demographics*, 41 percent of retirees say the adjustment was difficult. That's a huge percentage, given that only 12 percent of newlyweds thought marriage was a difficult adjustment and just 23 percent of couples thought becoming parents was tough.

So Americans bought the hype, and when they found out that the reality wasn't as fulfilling as the brochures promised, most bit their tongues and went along with the program. After all, it looked like the smart, upscale thing to do.

But now it's reality that's biting, in the form of demographics. The baby boomers haven't been saving like their parents did to help finance that retirement myth. And there are too many of them ready to collect benefits, with too few workers coming along the pipeline to help finance their payouts. In 1950, there were sixteen workers paying taxes for every retiree collecting benefits. Now just three workers support each pensioner, and by 2030 that will be down to two. At current tax and benefits rates, it can't be done—it's as simple as that.

So we're back to the bottom line: Even if you think you're going to love living the whitewashed, prefab version of the American retirement dream, forget it. You won't be able to afford it. You're going to need some other source of income to sustain a decent quality of life. And if you're one of those who just bit your tongue and went along with the program, now is the time to hop off the merry-go-round and set yourself on the right track for a fulfilling and profitable new stage of your life.

LOOK AT WHAT HAPPENED TO
MURIEL HARTMAN

Muriel Hartman fully expected to sail into a well-heeled retirement and was looking forward to it. She was born a golden
girl, the apple of her upper-middle-class father's eye. She was
the firstborn and very bright. Long before it became fashionable
to do so, her father treated her as he did his sons. He expected
her to excel at sports, academics, and, of course, in the social
arena as well. And so she did.

She was expected to marry well, too—just as a backup, so
she wouldn't have to worry about supporting herself in the
proper style. She excelled there, too. She married a proctologist,
Robert, whose income helped assure a well-cushioned life for
her and their two sons. Muriel and Robert argued a bit over
her determination to have a career of her own; he wanted her
to be at home with their children and available for midweek
sailing excursions when his office was closed.

She compromised, and instead of returning to her blossoming
career as a newspaper editor, she agreed to work at home, trying
her hand at writing plays. Again she was surprisingly successful, having two small openings off-off-off-off-Broadway. Robert's contacts helped. But such luck didn't last, and by the time
the boys hit their teens she was back at work full-time as an
editor in the news and information service at the local university. She really liked her job and was good at it. It didn't much
matter that it didn't pay all that well—Robert's was their primary income and would provide for them well in their golden
years.

If this story sounds too good to be true, you're right. The
god of misfortune was just waiting for the worst moment to
jump out and half scare Muriel Hartman to death. Last spring,
at age fifty-nine, Muriel decided to take the early retirement
option being offered by the university on a one-shot basis to
help curtail layoffs. The state had cut its education allocation
yet again, and the university was suffering. Muriel didn't mind.
Her pension would be less, but she had some Social Security
coming to her, and Robert, and their retirement dream of sailing
around the world, right?

Right. Until Robert fell over of a heart attack while tying up their forty-footer at the dock. And until she found he had made some bad investments and cashed in their insurance policies to cover his losses. And until she found that, ensconced in an apartment across town, there was a Ms. Faith Noble to whom Robert had been funneling much of his income over the past several years.

"I can't believe I was so naive," Muriel cried. "All this time I didn't prepare properly for my own retirement because I assumed Robert and I would live happily ever after. It's not like I didn't work. It's just that I never built up enough pension money or savings to see me through if I had to go it alone. It just never occurred to me."

Muriel's story may be headed for a happy ending after all. It was too late to cancel her early retirement. But the steps she took next helped her prepare for a more comfortable future than she was looking at when Robert died. First she took some time to calm down. Then she did a step-by-step assessment of her interests, her skills, and her needs, financial and emotional. Then she set herself up in a home-based business.

She started a book packaging and editing business based on the skills, wisdom, and contacts she had acquired over the course of her career. Turning her own unhappy experiences to profit, she sold a well-known paperback publisher on the concept of a series of self-help books for older women on a variety of topics. The idea is to help prepare them for an independent and successful life in the twenty-first century. The books are on how to buy and renovate your own home, how to start your own business, how to start and maintain an investment portfolio, and how to navigate the new information superhighway, for starters.

She's writing a couple of the books herself, but she's also hired other women to write some. And with the university as a source of clients, the editing portion of her new business seems to be thriving, too. The business won't make her a fortune, but it will bring in a comfortable extra buck or two. Enough for her to buy a small Sailfish of her own.

"You know, I feel better than I have in years," Muriel said recently. "I started life as a high achiever, but let that slowly peter out, living with Robert and working for someone else. I liked what I did, and I knew I wanted to be out in the workplace instead of at home or the country club. But I never had that sense of excitement I have now. I feel like a maverick, and it's really quite addictive.''

RIDE THE GRAY WAVE TO FUN AND PROFIT

Muriel not only chose the right career for herself in terms of her skills and interests, but without realizing it she chose the right market as well. Because there's good news, too, in that gray wave of baby boomers looming on the horizon.

Even before the boomer bump, the spending power of older adults is awesome. Although they represent only a quarter of the total U.S. population, Americans over age fifty now have a combined annual income of more than $800 billion and control 70 percent of the total net worth of U.S. households—nearly $7 trillion of wealth. Combine that with boomer spending power and you're talking a massive ''generational'' market.

Experts have predicted that by 2025 Americans over age sixty-five will outnumber teenagers by more than two to one; by the year 2050, it's expected that one in four Americans will be over sixty-five. For the mature, savvy entrepreneur, the aging boomers and other older Americans are a gold vein waiting to be mined.

They're a huge source of discretionary spending, and if you can tap into that source with the right product or the right service, aimed at the interests and needs of older Americans, you've got it made.

The needs and desires of the baby boomers have driven the machine called the marketplace since they were born. Millions of baby carriages, schools, and homes were built for them. They worshipped at the temple of youth, while health clubs, plastic surgeons, and sports gear manufacturers prospered with their homage. They turned supper into dinner and dining into an international gourmet experience that often cost the equivalent of their parents' weekly food budget.

Boomers learned early and well how to live the good life.

And despite the bleak future for Social Security and private pension plans, it's likely they'll do whatever it takes, including continuing to work, to maintain that good life. Boomers have been big spenders and poor savers all their lives, and they'll probably continue their spending spree into the years to come.

Now, as they age, boomers continue to dominate the marketplace, and you can bet we'll see the decline of the cult of youth. Businesses today already are beginning to understand the value and buying power of older people, who are remaining active far longer than earlier generations. What they haven't quite caught on to yet is that these older adults want to purchase products and services that meet their needs, not the needs of a twenty-five-year-old. And they want to buy these products and services from people like themselves, people who understand their needs and desires, people like you.

So what are you waiting for? By now you've thoroughly analyzed that queasy feeling in the pit of your stomach and decided you're not interested in retiring, at least not in the old, outdated sense of the word. You want to work. In fact, you suspect you might want to start your own business and have begun to see that gray wave as an opportunity rather than as a natural disaster ready to wash over you.

The next step is to decide exactly what you want to do with the rest of your life. In chapter 3 you'll take an attitudinal self-analysis test to help you sort out what you want to do in your next career and what you have to do to get there. What kind of job or business will work for you? Do you want to tackle your own business at this stage in your life or just put in time for a paycheck? Chapter 3 will help you answer these questions and take the guesswork out of your future.

⋘3⋙

WHAT SHOULD YOU DO
WITH THE REST OF YOUR LIFE?

Cheer up, there's hope for you yet. Retirement doesn't have to be a dirty word, and buying this book is the first step to a whole new, more challenging and rewarding phase of your life. Legions of people are redefining the words *retirement* and *work* and are finding fuller, more satisfying and more productive lives in their golden years than they ever thought possible.

They've learned they can take the wisdom, skills, and experiences from their younger years and mold their retirement into something new: into a nontraditional retirement offering exactly the kind of lifestyle they choose.

That's exactly what you can do, too. You've decided traditional retirement just isn't going to work for you. You want to chart a new course for yourself leading to greater financial and emotional riches in your golden years.

So what's next? The next step is to do a complete attitudinal self-checkup so you don't rush blindly down the wrong path. You need to determine what nontraditional retirement option is best for you. Do you want to keep or return to your old job or a similar one? How about changing careers? Should you take advantage of new, more flexible scheduling options at someone else's business, be a volunteer, or start your own business? Before choosing your own nontraditional retirement option, you need to answer the following questions.

But wait—before you sharpen your pencil and start answering these questions, get yourself organized for the step-by-step task of plotting your path to a financially secure and satisfying future. Remember, your answers to the questions will begin to build the foundation for your next career. You need to do it right. And that means you need to begin building what will become, in addition to this book, your nontraditional business bible.

Go out now to your nearest office supply shop and purchase an oversized, heavy-duty, three-ring binder. Over the coming months it will become both your resource and your guide. Get a good supply of paper and a couple of packages of dividers. There are lots of different areas we'll need to cover as we get your business off to a successful launch.

If you're on-line with a personal computer and a good printer, go ahead and set up an electronic file. But be sure to print out the answers to these questions and the other plans you will make as we go along, and put those into your notebook, too. It's going to be important for you to be able to carry that notebook wherever you go. You'll want to place it by your bed each night, because chances are you'll be waking at two A.M., excited by an idea you'll want to jot down immediately so it doesn't disappear in the night.

You can label this notebook "How to Ride the Gray Wave to Fun and Profit." Or "My Personal Business Bible." Or whatever else springs to mind. The important thing is to do it and do it now, then sit down and answer these questions. And be honest in your answers. This is one case where you'll truly hurt only yourself—and jeopardize your future success—if you fudge even a little bit.

QUESTIONS TO ASK YOURSELF

WHAT ARE YOUR INTERESTS?

- Did I enjoy my last job?
- Did I hate my last job but enjoy the field or business?
- Did any of my coworkers or friends in another field have the kind of job I dreamed of?
- What kinds of activities/subjects interest me most?
- What occupation or field would I most be interested in?

WHAT KIND OF WORK ENVIRONMENT DO YOU WANT?

- Do I want to be physically active or cerebrally active?
- Do I want to spend most of my time indoors or outdoors?
- Where would I most like to live?
- Do I want to work with other people or by myself?
- Do I want to work with a large group of people, many different kinds of people, or a small homogeneous group?
- What kind of people would I like to have as coworkers? Customers?
- What work hours/work schedule would I most like to have?
- Do I want to work full- or part-time, year-round or seasonally?
- Would I like to travel in my job?

WHAT IS YOUR GOAL IN YOUR "RETIREMENT CAREER"?

- Do I need the salary and benefits I currently have or had? Could I earn enough in some other field or area?
- How much money do I need or want to earn?
- Would I be willing to invest my time and money in the necessary training or retraining to make a radical change?
- What are the major reasons I would seek a change?
- Would I be willing to work without pay?
- Is there a cause I would be willing to support as a volunteer?

DO YOU WANT TO WORK FOR YOURSELF OR SOMEONE ELSE?

- Do I want to work for my former/current boss?
- Would my former employer be willing to hire me back on a more flexible or reduced work schedule?
- Do I prefer to be my own boss?

- Do I have a unique and marketable idea, product, skill, or service?
- Am I willing to take a risk with some of my savings?
- Am I willing to assume the full burden of responsibility for a business?
- Do I have sufficient financial resources to start a business?

Answer these questions honestly, then take a good look at your answers. They will help start you on the path to a satisfying retirement career. There's no question that you want to work. Now you need to define more fully what you want out of your retirement work—what kind of work environment will pay off for you financially and emotionally.

MCJOBS ABOUND, BUT MAY NOT BE RIGHT FOR YOU

First, you need to decide how much money you want to make. Do you need just a bit more cash to ease the strain on your pocketbook? To provide little luxuries like country line dance lessons and a weekend or two in the Poconos? Or do you want the potential for significant income so you can really live it up in your retirement years?

If you're only looking for extra cash, just about any part-time job will do. With the McJob approach you could go the fast-food, burger-slinging route or do occasional baby-sitting. Or you could drive a taxicab or sell Mary Kay Cosmetics to your friends. The list of McJobs is endless, and openings abound.

Don't forget, the pool of teenagers is drying up. In July 1983, the number of Americans over the age of sixty-five surpassed the number of teenagers. Although 76 million babies were born during the boom years, only 57 million were born from 1965 to 1985. There's a real labor shortage coming, and plenty of service businesses are beginning to look to older adults as potential employees.

But if you want to make more than bare minimum wage, think about doing something else.

Then there's the emotional factor. You didn't graduate to senior status just to end up slinging burgers at a McJob. Keep in mind, we're not talking rocket science here. Most of these jobs aren't going to challenge you or stimulate your interests. They're bone-chilling boring, boring, boring. If you want a challenge for your creativity, you're going to have to keep looking.

And although you can work at these McJobs part-time, you pretty much have to do it on the employer's terms, with a schedule determined by the business's needs, not yours. Some companies are beginning to come around, of course. McDonald's is trying to cater to older workers, putting them through a special "McMasters" training program and suggesting they be offered their choice in scheduling as much as possible.

But the pay's a joke, the work's not even amusing, and at a McJob you're just a small cog in somebody else's wheel. My advice? Forget the McJobs.

DETERMINE THE RIGHT COMBINATION OF WORK AND RETIREMENT

Remember, you're in charge here, so let's get back to aggressively plotting your own unique path. It's time to decide how much or how little you want to work in your nontraditional retirement career. Before you can decide on the job or business that's right for you, you have to decide what kind of work schedule you want. And that's really a lifestyle decision.

You started sketching a broad outline of your dream work schedule when you answered some of the questions in the attitudinal self-checkup earlier. But now it's time to flesh out that broad outline with more details. Maybe you still want to work fifty- or sixty-hour weeks. Maybe you're really a hopeless workaholic and that's all you want to do with the rest of your life.

So enjoy. Part II of this book, "Get Down to (Your Retirement) Business!" will be just as valuable for workaholics as it will be for those people who really want to change the concept of retirement, not throw it out altogether.

But many of you, I suspect, want to work a bit and play a bit in your nontraditional retirement. Right now, jot down the details of your dream work schedule. Do you want to work full- or part-time: fifteen hours, twenty hours, or forty hours a week? Do you prefer weekend work or weekdays only? Are you a night person or a day person who leaps out of bed at five A.M. and can't stay awake past nine at night?

Do you prefer working alone, or do you crave a close working relationship with a couple of other people? Do you want to work at home or do you need the discipline and companionship of leaving the house for your job? How do you feel about seasonal work only? Is that just about enough for you, or could it satisfy your financial needs but leave you feeling unfulfilled during your off-season?

Once you've filled in these details, you're ready to look at some options besides a McJob.

UNFORTUNATELY, SOME EMPLOYERS STILL EXPLOIT OLDER WORKERS

It's sad, but true. Older employees still are exploited. In this youth-worshipping nation, older people often do not command the respect they do in some other countries, such as Japan and China. It's beginning to change here with the aging of America, but as a society we have been thoroughly "gerontophobic." *Age* has been considered synonymous with *unattractive, used up, washed out, over-the-hill,* and *valueless.*

If you've ruled out a McJob and are thinking about mounting a search for a meaningful, challenging job that pays decently, you need to face this ugly fact: Some employers tend to look with distrust at older job applicants. They assume that if you're an older adult without a job and still in the job market, there must be something wrong with you. Either you have no usable skills, can't be trusted or have no relevant experience.

And if you can break down those barriers and convince employers you can do the job, they still assume you won't be around long and probably are a health risk. So they hire you to fill in gaps rather than fill meaningful posts. They may assign you the worst tasks and the worst shifts, assuming you'll be grateful just for the chance to work.

Okay, so a McJob isn't going to do it for you, and reentering the traditional job market could be problematic. But there's hope yet.

SOME EMPLOYERS ARE WISING UP TO THE VALUE OF OLDER WORKERS

Not all employers are Neanderthals. Some enlightened business owners and executives actually have looked at the new demographics and are beginning to see the handwriting on the wall. They recognize that older workers are a valuable resource they should be striving to retain. And that is opening up opportunities for older workers that didn't exist ten years ago. Sure, these opportunities are still tough to find, but their numbers are growing every day.

These enlightened business owners not only see older workers as a ready source of labor to fill a shrinking pool, they also realize that older workers bring added value to the job: experience, sound judgment, lower absenteeism, personal skills, and emotional equilibrium. American Airlines, for example, actively seeks older workers to retrain as flight attendants to make their graying customers feel more comfortable.

So if you can't stomach or survive on a McJob, how about a more meaningful job with an enlightened employer on a nontraditional scheduling basis? Instead of the nine-to-five grind, some employers are offering more flexible employment patterns. If you can find one it could offer you a better balance between work and leisure and a more relaxed pace overall. For example, some of the new options include:

- *Telecommuting*—which harnesses technology such as computers and fax machines to allow employees to work at home.

- *Flex scheduling*—which requires that employees work a specified number of hours but does not specify what those hours must be. If you're taking courses at the local university or prefer to be on the links during midday, you might choose to work from six to ten A.M. and from three to seven P.M.

- *Job sharing*—which allows two part-time workers to split a job, acting as a team to complete projects and job requirements.

- *Temp work*—which offers the opportunity to work at temporary jobs when and where you want, as frequently or infrequently as you like, in a variety of business environments. Such opportunities may range from highly specialized professional projects to routine clerical work.

- *Employee leasing*—which permits a company to have its employees rehired by an employee-leasing company, which then leases the employees back to the original employer for a service fee.

These kinds of options open up possibilities well beyond a McJob and may allow you to continue meaningful employment in a challenging job. They do, however, assume that you will be doing pretty much the same kinds of things you've been doing in your recent career, calling on those skills and experiences you have accumulated over your past work life.

But what if you're really bored with what you've been doing for the past twenty years?

MAYBE IT'S TIME TO RE-CAREER

We talked in chapter 1 about the linear lifeline traditionally followed by most Americans: the rigid sequential path through life from nursery to school, then to work, and finally to the long-sought reward, easy retirement.

Throughout history, when life was much shorter than it is now, it was necessary for both the survival of the species and for social order that important personal and social tasks be performed at specific ages. You were educated and prepared for a job; were married and prepared for parenthood; had children and provided for them while preparing them for the same cycle; then you retired, if only to a back seat in the scheme of things. Each of these tasks was performed in sequence and at specific ages. You had to do it and get it done, because along came forty, fifty, or sixty, and you died.

But think about choosing your life's work at age twenty in the context of living to seventy, eighty, ninety, or one hundred instead of to just fifty or sixty. Think about how your ideas and interests, your dreams and desires, might change over that longer, fuller lifetime. Many people get divorced during their middle years, after they have changed and grown and their interests and ideas have shifted. They don't intend to remain alone for their remaining years, assuming that one relationship is all they're entitled to.

Instead they remarry, some several times, at different stages of their lives and with different interests in mind. Why, then, should we be expected to embark on one long, single-path career that ends in midlife with enforced leisure? Why not try different careers at different stages in our lives, as our interests grow and change? Perhaps with varying levels of intensity, or with different ratios of work-to-leisure time.

Why not, indeed? The answer is that people *are* beginning to re-career at later stages of their lives, not just as they fumble around at the beginning of their work lives for that one true career path.

Maybe instead of resuming your old job, with shorter hours, no benefits, and lower pay, you want to take the opportunity retirement offers to start on a fresh career path. Community colleges have sprouted like weeds all over America in the past thirty years, and they offer more direct job-training skills at much cheaper rates than four-year universities and colleges do. They're also close to home.

But universities, including some of the best Ivy League institutions in the nation, also are getting with the new program, spurred by the new gray wave demographics. They offer continuing education programs, many of them free for their own employees, that can help open your horizons to new career opportunities. Some of these programs still stick to standard book and theory courses, but many are designed to provide more practical skills and information you can profit from in your next career. Often they are offshoots and extensions of research work being conducted at large universities.

For example, through Cornell University and its extension services, anyone can take classes in horticulture, landscape design, herbal gardening, herbal healing, dairy farming, farm finances, pet care, weatherproofing, composting, vegetable and fruit canning, and a thousand and one other subjects that could form the basis of a new career. And Cornell isn't alone in this.

If you're not quite ready for full, traditional retirement, recareering may provide you with the opportunity for the career of your dreams, offering greater creativity, flexibility, and job satisfaction.

HOW MUCH RISK ARE YOU WILLING TO TAKE?

Whether you prefer to stick to your former line of work or recareer, you can choose to do it one of two ways: for yourself or for someone else. And that partly depends on your answer to the question "How much risk are you willing to take?" We'll explore this question further in chapter 4, but it's time to pose it for a gut-level reaction.

Does the thought of flying solo cause you to dream of the Goodyear blimp crashing and burning? Or does it make your nerve ends tingle with anticipation, like when you're reading that green for a six-inch birdie putt?

And what about the financial picture? Are you living or about to live right on the financial edge, with no comfortable cushion to play around with? Or do you have a bit of savings or a severance package that could be the ticket to your own nontraditional retirement business? Maybe you have an insurance policy you could borrow against or are ready to think about remortgaging your house.

But even that may not be necessary, because here's the secret to starting your own successful business in retirement: We're not talking traditional, high-volume, high-overhead business here. We're not talking megahours and megastress. As you'll find in Part II of this book, "Get Down to (Your Retirement) Business," the beauty of starting your own nontraditional retirement business is that you can do it on the fly, with minimum cash outlay and maximum fun.

We're talking gypsy retailing, without a traditional, high-rent, money-sucking shop to consume overhead. And home-based consulting and roving service businesses. You choose the time, place, and season for your business. All you really need is your lifetime of skills, common sense, and a sharply focused concept of how to bring a very specific target market exactly what it wants or needs.

LOOK AT HOW MAXINE WEISENFELD IS MAPPING HER FUTURE

Unlike Alexander Faulker and Muriel Hartman, Maxine Weisenfeld took charge of her retirement future early in the game. At age fifty-four, she's still quite a few years away from the traditional retirement age of sixty-five, but Max likes to plan ahead.

She's observant, too, and about a year ago she noticed some signs that a major merger might be in the works for her company, a manufacturer of medical supplies. As a vice president for marketing, Max suspects she might find herself a redundancy in the merged corporate giant, and as such she would be a prime target for downsizing. She feels it may be a good time to jump ship with an early retirement incentive package. So for the past year she's been getting ready to jump—into her own well-stocked retirement lifeboat.

She says she's too young to retire—and besides, she's got too much energy. And she's always liked the idea of working for herself. It's something she wanted to try someday, and it looks like someday might be now. Here's what she's done. For years, Max and her partner, Alice, have been spending summer weekends and vacations at the Jersey shore in a weathered, rambling house on the bay near the Barnegat lighthouse. Max's parents left her the house when they died a few years ago, but Max has been going there since she was a little girl, and she jokes that she has baywater instead of blood in her veins.

Since her parents died, Max and Alice have rented out the house a good portion of each summer to help pay the taxes and upkeep, but they still spend at least several weeks and odd weekends there. They feel comfortable at the beach, they say, and are part of a small but closely knit gay community there.

As a young girl Max told her parents firmly that she wanted to live year-round at the shore house, and they pooh-poohed the notion. It's cold and lonely and too quiet, they said. Besides, what would you do for a living, with all the summer people gone? they asked. Max grew up, saw the rationality in that, and gave up her dream of really living at the beach.

Until she saw the handwriting on the wall at her "real" job. A year ago, just after Labor Day, Max and Alice were preparing to close up the beach house for the winter, cleaning and shuttering and mending screens. Max stopped and called Alice out to the deck overlooking the dock and bay, sat her down, handed her a rum punch, and said it was time to start planning their future.

Max said she thought her job at the medical supply company was in jeopardy and that instead of waiting for the big blow they should figure out exactly where they wanted to spend their golden years and how they wanted to spend them. Then they needed to decide how they could adequately finance those years without dying of boredom, she added.

The answer to the "where" question was easy. By this time they both had baywater in their veins and friends they didn't want to leave. They decided they would winterize the house and move to the beach year-round.

The next part wasn't quite so easy, but it wasn't too difficult, either. Max was a list maker by nature, as well as an observer. So she and Alice made lists. Lists of their interests, lists of their skills, lists of the kinds of schedules they liked to keep, the hours they were freshest. Then they made lists of changes they had seen at the Jersey shore over the years—changes in the kinds of people who vacationed there and in their needs and interests. And changes in the shore community itself and what it offered those vacationers—what kind of shops, conveniences, and services had filtered in from the city and what was still missing.

Then they put the pieces of those lists together something like a jigsaw puzzle. The completed puzzle guided their actions over the next year. In essence it became the map for their future. This is what they decided: Max had noticed the beach becoming more "yuppified" each summer. The old fishermen still rode the waters, catching fresh fish for the markets and restaurants. But newer, fancier fishing fleets had invaded to cater to the vacationers, day-trippers, and weekend warriors who wanted to go deep-sea fishing and bag something big to brag about.

At the same time, their wives, children, and friends were lying on the beach and riding the waves, getting hungry and thirsty. To supply their dining-out needs, new, gourmet-style restaurants were replacing the old taprooms and crab shacks with newspapers on the tables. A couple of gourmet delis with exotic prepared carry-out salads, cheeses, breads, and desserts had even cropped up, so these upscale beachgoers could dine on their own decks at their leisure.

But these new-style fishermen and women and their families on the beach weren't getting the kinds of gourmet foods they were used to before and during their fishing expeditions, or as they lay on the beach. This, Maxine and Alice decided, was their window of opportunity. These yuppie vacationers with seemingly bottomless pocketbooks and discerning palates would be their ticket to a comfortable retirement business they could operate just five or six months a year—say, May through September or October.

They decided to buy a couple of mobile carts, like the ones you can buy hot dogs from on city streets, and take gourmet breakfast, snack, and luncheon treats to the fishing docks and beaches.

During the winter they bought the carts and restyled them with a country café motif—lots of wicker and paisley drapes. Alice quit her job as a computer programmer and started cooking up a storm, experimenting with a variety of muffins, breads, salads, and outrageous sandwiches. Cooking had always been her avocation, and she would be the chief chef.

Last summer they did a test run, thinking they could easily resell the carts if the business was a bust. Max kept her job at the medical supply company but took her vacation on Fridays and Mondays. Alice cooked and baked all week, and Max and her niece, who needed a summer job, operated the carts from Friday through Monday.

To put it mildly, their test run was a home run. The main problem was keeping up with the healthy appetites of hungry vacationers determined to treat themselves and their families to the best for at least a week or two every summer. The new business even started getting requests for home delivery and party catering.

Max and Alice weren't sure whether their business would really take off—or how they felt about expanding if it did. After all, they were planning this as a semi–leisurely retirement business. Now Max is hoping that corporate merger her and early retirement incentive come through soon, so she can jump into their new business full-time during the summer season.

They're still deciding about whether to expand next summer or take it a bit slower for a while. But they're happy with the choices they've made about their future and are confident they can live well in the place of their choice well into their golden years—and with the challenge and fun of a small, home-based business to run.

SO WHAT SHOULD YOU DO WITH THE REST OF YOUR LIFE?

The key to Max's success is she took charge of her nontraditional retirement early in the game; analyzed her options, needs, and desires, and then carefully crafted exactly the kind of future she wanted. Now she and Alice are ready to live happily ever after.

So what should *you* do with the rest of your life? Only you can decide. But if, like Alexander, you get depressed at the thought of traditional retirement; or if, like Muriel, you're suddenly thrown a financial curveball and have to earn some money just as you were set to retire; or if, like Maxine, you're about to face a forced early retirement and always hankered to be your own boss—if you fit any of those "ifs" or a million and one others, it's time to take charge of your retirement future.

We've discussed a number of options in this chapter. You could try a McJob, or try a new, more flexible scheduling option at your former place of employment. Or you could re-career and try to find a whole new job. But maybe those options just don't do it for you. Maybe, like Maxine, the idea of working for yourself brings a tingle to the tips of your toes instead of striking fear in your heart. If so, you probably answered "Yes" to that last series of questions in the attitudinal self-checkup at the start of this chapter. In that case you'll definitely want to read on to determine once and for all whether you really are entrepreneurial material.

⋰4⋱

———————

ARE YOU REALLY GRAY WAVE
ENTREPRENEURIAL MATERIAL?

This is it. It's fish-or-cut-bait time. Time to decide once and for all whether you really have what it takes to become an entrepreneur, on whatever scale, at this stage of your life. Being an entrepreneur, after all, takes some pretty special qualities. Think about it. These are the men and women who made America great, the folks who came to this country dirt-poor, like Alexander Faulker's father, and built vast financial empires.

They started with pushcarts peddling potatoes and built nationwide grocery chains. They started with small bottles of home-brewed tonic and built international drug and medical conglomerates.

They also built small general stores that served as the unofficial town halls of countless small towns across the country. And those general stores became mom-and-pop corner groceries serving the needs of towns and small cities throughout America. Every business you see on every street corner—every restaurant, every store, every market, and every factory—was started by someone, sometime. And each of those people had some things in common.

They all had an idea, something they wanted to do with their lives that, perhaps incidentally, could earn them a living. Then, each of them had the determination—the stubbornness, perhaps—to stick to that idea, that dream, and make it a reality. Or maybe it happened another way for some of them—maybe they didn't start with an idea of what they wanted to do. Maybe they just knew they wanted to be independent, to work for themselves rather than for someone else. Maybe that was such a strong conviction, so firm an idea in and of itself, that they searched and searched and researched and researched until they found an idea they could make their own, a business they could found for themselves.

It doesn't matter which way it happened. Either way worked for those earlier entrepreneurs and will work for you. You can come to the entrepreneurial starting gate with a burning desire to make something or sell something or do something specific and then decide to do it on your own, in your own business. Or you can come with the burning desire to start a business of your own and then seek a product or service to deliver. Both ways work, provided you have the traits of a true entrepreneur. And that's what we're going to determine in this chapter, once and for all. But first, let's take a look at the pros and cons of starting your own business.

THE PROS OF BECOMING A GRAY WAVE ENTREPRENEUR

- This may be your last opportunity in life to create something substantial, something successful, from scratch—literally, from nothing. It could be a successful product or service, but whatever it is, it's all yours, and you'll have that knowledge to warm you as you age.

- You may be fulfilling a lifelong dream, and nothing is quite so rewarding as that. Some people never have the chance to fulfill their dream, others let the chance slip away and regret forever that their dream remains unfulfilled.

- You, and only you, will be determining your own life and your fate, from workday to financial reward. And for the true entrepreneur, there's nothing like being your own boss.

- Speaking of financial rewards, when it's your business, you reap the profits. And with the right business and the right management, the profits can be great indeed. In fact, the profits can be as substantial or as minimal as you choose to make them.

- Starting your own business has the advantage of making you immune to the sudden onslaught of corporate downsizing that's so virulent in today's business climate. If there's any downsizing to be done, you'll be the one making the decisions.

- You can make the mental and emotional switch from being a mere user of goods and services to being a producer—both essential elements in society, but offering different perspectives. And instead of taking a job, you may be able to create a job or two for someone else who needs one.

- As a mature, small businessperson you can help reestablish a sense of community, so sadly lacking in this country. Chances are you'll be dealing one-on-one with your neighbors, family, and friends in your new business, and those regular human contacts just don't happen at Wal-Mart, Costco, and Price Club megamarkets.

- Finally, in your own business, you set the tone, the ethical climate. And even in a small business today, you can take steps to help safeguard the environment in countless little ways that many large companies still ignore—such as recycling paper products, buying recycled goods, and using biodegradable cleaning products, to name a few.

These are just a handful of the pros I can list about becoming an entrepreneur. You can probably add a dozen more to the list from your own personal point of view. But there are some downsides, too.

THE CONS OF BECOMING A GRAY WAVE ENTREPRENEUR

- You'll need to invest some money in your venture, and that entails some risk. You might lose it, after all. Worse, you might end up with some serious new debts. Are you ready to bet your financial stability on your dream?

- You need good health, high energy, and ongoing enthusiasm for your venture. If any of those fluctuate for you greatly, you'd better think twice before becoming a Gray Wave entrepreneur.

- You'll be restricting your life in many ways, even with a nontraditional retirement business based on some flexibility. Let's face it, the boss just can't decide to call in sick when he or she wants to, assuming someone else will pick up the slack. You can't disappoint your customers too often without losing them.

- You and you alone will be responsible for your fate. We listed that as a pro, but it can also be a con. If that thought scares you, think twice before you leap into business ownership.

- Not everyone has the right personality, the right characteristics, to be a successful entrepreneur.

We're going to discuss those characteristics right now. Then, further on in this chapter, you can take a Gray Wave entrepreneurial aptitude test to see if you fit the mold. By the time you're done reading this chapter you'll be able to make a fully informed decision about whether entrepreneurship is right for you—whether, in fact, you should start now, learning all you need to know to start your own nontraditional retirement business.

PICTURE MEL GIBSON IN "THE ROAD WARRIOR"

So what are the key qualities of a successful entrepreneur? Think for a minute about Mel Gibson in *The Road Warrior*. Or if you're an old movie buff, think about John Wayne in just about any movie he made. Or Clint Eastwood. Visualize this Road Warrior, this tough-guy hero who makes it all happen and happen right. Got the picture? Take a mental snapshot and let's talk about this guy for a minute. What exactly is he like? What are his key traits?

CONFIDENCE

Probably the first thing you notice is confidence. This guy exudes confidence from every pore. He straddles the highway or corral looking ten feet tall, with the air of someone who can easily defeat the bad guys without ever firing a single shot. Chin up, he looks you squarely in the eye, shoulders straight and set, watchful yet at ease. He's ready to take on the world and win. He is, in short, a winner and he knows it. To be a successful entrepreneur you have to believe in yourself, believe unflinchingly you can do what you set out to do.

DRIVE

Nothing, but nothing, stopped Mel Gibson in *The Road Warrior.* Not the Humongous and his entire army of bad guys, not an arsenal of weapons. The Road Warrior had drive, and his natural energy fueled that drive. He was driven by his mission. He was single-minded and committed to his goal, and he marched relentlessly toward victory. That energy and drive are essential for the successful entrepreneur.

DETERMINATION

Just as the entrepreneur's natural energy fuels his drive, that drive fuels his determination. Despite minor or even more significant setbacks, Mel Gibson and John Wayne never seriously falter in their march to victory. They set their square jaws and persist, refusing to let stumbling blocks deflect them from their path. Instead, they consider each problem carefully and devise a solution, always with their eye on their main goal. They can do anything they set their minds to, anything they're determined to do. It's just a question of making the mental commitment, of digging in their heels and deciding to do it—and do it right.

INTEGRITY

Picture John Wayne straddling a town's single dusty street in front of the swinging doors of the saloon. Look into his eyes. You know instantly that whatever else you might discover about this man in the confrontation to come, he's a man of integrity.

He's a man you can trust with your life, if it should come to that. That sense of personal integrity that shines through all your actions is key to being a successful entrepreneur. When you own your own business, customers and clients look into your eyes and no one else's to decide whether to entrust their business to you. They're seeking a sense of your personal integrity. They want to be assured that you're honest and honorable and trustworthy—in short, a person of integrity.

EXPERIENCE

You don't have to know all the answers. This isn't really a movie, after all, and even Clint Eastwood makes some mistakes. But few green, unseasoned entrepreneurs have what it takes to succeed in their own business. To be successful, you need those years in the field, or simply the many lessons of a long life, to help you overcome the obstacles that inevitably will fall in your path. This is one of the secrets of your future success. You've lived a long time and have learned much over the years. Now you can distill that experience and those skills you've honed and put them to use in your own business.

COMMON SENSE

Hand in hand with experience goes common sense. As an entrepreneur you need to stay grounded in reality, like John Wayne's characters. Those guys stayed alive by knowing instinctively when to duck, when to check their backs, and when to shoot first. Common sense is all about trusting your instincts and not relying on pat formulas and rote learning as a new entrepreneur. When the going gets tough or you make a mistake, chances are you're not going to find the solution in a textbook for Business Management 101. The best solution probably is right in your head, waiting for you to just figure it out.

CREATIVITY

You may think Mel Gibson's Road Warrior an unlikely source of creativity, but think again. The Road Warrior survived by finding food and fuel in a burned-out desert landscape in the most unlikely places. And he patched and protected and armed his vehicle by thinking creatively and using common, everyday, household items creatively. Common sense and experience are essential for the budding entrepreneur, but they'll take you only so far.

Creativity means thinking new thoughts, having new ideas, going beyond the known to the unknown and transforming it—harnessing it. Webster's defines creativity as "artistic or intellectual inventiveness."

To be successful you'll need creativity to find just the right business or product for you as a semiretired Gray Wave entrepreneur. And you'll need creativity to find customers and clients—the absolutely right market—for your business, and then to keep them.

FLEXIBILITY

Finally, Mel Gibson's Road Warrior had to be flexible, and so do you if you intend to make it as an entrepreneur. If an idea or plan doesn't work, you can't let yourself waste time, energy, and emotion bemoaning that failure. You need to be able to learn from that failure and quickly come up with an alternative solution. You have to be adaptable and throw your ego out the door, so you can continue to move forward when things don't go quite as you expected. While you'll need to stay focused to achieve your goal, you may need to try several different means to get there in the end.

For example, one marketing approach may work for a while and then stall. At that point you'll need to be flexible and come up with something new. Remember, every business plan and every business can benefit from a fresh look and a few minor adjustments every once in a while, even if things seem to be going just right.

So now you've got a good snapshot of what an entrepreneur looks like, and how that translates into the key character traits necessary for a successful entrepreneur. But we were talking about Mel Gibson, John Wayne, and Clint Eastwood—movie stars, after all. Maybe you're wondering what a real-life semiretired entrepreneur looks like.

MEET REAL-LIFE ENTREPRENEUR "DANGEROUS DAN" MARVIN

Col. "Dangerous Dan" Marvin is retired from the U.S. Army Special Forces. But Dan's still a Clint Eastwood kind of guy. He even looks a little bit like the actor, all sinew with a square jaw and steely blue eyes.

Dan's a grandfather, and dotes on his eleven grandchildren, his three daughters, and his wife, Kate. But in his heart Dan is and always was a soul-fired crusader. Had he been born centuries ago he would have been a knight in armor, searching for the holy grail.

Dan was born in Detroit in 1933, into poverty and injustice; it was the injustice that lit a fire in his soul. His father, a vain, inglorious, hard-drinking womanizer, left his wife when Dan was born—and that abandonment led Dan to become a crusader. At age eleven he formed his first gang, the Blue Jackets, to protect little old ladies on Chicago's mean streets. Today he's still crusading, and, frankly, it gets expensive.

Dan quit school on his sixteenth birthday, while in the tenth grade, to help support his mother. He worked as a busboy, janitor, and short-order cook for the next three years. He enlisted in the U.S. Army at age nineteen as a private. But Dan is a man of strength and character, and he was fearless. He also put work, and the army, ahead of everything. And in his single-mindedness and determination, he excelled. He was promoted time and time again.

In February 1964, then-Capt. Daniel "Dangerous Dan" Marvin, U.S. Army Special Forces, believed it was his duty to protect his country against its enemies. He was trained by the CIA in assassination and terrorist techniques and performed numerous covert missions for the CIA over the next four years.

In June 1966, during the Vietnam War, Captain Marvin accepted a special CIA mission in Cambodia. He accepted the mission on the basis of stipulations that would have guaranteed his team medical evacuation and air support. When his stipulations were denied, he aborted the mission. Dangerous Dan was declared a renegade Green Beret.

Dan and the 509 men under his command eventually got out of that death trap with the help of a Vietnamese general named Quang Van Dang, and Dan's military career got back on track. He retired from the army in 1973 with the rank of lieutenant colonel.

The year before he retired from the military, Dan awoke one morning from his usual four-hour nightly sleep with his whole left side numb. A doctor took X rays and diagnosed severe bone deterioration due to "continuing psychological and physical stress." Dan was working too long, too hard, and too intensely. The doctor ordered him to find a hobby, pronto.

Dan and Kate had just taken an old piece of furniture to Gerry Davis, whose business was called the Colonial Craftsman, in nearby Pennsylvania to be restored. Davis did antiques repair and restoration and was considered among the best in his trade. He was also a retired military man who, like Dan, smoked cigars, so he and Dan had much in common. Dan decided right then on his hobby. He began an apprenticeship with Davis and worked with the older man every weekend for a year until he, too, had mastered the craft.

"I just loved it," Dan said. "And would you believe, in six months my bones were right back where they should be."

When he retired a year later at age thirty-nine as a lieutenant colonel, his pension was $1,000 a month. "It just wasn't enough to live on," Dan said. He tried a couple of different jobs to supplement his income, but didn't much care for working for someone else. By 1974 he had decided to go into the antiques repair and restoration business for himself.

Today, at age sixty-two and a full colonel, he's still at it, working in his basement shop about six hours a day. He still does it because he loves it and because psychologically he needs to work. But he also needs the extra $1,000 a month his shop brings in. Even now, at $2,974 a month, his army pension can't support his mortgage and his crusades.

In 1984, Dangerous Dan was born again and became a soldier in Christ's army. He now crusades vigorously against government-sponsored terrorism and assassination, spending hours every day, when he isn't in his shop, writing and mailing articles and letters, trying to tell the world the ugly truth about the government's covert operations. He also campaigned for several years to get his old friend General Dang, who once saved his life, permission to emigrate to the United States.

Dan said his crusades cost him about $200 a month just in mailing and copying costs. His phone bill, too, is enormous. So his business helps offset those expenses.

Dan got started in his retirement business by going door-to-door in his neighborhood and by placing his business cards in a friend's Ethan Allen furniture store. He boasts proudly that he has never advertised. His business comes, by word of mouth, from all over the Northeast. "I never had a customer that I didn't get another customer from," he said.

He also admits that when he takes on a restoration, even one he's never encountered before, he won't let the customer tell him how to proceed or what to do. Instead, he feels he has to do what's right and natural for each piece, and he has to find that way for himself.

"I'm so darn stubborn, I just can't let anyone tell me what to do. And I want it to be right, just like it was supposed to be. I just close my eyes and think about it, and with the Lord's help, it comes to me," he said. "If they want some particular finish or some decorator thing that isn't right, I send them to someone else."

Two years ago his oldest daughter apprenticed with him for a while, then opened her own shop. And now two of his grandchildren are working with him a couple of hours every two weeks, learning the craft. That way, Dan said, he'll have somebody to take over when he's ready to slow down. But right now he's busy restoring a 200-year-old papier-mâché toy horse for a devoted customer several hundred miles away in New Hampshire.

IT'S TIME TO TAKE THE GRAY WAVE ENTREPRENEURIAL APTITUDE TEST

Dangerous Dan didn't carefully weigh the pros and cons of being an entrepreneur. He certainly didn't take an entrepreneurial aptitude test before he decided to set up shop, following in the footsteps of the Colonial Craftsman. At the time Dan did what the doctor told him to do to get healthy, and then one thing followed another. Dan eventually found himself in business and his own boss, which was exactly the right thing for him. As Dan said, he really isn't capable of working for someone else.

But what about you? We know you're suffering from RPRS—after all, you're reading this book. We talked about the pros and cons; we outlined the key character traits of an entrepreneur. You're thinking about committing serious time, energy, and financial resources to your retirement career and you don't want to make a mistake.

So let's find out, once and for all, if you're really Gray Wave entrepreneurial material, if you have what it takes to start up a business at this stage in your life and run with it. Sharpen your pencil, get out your Gray Wave notebook, and start a new section labeled "Making of an Entrepreneur."

First, divide one sheet of paper in half and label one column "Pros," the other "Cons." Then number and list the pros I enumerated earlier in this chapter and add your own. Do the same for cons.

Take another sheet of paper and head it "Entrepreneurial Character Traits." Divide it in half and head one column "Entrepreneur," the other column "Me." In the first column, list the eight entrepreneurial character traits I mentioned earlier. In the second column list your own key personality traits, as you have come to understand them over the years.

Now, on a third sheet of paper, list some of the heroes and heroines from recent or favorite movies you have seen. Do you resemble, in real life, any of those stars of the silver screen? Are you Thelma or Louise in *Thelma and Louise*? Are you Bruce Willis's character in *Die Hard 2*? List some of the ways in which you resemble those heroes, or jot down ways in which you differ.

Finally, take another piece of paper and copy the questions in the test below. Then answer them carefully and thoughtfully. Remember, be honest. There are no right or wrong answers, but there are pitfalls and wrong paths, and honest answers to this test will help you avoid them.

1. I would readily give up my daily 18 holes of golf to start my own business, even if it meant exchanging a lifestyle grounded in leisure for one based on hard work.
   A. strongly agree
   B. moderately agree
   C. moderately disagree
   D. strongly disagree

2. I've found over the years that I'm more determined than most people and can do just about anything I set my mind to.
   A. strongly agree
   B. moderately agree
   C. moderately disagree
   D. strongly disagree

3. My supervisors and others have said I have a sharp, analytical mind.
   A. strongly agree
   B. moderately agree
   C. moderately disagree
   D. strongly disagree

4. In my previous careers I worked long, hard hours for long periods of time, and I would still be willing and able to do so if necessary.
   A. strongly agree
   B. moderately agree
   C. moderately disagree
   D. strongly disagree

5. I've always felt compelled to be the best in everything I do.
   A. strongly agree
   B. moderately agree
   C. moderately disagree
   D. strongly disagree

6. I get frustrated easily.
   A. strongly agree
   B. moderately agree
   C. moderately disagree
   D. strongly disagree

7. At this point in my life I savor a challenge and don't want to waste my time on routine tasks.
   A. strongly agree
   B. moderately agree
   C. moderately disagree
   D. strongly disagree

8. I've learned to value competency over personality, and prefer to work with a difficult person who is very competent rather than one who's very congenial but less competent.
   A. strongly agree
   B. moderately agree
   C. moderately disagree
   D. strongly disagree

9. I usually am the one to organize a group of people and take charge.
   A. strongly agree
   B. moderately agree
   C. moderately disagree
   D. strongly disagree

10. I had enough of taking orders in my previous career and never have liked being told what to do.
   A. strongly agree
   B. moderately agree
   C. moderately disagree
   D. strongly disagree

11. I've learned to be efficient and to stick to a strict timetable in order to complete tasks in a timely way.
   A. strongly agree
   B. moderately agree
   C. moderately disagree
   D. strongly disagree

12. I would value my employees' well-being, but not at the expense of my business.
   A. strongly agree
   B. moderately agree
   C. moderately disagree
   D. strongly disagree

13. Given reasonable odds, my efforts usually can successfully influence the outcome of an endeavor.
   A. strongly agree
   B. moderately agree
   C. moderately disagree
   D. strongly disagree

14. My energy level is higher now than it was in my younger years, when I sometimes lacked focus, and seems to be higher than that of most people.
   A. strongly agree
   B. moderately agree
   C. moderately disagree
   D. strongly disagree

15. I have seen and encountered a variety of problems over the years, and most things do not fluster or unnerve me.
   A. strongly agree
   B. moderately agree
   C. moderately disagree
   D. strongly disagree

16. I've learned to be patient, that everything takes a certain amount of time and can't be rushed.
A. strongly agree
B. moderately agree
C. moderately disagree
D. strongly disagree

17. I love the challenge of analyzing, attacking, and completing a complex task.
A. strongly agree
B. moderately agree
C. moderately disagree
D. strongly disagree

18. In both my previous career and in my personal life I've often led and directed projects and groups.
A. strongly agree
B. moderately agree
C. moderately disagree
D. strongly disagree

19. I tend to be somewhat inflexible, and find it difficult to change course once I've started a project, even if it begins to look as though success is unlikely.
A. strongly agree
B. moderately agree
C. moderately disagree
D. strongly disagree

20. I know I'm capable of firing an unproductive employee, although I wouldn't be happy at the prospect of doing it.
A. strongly agree
B. moderately agree
C. moderately disagree
D. strongly disagree

21. I like to experiment and try new things—from wine, to food, to meeting new people and trying new activities.
A. strongly agree
B. moderately agree
C. moderately disagree
D. strongly disagree

22. I have had _____ year(s) of experience, either in business or as a hobby, in the field in which I plan to start a business.
A. 0
B. 1/2 to 1
C. 1 to 2
D. more than 2

23. I've had the following business experience:
A. a management position in a successful firm
B. a management position in any firm
C. no management experience

24. I've been ill to the extent that it curtailed my activities _____ days over the past three years.
A. 0 to 5
B. 6 to 10
C. 11 to 15
D. 16 or above

25. I function most effectively if I get at least _____ hours of sleep a night.
A. 8
B. 7
C. 6
D. 5 or less

Scoring Your Answers

Now, check the answer you marked for each question and see how many points it's worth. Put that number next to your answer. When you're finished you're going to add your total score, then find out just what that suggests about your chances of becoming a successful entrepreneur.

1. Need for leisure—entrepreneurs are willing to forgo a lifestyle based on leisure (a = 4, b = 3, c = 2, d = 1)

2. Self-confidence—an obvious necessity (a = 4, b = 3, c = 2, d = 1)

3. Conceptual ability—successful entrepreneurs are stars at this (a = 4, b = 3, c = 2, d = 1)

4. Energy level—it must be high (a = 4, b = 3, c = 2, d = 1)

5. Need for achievement, as opposed to status (a = 4, b = 3, c = 2, d = 1)

6. Emotional stability—the more stable the better (a = 1, b = 2, c = 3, d = 4)

7. Attraction to challenge, opportunity—otherwise, why start your own business? (a = 4, b = 3, c = 2, d = 1)

8. Objective approach to interpersonal relationships—entrepreneurs sometimes have to regard people as a means to an end (a = 4, b = 3, c = 2, d = 1)

9. Need for power—a strong one is essential (a = 4, b = 3, c = 2, d = 1)

10. Need for power (a = 4, b = 3, c = 2, d = 1)

11. Sense of urgency—a powerful one is a prerequisite (a = 4, b = 3, c = 2, d = 1)

12. Objective approach to interpersonal relationships (a = 4, b = 3, c = 2, d = 1)

13. Internal locus of control—believing you control your own destiny—a must for successful entrepreneurs (a = 4, b = 3, c = 2, d = 1)

14. Energy level (a = 4, b = 3, c = 2, d = 1)

15. Emotional stability (a = 4, b = 3, c = 2, d = 1)

16. Sense of urgency (a = 1, b = 2, c = 3, d = 4)

17. Conceptual ability (a = 4, b = 3, c = 2, d = 1)

18. Need for power (a = 4, b = 3, c = 2, d = 1)

19. Realism and flexibility—entrepreneurs cannot be rigid when seeking solutions to problems (a = 1, b = 2, c = 3, d = 4)

20. Objective approach to interpersonal relationships (a = 4, b = 3, c = 2, d = 1)

21. The most successful entrepreneurs are open to new experiences, opportunities, and challenges—they like to try new things (a = 4, b = 3, c = 2, d = 1)

22. The more business experience the better (a = 1, b = 2, c = 3, d = 4)

23. A management position in a successful company is the best experience to prepare you to succeed as an entrepreneur (a = 4, b = 3, c = 1)

24. Regardless of age, the healthier you are the more you will be able to handle the stress and long hours that come with entrepreneurship (a = 4, b = 3, c = 2, d = 1)

25. Energy level (a = 1, b = 2, c = 3, d = 4)

WHAT YOUR SCORE MEANS

Add up your total score, then check out where your score falls in the categories below. If you score 85 or above, you're on your way and it's clear sailing. If you scored below 85 . . . well, read on.

94–100: What are you waiting for?

You possess most, if not all, of the key personality and behavioral traits of the entrepreneur. You have the best chance to succeed.

85–93: Go for it.

You possess most of the characteristics of an entrepreneur. If your score on the last five questions was 23 or above, your behavioral attitudes could compensate for any personality traits you are lacking.

75–84: Think again.

You possess some entrepreneurial traits but probably not to the degree necessary to buck the daunting odds and be successful. If your score on the last five questions was 22 or below, the risk is even greater. Remember: Entrepreneurs are not attracted to risk, they are attracted to challenge and opportunities. Go back to working for someone else or relax and enjoy your life of retired leisure—you probably aren't cut out to be a Gray Wave entrepreneur.

Below 75: Stay right where you are.

You possess an insufficient number and degree of those personality traits and behavior patterns common to entrepreneurs.

So you don't look like Mel Gibson's Road Warrior and you're not a crusader like Dangerous Dan. You've taken the Gray Wave Entrepreneurial Aptitude Test, but even that is only a guide. Only you can answer the question of whether you're truly an entrepreneur.

So, look into your own heart—do you like what you see? Do you feel strongly that, at least partly thanks to your years of experience and character building, you *are* Gray Wave entrepreneurial material? If so, then you, with the help of this book, are ready to become the master of your business future.

❖ 5 ❖

EXPLORING YOUR OPTIONS

You're on a roll here. You've figured out you're suffering from RPRS (Repressed Pre- or Postretirement Syndrome). That means you're a person of maturity, energy, and experience who just isn't ready for the traditional retirement role. You've found you're not alone. You've learned about scientific advances, social dynamics, and the new Gray Wave demographics that are changing the way people think about aging and work— changing them in ways that will alter forever the retirement landscape of the twenty-first century and beyond.

And finally, you've made the most exciting discovery of all. You've sailed through the Gray Wave Entrepreneurial Aptitude Test and have decided in your heart of hearts that *you* are ready to become a Gray Wave entrepreneur. You're going for it.

The question now is: What, exactly, is *it*?

The answer is that your options are limited only by your imagination, energy, and resources—and the last is limited only by the first two. You can start your own business from scratch, buy an existing business, or buy a franchise business, which combines elements of the first two. You can become a retailer, selling just the right product to a carefully selected target market. Or you can start a service business, helping others get through their daily lives a little easier by doing for them something they haven't the time or skill to do for themselves.

To help you narrow your choices, here are some basic facts that will provide a broad outline of five specific options. Don't worry about filling in the details yet. Subsequent chapters in this book will give you step-by-step instructions on how to start each of these kinds of businesses. For now, check out these options to determine which might suit you best. And get your Gray Wave notebook ready. Make notes on each option as you read about it, and at the end of each section summarize the pros and cons as they strike you, while they're fresh in your mind.

BUYING A FRANCHISE BUSINESS

Franchising is the fastest-growing segment of American business today, and buying a franchise business may offer you the quickest, most straightforward, most surefire path to becoming a successful Gray Wave entrepreneur.

Just take a look at these statistics: A franchise owner has a four times greater chance of success than someone who starts a business from scratch, and twice as great a chance as someone who buys an existing business. A recent study of the franchising industry found that almost 97 percent of all franchises opened during the previous five years were still in operation, and that almost 86 percent of those businesses were still owned and operated by the original franchise buyer. Contrast that with studies that show four out of five independent businesses shut their doors within five years.

So what's a franchise, exactly? And why does it work so well?

Franchises can be anything from toy stores to yogurt stands to car washes, and many of their owners are over fifty, among the ranks of the pre–Gray Wave pioneers who refused to buy the retirement sales pitch. To put it simply, a franchise is a financial partnership between a large organization and an independent entrepreneur that works to the benefit of both. The large organization—the franchisor—sells you—the franchisee—the right to conduct business using the organization's name, trademarks, products, business procedures, marketing strategies, and advertising.

One of the biggest franchise businesses of all was started by seventy-two-year-old Col. Harlan Sanders, who had lost all his money before he started experimenting with his mother's fried chicken recipe. Colonel Sanders not only turned Kentucky Fried Chicken into one of the most successful franchise businesses today, and himself into a very wealthy man, but his franchises opened up opportunities for others to take their shot at the American entrepreneurial dream.

Buying a franchise offers some unique benefits. You'll be starting a business from scratch because, strictly speaking, you'll be opening a business where none existed before. But you'll also be buying a well-tried and tested business concept that has proven successful. Even better, you'll be backed by the accumulated knowledge, skills, experience, and financial strength of a parent company that can help guide you through the pitfalls that beset the start of any new business venture. It'll be your business and yours alone, but in a sense big daddy will be standing in the shadows behind you, ready to lend a helping hand.

Franchising is *the* business success story of the tail end of the twentieth century, and a sure recipe for success as we start the twenty-first century. Right now there are more than 540,000 franchises in the United States, and the number is growing fast. In fact, the franchise industry seems to thrive regardless of whether the rest of the economy is withering. In 1992, when the economy stumbled, the franchising industry created 20,000 new businesses, which generated a total of 100,000 new jobs. While many other companies were downsizing and closing divisions and branches to help stem the flow of red ink, franchises experienced a 6 to 8 percent growth in revenues.

Franchises work well because both parties benefit from the other's success. To the franchisor, the successful entrepreneur is a source of income. The more successful you are, the more popular and sought after the company's franchises become, and that in turn brings the franchisor more money from higher royalties and from the increased prices he can charge for his franchises.

You, in turn, reap the rewards of the franchisor's success. The bigger the organization grows, the more money it can—and should—spend on long-range planning, product research and development, and the creation of promotions, advertising, and marketing plans. In the long run, all of these can help your individual franchise operation through better products and bigger, more potent name recognition.

Remember—in a nation where businesses come and go, making barely a ripple on Main Street America, much less Wall

Street—name recognition can go a long way toward helping push your business into the black. Just think about McDonald's golden arches. Almost before they can even talk, kids can spot those golden arches miles away and shout out a garbled, toothless "Big Mac." They know that sight—and the name McDonald's—means fast-food satisfaction.

Today, franchises account for fully a third of all retail sales, with annual revenues of more than $760 billion. And if this phenomenal growth rate continues, franchises will account for half of all retail sales by the turn of the century. That's a success rate unbeatable in American business. It might just be your ticket to Gray Wave entrepreneurial success, too.

And you don't have to be a budding shopkeeper to take advantage of the franchise trend. In fact, in today's hectic world, as more and more people opt to pay someone else to perform basic tasks for them, the opportunities for service-based business franchises are exploding. After all, a lot of people need their cars washed, their houses cleaned, and their taxes calculated. These are just a few of the countless service-based franchise business opportunities out there for enterprising entrepreneurs.

Is there a downside to buying a franchise business at this stage in your life? You bet. The biggest negative by far is the price tag. Most franchises, because they come with more backing and support than most businesses, come at a pretty hefty cost. Standard start-up for a Cafe Classico, a European-style café offering gourmet coffees, sandwiches, salads, espresso, and gelato (Italian ice cream), is about $200,000. Cafe Classico is owned by the Baskin-Robbins franchise company and is based in Brea, California.

When you pay that kind of a start-up cost for your franchise, you definitely want to work hard to make sure it succeeds. That probably means working longer and harder than you may envision in your semiretirement mode, unless you cut into your profits by putting others to work in your place. Maybe that'll work for you. But it's something you'll need to look at closely as you draw up your business plan and before you decide to go the franchise route.

There's also the question of who's the boss in a franchise business. Of course, the answer is you, but there are strings involved in owning a franchise business. Through years of trial and error, the franchisor has created a finely tuned business that runs just the way he wants it to. To make sure that you succeed as well, and that you fuel his own success, he'll insist you do certain things his way.

Franchise contracts contain many stipulations on how the business will be run, and you'd better look at that contract very carefully before signing on the dotted line. You don't want to sign away the very autonomy you hope to enjoy in your golden years.

Consider also how you scored on the Gray Wave Entrepreneurial Aptitude Test. If you ranked at the top of the chart as a very highly motivated future entrepreneur, keep in mind that franchising is in some ways the side-door entrance to entrepreneurship. As a franchisee, you aren't really starting a business from scratch, creating something from nothing but an idea in your own head. It can be fulfilling and financially rewarding, but it can't be considered truly creative.

And most important of all for a budding semiretired entrepreneur, most franchise contracts run for a specified number of years, with the minimum usually ten and the average fifteen to twenty. At this stage of your life, that may be longer than you care to commit to.

So before we look at your next option, take out your Gray Wave notebook and start a new section labeled "Business Options." On a fresh sheet of paper list "Franchise Business" as option number one, and jot down your reactions to some of the pros and cons we've discussed in relation to a franchise business.

In chapter 6, I'll detail how to buy and operate the perfect franchise business for a Gray Wave entrepreneur. I'll take you through the process step-by-step. So if you think a franchise business might meet your needs, turn to page 81, and let's get started. On the other hand, why not check out the other options first?

OPERATING A GYPSY RETAIL BUSINESS

Owning and operating your own retail business—your own store—remains one of the best opportunities for an entrepreneur today, as it has practically since human beings first stood up on two feet and started trading.

Think about it. From the very birth of this country there were hunters, there were farmers, and there were traders—the earliest retailers—who bought and resold the goods and services of everyone else. These early retailers were independent-minded pioneers who blazed paths through the heart of the new country, bringing their goods with them in carts and wagons and on their backs.

As settlements grew into villages and small towns and later cities, retailers settled in, too, building impressive shops and stores and even more impressive fortunes for their futures and the futures of their heirs. They put down their business roots in the early or middle stages of their lives, and their solid business establishments were testimony to the strength and soundness of their business skills. Their places of business were themselves advertisements that they were there to stay, invitations to enter into a business relationship with a retailer who wouldn't pack up and disappear overnight.

But you're no longer in the early or even middle stage of your life. You're in a more seasoned stage, facing retirement. And although you want to start a new career as an entrepreneur, and a retail operation sounds exciting, the last thing you want to do is burden yourself with so fixed, immutable, and expensive a structure as a store. For most retailers, the biggest expense item is associated with their place of business—their rent or mortgage.

And that high, fixed building cost means that you have to work longer and harder, and earn more revenue, in order to pay off that rent or mortgage. A fixed place of business carries with it the necessity of a certain level of relentless effort, income, and success.

So what's a Gray Wave wannabe retailer to do? Become a gypsy retailer, of course. A gypsy is a person who wanders, carrying his possessions with him wherever he goes. The country's earliest retailers, those traders who roamed the wilderness with their goods in wagons and on their backs, were gypsies of a sort. They took their goods and services to their customers, maximizing their profits and minimizing their overhead. You can do that, too.

Independent retailers provide an essential service to the community and its members. Your mission as a retailer, regardless of what you're selling, is to provide members of the community, the buying public, with access to goods and services. People pay handsomely for that access in shops in malls and on Main Streets all over the country. Think how happy those busy consumers would be if that access was even more convenient—right in their living rooms, or outside their places of business, or on their beaches or near their school yards.

In today's busy, high-pressure world, people are putting their energy into work and into play, and they don't want to have to work too hard to accomplish the basic necessities of life, like grabbing lunch or buying a bouquet of flowers for dinner with a business associate or picking up a fancy dessert.

As a gypsy retailer you'll have the opportunity to provide customers with better service, greater access, and lower prices simply because you *are* a gypsy retailer and therefore *don't* have a fixed store.

Perhaps even more important, as a Gray Wave gypsy retailer you can provide the perfect antidote to the chilling, numbing sterility of today's impersonal megamalls, superstores, and warehouse clubs. You've lived many years and value human beings. You can talk to people, and better yet, you know how to listen. You know good service and can deliver it with a personal touch, and that's just what you'll be doing as a gypsy retailer.

You'll be bringing the goods—whatever they are—right to your customers, where they need them and want them. You'll provide convenience and service, and at a lower cost than would be possible for such quality at a fixed storefront. And as you do it you will be able to look your customers straight in the eye, smile, shake their hands, and get instant feedback on your product and your delivery. Better yet, you'll be adding just a tiny bit of human contact and warmth to what for many has become a very impersonal way of life. That's something K mart can't compete with.

And here's another plus: A gypsy retail business can provide the perfect outlet for your creative energies, both in terms of your mobile cart or booth and in the range of your stock. So, let your imagination and creativity roll, and you'll see the return at your cash register.

Is there a downside to operating a gypsy retail business? Sure there is. First, we're talking about sales here. And some investment in inventory, which involves risk. It also involves hard work. If you're not out on the street, or at those flea markets selling, forget it. You're just not making sales and you're not making money. It's as simple as that.

And depending on what product you decide to sell, you will have to invest some money in inventory. So, what if you guessed wrong and nobody wants stuffed monkeys this Christmas? Let's face it, if you guess wrong, or don't fully research your market and your product, you could be up the creek and your investment down the drain.

Then there's the question of travel. Depending on how much of a gypsy your business is structured to be, you may have to be on the road a bit. If you decide to set up as a gypsy antiques dealer, for example, you'll probably need to travel from show to show, and that can entail spending a good portion of your time away from home. That could be either a plus or a minus, but chances are those fast-food burgers that come with the itinerant life will wear on your stomach.

And if you decide to set up a gypsy cart outside a busy office building and serve gourmet muffins and hotdogs, you'll have Mother Nature to contend with. And she can be *trés formidable*. She also can cut into your profits with a prolonged spell of bad weather when people won't want to leave their buildings, much less stand in the driving rain waiting for a hotdog.

So right now, before we move on to your next option, take out your notebook, turn to a fresh page, head it ''Gypsy Retail Business,'' and list what you perceive to be the pros and cons of this kind of operation. Then jot down any other thoughts that come to mind.

In chapter 7 I'll give you detailed instructions on how to start a gypsy retail business. I'll take you through the process step-by-step. So if you think a gypsy retail business will suit you just fine, turn to page 115 right now. On the other hand, why not check out the other options first?

STARTING A MOBILE SERVICE BUSINESS

Since the end of World War II, America has been moving from a manufacturing-based economy to a service-based economy. Virtually all of the almost 70 million new jobs created since World War II have sprung from the service industry. And according to experts, almost 90 percent of all jobs will be service-based by the twenty-first century.

The high cost of labor and raw materials crippled the manufacturing industry in this country. And we're just beginning to see the backlash of consumers—sick of the impersonal, antiseptic uniformity of huge superstores—turning to small gypsy retailers. But even gypsy retailers need to buy inventory, and that takes some bucks.

By contrast, a mobile service business—one in which you sell your time, effort, and expertise rather than a specific product, and bring your service directly to your client—is less expensive and easier to start. Your overhead is low because you have no fixed place of business on which to pay rent or a mortgage. You can run your business out of your home and the trunk of your car.

All you really need is yourself, your energy and enthusiasm, a basic skill, and maybe a few simple pieces of equipment. More than ever before, people are willing and eager to pay someone to do for them what they no longer have the time, energy, or expertise to do for themselves.

Think about it—the growth of technology and the birth of the new information age have increased the already frantic pace of life and work for just about everyone. We're all struggling to get ahead and stay there. And in that daily struggle we've learned to make choices about what's important and what's not, about what we need and want to do and what we are willing and able to pay others to do for us.

The perfect Ozzie and Harriet nuclear family that sat down to pot roast at six every evening to share dinner and their stories of the day is dead. Harriet went back to work several years ago to help put little Ricky through college and pay for a vacation in the Bahamas. And dinner is more like take-out Chinese or pizza delivered to the door at eight, when everyone finally has gotten home from work, teams, and lessons.

And that's where your mobile service business could come in. Why should Domino's get all that home-delivered pizza business? Maybe today's Ozzie and Harriet are sick of pizza but still don't have the time to cook for themselves. They'd probably jump at the chance to buy home-cooked meals like Harriet used to make, delivered to their door with a friendly smile three nights a week.

And Ozzie's hardly home weekends, what with his new high-profile job. And when he is he's got his nose buried in his computer. He doesn't have time to wash and clean the car anymore, and he doesn't even want to waste ten minutes taking it through the car wash when he could be watching Ricky scoring on the ice or breezing through the *New York Times Book Review* section.

Ozzie would be happy to pay some conscientious Gray Wave entrepreneur to set up a regular cleaning and maintenance schedule for his two cars, so he can just put the whole thing out of his mind and concentrate on that report he's got to write.

The possibilities are endless for enterprising Gray Wave entrepreneurs who are ready and eager to start a mobile service business. Almost everything that needs doing around your home and yard and for your personal possessions can be turned into a service that you do for others all over your town and county.

These are not the kinds of businesses that are necessarily going to lead to fortunes or megabucks empires. But that's not what you're looking for at this stage of your life anyway, remember? The kind of reduced need and reduced expectation you feel as a semiretired future Gray Wave entrepreneur is very freeing. When your whole livelihood isn't riding on the outcome of your new business idea, you can give it a try and just enjoy the extra bucks it brings, as well as the social interaction with friends, neighbors, and (ultimately) clients.

And that's just the start. The nationwide trend in corporate and business downsizing that has reduced workforces and left thousands without full-time jobs also has created opportunities for ambitious would-be entrepreneurs. Large corporations are balancing the books by cutting the payroll and filling in the gaps with part-time or temporary workers who can perform specific skills as needed. These companies realize it's cheaper to employ someone part-time, or hire an independent contractor—which is what you would be as an entrepreneur with a mobile service business—than it is to pay for a full-time employee with costly benefits.

The opportunities and ideas for starting a mobile service business are endless in today's highly specialized, high-stress, frenetic world. And the more specialized, competitive, and fast-paced the world becomes, the more opportunities open for a Gray Wave entrepreneur like you.

So, what's the downside to this? Frankly, you're on your own on that one. I can't think of any way to lose by starting a mobile service business. Unless, of course, you are totally, completely unrealistic and come up with a service that absolutely no one wants. So to avoid that remote possibility, turn to your Gray Wave notebook, sharpen your pencil again, and label a new page "Mobile Service Business."

First, list all the plusses. List any negatives you can dream up in addition to the one above. Then, do two things. First, list all the tasks people need to accomplish, big and little, in a day, a month, a year. Everything from doing the dishes to twice-a-year silver polishing to weekly grocery shopping. Get creative; be exhaustive. See how long a list you can create.

Second, put a check next to some of those tasks you wouldn't mind doing for other people. For each task, calculate roughly how much time it would take to do that task for a single client, then how much you could reasonably charge that client for that task. Keep figuring. How many such jobs would you need each week to make the level of income you want to make? Finally, is it worth it to you? Are you willing to do this kind of job, for that much time, for this amount of money? Only you can answer that.

In chapter 8 I'll tell you exactly how to start a mobile service business. I'll take you through the process step-by-step. So if you're sure you want to start a mobile service business, turn to page 141 right now. On the other hand, why not check out the other options first?

ESTABLISHING A HOME-BASED CONSULTING BUSINESS

More and more Americans of all ages are working at home. Some have been displaced from business and corporate workplaces by the trend toward downsizing, but many others are choosing to work at home as a deliberate lifestyle choice. And the new age of high-tech but affordable personal computers and easy-to-access information technology has made such choices not only possible but the smartest option in many cases.

In a sense, those working at home today have come full circle, back to the preindustrial age in this country, when just about everyone worked at home. It was a time when life and work were intertwined and centered around the home, rather than being split into two separate and often competing existences.

One of the chief sources of satisfaction for the worker in those days was that he controlled his own work environment and his destiny. And that's exactly what many are looking for today when they choose to work at home. Particularly when they become home-based entrepreneurs. And as a future Gray Wave entrepreneur, that's exactly what you're looking for: control over your work environment and your destiny.

You're not alone. According to Link Resources, a technology-research company, the total number of Americans who work at least part of the time at home, for themselves or for someone else, rose to almost 45 million in 1994 from fewer than 25 million in 1987.

And many of those working at home have become consultants. Consultants provide professional advice and services to businesses and consumers. You don't have to be an expert in your field to be a consultant, but you do have to know how to find answers and solve problems. But for someone of your years of experience in your field, that shouldn't be a problem, right?

Clearly, there's money to be made, and creative energy and skills to be tapped, with a home-based consulting business. According to a recent article in *The Wall Street Journal,* income from part-time home-based consulting businesses has zoomed from just over $6 million in 1989 to about $10.5 million in 1995. And consulting itself is a $17-billion-a-year business today.

As is the case with a mobile service business, a home-based consulting business—operated by an experienced, well-seasoned Gray Wave entrepreneur—can fill a gap created by the corporate housecleaning and lifestyle trends sweeping the country today. As the statistics cited earlier show, a multitude of businesses, large and moderately sized, have lost key skills, knowledge, experience, and services in the past ten years. Some of what they've lost, you've got. And that inventory of yours is stored in a convenient place—in your brain, not in an expensive warehouse.

The advantages of operating a home-based consulting business are obvious. Working at home reduces your overhead considerably while giving you maximum control over your working environment. You also can say farewell forever to the frazzle and stress of commuting. And depending on how you prefer to structure your time, if your office is in your home you can cut the frustrating downtime every consultant experiences while waiting for calls to be returned or reports and proposals to be approved. Instead, you can put that downtime to work in your garden or at other tasks around your home.

There are tax benefits as well. For most of us, our home already is our biggest investment and biggest tax-saving device. A well-designed and well-operated home-based business can enhance those tax savings considerably.

There are some disadvantages to working at home. If one of your goals in starting a retirement business is to assure yourself regular daily contact with people, working at home might not work for you. In a home-based consulting business, most of your contact with people may end up being electronic—via E-mail, the telephone, or the fax.

And if you work best in a structured setting with set hours, and prefer to keep your work life and your leisure time separate to do justice to each, you could be in trouble (although that problem can be solved with some self-discipline and a detailed daily planner and schedule).

Before you go further down the road to a home-based consulting business, you should assess whether this option is right for you. So get out your Gray Wave notebook and start another clean page labeled "Home-Based Consulting Business." Jot down the pros and cons we have discussed, adding more personal and specific ones as they relate to you.

Next, write a paragraph or two describing your work history and defining your skills and fields of knowledge. List what specific tasks you can perform and can train others to perform. Then answer these questions: What kinds of problems can you solve for businesses and/or consumers? Do you think there's a market for this kind of skill and knowledge? Who might your clients be?

Chances are there are far more possibilities here than even the most creative of you have come up with. So if you're still interested in home-based consulting after that little exercise, I'll give you step-by-step guidance in chapter 9. You can turn to page 168 to get started. But first, why not check out one last option?

BUYING AN EXISTING BUSINESS

By now you're probably asking yourself: Why not just buy an existing business? Why should I go through all these hassles, jump all these hurdles? Why don't I just save myself some steps and some headaches and buy somebody else's business?

Good question. And the answer is that you *can* save yourself some headaches and take a reasonable shortcut by buying an existing business. On the other hand, you also may be buying yourself additional headaches—someone else's headaches—the likes of which you have never known.

And depending on how you scored on the Gray Wave Entrepreneurial Aptitude Test, this option may not quite fill the creative, inventive urge of the hard-core, baseline, budding entrepreneur. After all, you would *not* be starting a business from scratch. But you *would* be your own boss, running your own business on your own terms. And that can be just as satisfying for some Gray Wave entrepreneurs.

So while it doesn't fit the classic picture of an entrepreneur, buying an existing business does have definite advantages. It's certainly less risky than starting a business from scratch. And you'll start ringing up sales or bringing in clients, and therefore realizing profits, quicker. You'll get a faster return on your initial investments of time and money.

An existing business also has a track record, a customer base, inventory, location, equipment, name recognition, business and marketing plans, and staff. All you have to do is sign on the dotted line, dig into your pockets, and in one transaction you can step into the owner's shoes.

Of course, all of those positives could just as easily turn out to be negatives. The business's track record may be abysmal—after all, the guy wants to sell, right? Maybe the inventory is dated and the equipment's falling apart. The location may be slated for purgatory when the highway's realigned next year. And depending on the business skills of the current owner, that name recognition may be mud.

But the perfect opportunity might be out there on the market, waiting to fall into your lap. So just to cover your bases, take a stroll through the businesses-for-sale ads in your local and regional newspapers. In your Gray Wave notebook, make a list of anything that catches your eye as a possible prospect. You might also call some real estate agents to see what they have listed; many businesses that are for sale never make it to the want ads but are snapped up before that by smart, aggressive entrepreneurs.

And keep in mind: If a business catches your eye but isn't on the market, you may be able to convince the owner it's time to sell, even if she's never thought about it.

Before you proceed any further down this road, you'll want to read chapter 10 of this book to insure that you make the right purchase with the right terms—terms that will go a long way to assuring your success.

But first, read about Rosie Cordera and learn a bit more about the right—and wrong—way to proceed.

HERE'S WHAT HAPPENED TO ROSIE CORDERA

Rosie Cordera now says she probably was suffering from the same sickness that afflicted many Vietnam veterans when they returned from the war—post-traumatic stress syndrome. Rosie, fifty-five, had been a winner all her life—and the family's main breadwinner by a long shot during her marriage. Until she became another casualty in the corporate downsizing war being waged across America today.

Rosie and her husband, Marcus, had their two children late, when Rosie was thirty-eight and forty, partly because of a fertility problem that needed medical attention and partly because early on they had decided to follow Rosie's career as a graphic artist as far as it would take them. And it took them pretty far. Not only was Rosie a talented artist, she was also very smart, very good with people, a natural leader, and pretty astute politically.

With that mix, you guessed it, she didn't remain in the rank-and-file very long. Early on in her career, Rosie had joined a company that published a growing collection of craft and hobby magazines in the Northeast. As the company added new products to fill new reader niches, Rosie rose through the ranks, and by age fifty-five she was director of graphic design for the relatively small but still-growing company. Her salary, including annual bonus, had just hit six figures.

And while many people her age were beginning to think about retirement, Rosie's children were just getting ready for college at ages seventeen and fifteen. The family definitely needed her full income—at least—to put the kids through college and maintain their standard of living, which was quite nice, if not deluxe.

Marcus was an artist, too, a painter, and they had agreed at the beginning of their relationship that Rosie would be the career-builder while Marcus would dedicate himself to his painting. His paintings sold, too, sporadically, but they had faith that someday his art would be worth a fortune and Marcus would be famous. Over the years, he also tended bar part-time to help make ends meet.

The boom fell when a larger, nationally based publishing company bought out Rosie's company. Rosie was one of those at the higher-paying end of the salary scale who was told her services were no longer needed. Her vision, she was told, didn't fit with the long-term vision of her new employer—although its representatives had never had the courtesy of asking her just what her vision was. Her artistic approach was dated, they said, which really ticked her off, since she had constantly argued with her boss about redesigning and updating the magazines' look.

So Rosie was on the street with six months' severance, eight years of college tuition ahead, and no savings to speak of. She and Marcus lived up to and even a bit beyond their income. She needed to find work and find it fast, but she was bitter and demoralized and downright determined never to work for anyone else ever again. Not ever. She decided to become an entrepreneur. She started looking around for a business to buy, knowing she could use the severance and get some additional financing from family, if necessary. Better, she said, she wanted something she could continue running when the kids finished college and she was able to semiretire.

The first business she heard about, by word of mouth, was a franchise mailing and packaging business on the north end of town near the mall. The business, owned by an older couple who both were having health problems, was on the downslide. They had reduced the price and almost sold it a couple of times, but each time the deal fell through for one reason or another. They were getting sicker, less able to work, and, frankly, desperate. They even were willing to a hold a mortgage in the deal if necessary.

A friend of a friend had looked at it and thought it seemed like a great deal, but had decided to stick with his own field—insurance. Rosie, never one to waste time, liked the sound of it and decided to charge ahead. Within days she and Marcus had looked at the business, examined the books, hired a lawyer and an accountant to help them investigate even closer, and talked to Rosie's father about a loan. Rosie was ready to sign.

That's when Marcus stepped in with a reality check. "Rosie, look at you. You're five-foot-two, a hundred and ten pounds, and an artist, even if you have been mostly a manager the past ten years. You'd hate this work," he said. "It's backbreaking, boring as hell—nothing but wrapping and packing boxes of all shapes and sizes—and you'd be working alone. You'd be totally tied to the shop. You'd have no life."

Her father joined in the chorus. It wasn't that he was unwilling to lend them the money, but like Marcus, he could see that Rosie was ready to leap at the first business she had stumbled over out of desperation and defiance, not because it was right for her or even, necessarily, a viable operation.

Rosie kicked and screamed, argued and sulked, said her life was over and it didn't matter what she did anymore, as long as she made money. That's about the time the accountant called her and told her about another business for sale but not yet on the market. The accountant said he had called her, although he knew she was still debating the packaging business, because this one sounded so much like her—a small but exclusive decorating business in the plush part of town.

"You don't really have to be a decorator," the accountant assured her. "All you have to have is good taste, an eye for color and design—you're selling the best in wall coverings, drapes, carpeting, and some specialty furniture items which people can't buy anyplace else in this area. You'd love it. Just take a look."

To make a long story short, Rosie took a look, met the fashionable woman who owned the business and had run it as a part-time hobby for her wealthy acquaintances, and fell in love. It really was love at first sight. Rosie remembered the minute she walked into the small, beautifully decorated shop how she had spent hours as a young girl dreaming about being an interior decorator and drawing room after room with multicolored pencils and pasting on bits of fabric and wood.

The deal isn't signed yet, but Rosie and Marcus have been taking this one slower, looking very carefully into the books and into the market potential. After all, Rosie doesn't have a closet full of rich friends, but she does have the goodwill of the already established client base and a lot of ideas about widening the target market without losing the exclusive look.

It looks as if she and Marcus will go for it, and Rosie is bubbling with anticipation again. She realizes now that she was ready to leap too soon with the packaging business, that it wasn't right for her at all.

"This one, though, is a perfect fit. It's me. I feel it in my bones," she said recently. "But I'm not going to let my heart alone rule me on this one, either," she added.

"We're doing it right. We're doing a whole business plan— the operation needs to be computerized, for example—before we take another step. I'm not in such a rush anymore. This business is going to last me well into my retirement years," she said with a big smile.

SO WHERE DO YOU GO FROM HERE?

By now you've diagnosed that you're suffering from RPRS, and you're already on the road to recovery. You've taken the Gray Wave Entrepreneurial Aptitude Test and have figured out that for you the correct prescription is to become a Gray Wave entrepreneur. In this chapter we've outlined five sound and exciting business options that can spell success and years of satisfaction for an ambitious and hardworking Gray Wave entrepreneur.

The next part of this book, "Get Down to (Your Retirement) Business!" will offer detailed instructions on how to proceed with planning and launching each of the five business options discussed above. I'll give you tips, do's and don'ts, and lists of additional resource materials appropriate for each option. I'll also list ideas for specific businesses that are perfect for the twenty-first century Gray Wave entrepreneur. You can simply steal them, adapt them as you like for your own use, or use them as a starting point to get your own ideas flowing.

Before you finally start narrowing your choices, you'll want to be sure the business format you choose matches your person-ality traits. Think about it. By this stage in your life, you know yourself pretty well. And the tests you've taken earlier in this book have helped to refresh your memory about yourself, your likes and dislikes, your strengths and weaknesses.

If you're a real people person who thrives on interacting and socializing with people every single day, a gypsy retail or mo-bile service business would suit you fine. You'd probably wither with a home-based consulting business. If you're a straightforward, no-nonsense management type, but not very creative or flexible, think about buying a franchise or an existing independent business. You probably wouldn't feel comfortable or have much flair as a gypsy retailer. And if you're really something of a stay-at-home and don't like having to deal with people on a daily basis, a home-based consulting business would be perfect for you.

So be realistic about matching your future business's personality with your own. It's kind of like a good marriage. While a union of opposites has been known to work, experts agree that the chances of success are greater in a marriage where some key personality traits are shared.

By now you may have decided which business option is best for you. In that case, you can turn directly to the appropriate chapter. But in all fairness, you would be doing yourself a disservice if you failed to at least thumb quickly through the other chapters. I can guarantee that if you do, you will find some nuggets—some tips and suggestions—that will be helpful in your own type of venture as well.

And if you're still not quite certain which business structure is the right one for you, read each of the following chapters carefully. For many people, several of these business structures can work. As you read the details describing each business start-up your ultimate choice will become clear. So grab your Gray Wave notebook and a handful of pencils. The final path to your successful Gray Wave entrepreneurial future starts here.

II.

GET DOWN TO
(YOUR RETIREMENT)
BUSINESS!

⊰❦6❦⊱

HOW TO BUY A FRANCHISE BUSINESS

A franchise business is a very smart choice for some semi-retired Gray Wave entrepreneurs. In today's fast-paced world a franchise gives you a head start on launching a proven business operation. Since you don't have to start from scratch, you minimize your risk right from the starting gate. You also minimize your start-up time.

A franchise is a mutually beneficial financial partnership between a large organization and an independent entrepreneur. The large organization—the franchisor—sells you—the franchisee—the right to conduct business using the organization's name, products, business plan and procedures, trademarks, marketing strategies, advertising, and other factors that set the business apart from others of its kind. All that business planning and process is done *for* you.

THE ADVANTAGES OF FRANCHISING

With a franchise business, you can take your years of business savvy and life-honed managerial skills and apply them to a pre-packaged business with a track record of success. Even better, you don't have to go it alone. You've got a partner with plenty of business muscle standing right behind you, ready to guide you past the potholes that can beset any new business venture.

When you buy a sound franchise, you're buying a share of success. The parent company is structured to assure your success.

81

In fact, the franchisor is selling you the formula that made her a success in the first place and works closely with you to help translate that formula into your own prescription for success.

So what is it about franchises that assure success? There are three main elements to most successful franchises. The first is a well-established identity, which brings name recognition. Everyone recognizes Burger King, Pizza Hut, Hertz, Dairy Queen, and Agway, to name just a few. The second element is a carefully orchestrated, finely tuned business format that has proven successful in different markets. The third is a long-term financial partnership with the franchisor. Usually the franchisee makes a lump sum payment to the franchisor at the start of the relationship, then makes ongoing royalty payments based on a percentage of the business's gross sales.

The franchisor makes money by letting you in on her good idea—for that initial franchise fee and for the continuing percentage of your profits. Many franchisors also make money by selling franchisees their own lines of products and supplies.

In return for your investment you get a prefabricated, fast-track business that offers a service or product in proven demand, a high-octane identity, and a supercharged marketing strategy. The franchisor also provides training. Many will help you select a prime location. And a third of all franchisors are willing to provide some financing. With this kind of arrangement, each party stands to benefit from the other's success. It's a win-win prescription.

THE DISADVANTAGES OF FRANCHISING

You're probably wondering why, if a franchise is such a dynamite idea, I don't end this book with this chapter. That's because there are plenty of downsides to buying a franchise business, especially for a Gray Waver. Those downsides include:

THE COST

When you buy any franchise business you pay an initial franchise fee and then make royalty payments based on your gross sales. That franchise fee varies greatly, depending on what business you buy. But be forewarned: The better-known franchises are extremely pricey.

Take a look at the most popular franchise businesses, restaurants. Full-service restaurants are the most expensive, with a TGI Friday's, for example, requiring liquid capital of $1 million and net worth of from $3 million to $5 million. The initial price tag for a Perkins Family Restaurant is $250,000 cash and almost $2 million for total project costs.

Smaller fast-food operations, like an Arby's, are more reasonable, costing $100,000 to $200,000 in start-up cash and a total price tag of $550,000 to $850,000. A real bargain may be Subway Sandwiches and Salads, which only requires an investment of $48,000 to $81,000.

So if you've got a lot of extra cash collecting dust or even an uninspired rate of interest, try a franchise. If not, think again.

THE COMMITMENT

This may be the biggest drawback for a Gray Waver. Most franchisors require a long-term commitment. I know you're committed to hard work—you wouldn't have read this far if you weren't. But are you committed to ten or twenty years of hard work? At your age, you may not want to make that kind of long-term legal commitment.

And if you have any notion of a semiretired existence as an entrepreneur, forget buying a franchise. You just won't be able to run one part-time. The franchisor wants the franchise to generate the maximum income, so she'll want it open as many hours as possible. You can work part-time in the franchise as long as that's approved by the franchisor, but it still will have to be open. So you'll have to get someone else to run it when you're not there.

Remember, the franchisor looks on her franchises as little cash cows. She wants a franchisee who works long, hard hours and who is eager to make a long-term commitment to keep that cash coming in with minimum fuss and bother to her.

THE LACK OF AUTONOMY

The franchisor has carefully crafted and fine-tuned her little cash cows over the years and has them running just the way she wants them. To insure your success, as well as her own, she'll insist you do things her way. And don't forget, that's why you want to buy her franchise in the first place—because it's a great business.

But franchise agreements contain many stipulations on how the business will be run, right down to a dress code in some cases. Do you really want someone else to have the right to tell you how to run your own business?

THE POSSIBLE TREACHERY

Franchises are big business, and many people are trying to make a buck out of them today. Some are plain dishonest, so be careful.

You've got some protection. Today the Federal Trade Commission requires that franchisors provide a potential franchisee with a written disclosure statement that details certain kinds of information. In addition, many states have their own disclosure requirements. Disclosures are designed to protect you, but ultimately you have to protect yourself.

A FRANCHISE COULD BE JUST RIGHT FOR YOU

Now, get out your Gray Wave notebook and list the franchise pros and cons. But to thine own self be true. That means you have to weigh those pros and cons against who and what you are and what you honestly want to be in the next decade or so of your life.

Frankly, a franchise business will work best for a Gray Waver on the younger side of the wave—maybe one taking an early "retirement." If you want to buy an income and have the resources to do it; if you want to stay quite active; if you're healthy and have a high energy level; if you really aren't very creative; and if you don't mind another businessperson meddling in your business, a franchise might be just right for you. But it *must* be the *right* franchise. More about that later.

WHAT'S AVAILABLE?

So what's available for the future Gray Wave franchisee? The answer is: Just about anything. It's almost impossible to find an industry today that doesn't have some franchised companies. So whatever your interests and skills, you can bet a franchise opportunity is out there waiting for you.

Franchises now account for more than a third of all retail sales and will account for more than half by the year 2000. When that happens, America's franchises will be earning more than a trillion dollars a year in sales.

Those megasales will be spread over a multitude of industries, but two of the hottest franchise businesses are restaurants and convenience stores. Let's take a quick look at them.

RESTAURANTS TAKE A BIG BITE OF THE FRANCHISE BUSINESS

More than 40 percent of the people employed by franchises work in restaurants, and they ring up sales of nearly $100 billion a year. Although there's plenty of competition for those bucks, there's still plenty of opportunity as well, especially for the right specialty product for just the right market.

Today, McDonald's has more than 10,000 restaurants around the world, including more than sixty foreign countries. More than 500 new restaurants are opened each year. Company sales top $20 billion, and each restaurant averages more than $1 million a year in sales. Ninety-six percent of Americans eat at McDonald's at least once every year. Every day 7 percent of the population eats under the golden arches.

The McDonald's concept was such a successful sales machine that copycat fast-food chains mushroomed, selling everything from pizza to chicken to tacos and subs.

But fast food isn't the only segment of the food industry with successful franchises. There's Friendly's, the Ground Round, Ponderosa, TGI Friday's, and Perkins Family Restaurant, to name a few. All offer full-service, sit-down dining in a casual, family-oriented atmosphere. Each has its own gimmick or theme, but they're all franchises, and as such, all of their restaurants have the same menus, look, and general quality as the others in the chain.

CONVENIENCE STORE FRANCHISES ARE BIG, TOO

There's no question convenience stores ring up big sales, precisely because they're convenient. Annual sales have averaged 4 to 5 percent growth in recent years and now exceed $16 billion. The number of stores also has increased at about the same rate.

Perhaps the biggest advantage of a convenience store franchise is the outlook for the future. You can count on consumers of the twenty-first century to be as sold on convenience as consumers are today. You can also count on harried businessmen and businesswomen, who are trying to care for families while getting ahead, to forget some basic necessities when they do their weekly grocery shopping. That means a well-operated franchise convenience store, designed to provide customers' basic needs twenty-four hours a day, seven days a week, will continue to thrive.

Convenience stores serve a clearly defined market niche. The average convenience store provides the basics, such as milk, bread, soda, beer, cigarettes, pretzels, toilet paper, paper towels, toothpaste, lightbulbs, Pop-Tarts, disposable diapers, a ham sandwich, and coffee. And in many cases, of course, that very basic necessity, lottery tickets. As with restaurant franchise menus, the inventory is dependable—you know pretty much what you're going to find when you enter the front door.

BUT, HOLD ON A MINUTE

Don't leap too soon. While restaurant and convenience store franchises are extremely popular, they really aren't good bets for Gray Wave entrepreneurs.

Think about it. Restaurants are among the most labor-intensive businesses out there. And the most competitive. You certainly can't run one part-time, and to be assured it runs properly you need to be there yourself during business hours or hire a very reliable, energetic manager (then watch closely over his or her shoulder). A restaurant franchise is not ideal for this time in your life, when you're looking for a more relaxed business that can be part of your retirement, not end it altogether.

The same is true of convenience stores. While they certainly require fewer employees, they're open 24 hours a day. If a clerk decides to call in sick at 2 a.m. on Christmas morning, chances are you'll have to fill in. Is that your idea of a retirement business? It sure isn't mine.

MATCH THE TRENDS TO YOUR OWN NEEDS

So forget restaurants and convenience stores. Instead, consider the demographic, lifestyle, and workplace trends I cited earlier. It's clear that in the coming years—into the twenty-first century—service-based franchise businesses will flourish.

Remember, our lives are becoming ever more fast-paced, more specialized, and more compartmentalized. In order to succeed, and even just to survive, people are making lifestyle choices that impact their daily lives. They're assigning priorities to basic, everyday tasks. They're doing only what they absolutely need or want to do. Everything else—everything they can afford and are willing to have others do for them—they're paying to have done. That's a growing range of service business franchisors, and franchisees are cashing in.

Service business franchises are available in many different formats offering a variety of work style and workplace configurations. Some require storefronts, some work successfully from your home, and some can be operated quite effectively from the back of your automobile.

The key is to find exactly the right franchise for you. You want to find the franchise that offers the right workplace format for you, matching demographic trends to your own needs. All of the options have plusses and minuses, depending on your personality, your interests, your location, the market, and a million other factors. Some require a number of employees; others don't. Some are targeted toward specific age or interest groups. Some require very physical labor; some are purely desk jobs.

The first thing you need to do before you check out the list of business options below is to pull out your Gray Wave notebook and turn to your answers to "Questions to Ask Yourself" in chapter 3. Refresh your memory about how you defined your ideal future work environment. As you consider each industry, look at the answers to those questions and weigh what you learned about yourself—your likes, dislikes, and goals for the future—against the needs of that industry.

HERE'S A LIST OF POSSIBLE FRANCHISE CHOICES

All of these fields have possibilities for the ambitious Gray Wave entrepreneur.

Accounting

Advertising

Automobile/truck rentals

Automotive products/services

Beverages

Bookstores

Business broker

Business services

Campgrounds

Children's services

Cleaning services

Clothing and shoes

Computers

Construction/restoration services

Cosmetics

Dating services

Dental centers

Drugstores

Educational products/services

Electronic products

Employment services

Financial services

Fire protection

Florist shops

Food (retail)

Formal wear rental

Hair salons/services

Health aids/services

Home appliances

Home furnishings

Home inspection

Hotels/motels

Insurance

Janitorial services

Jewelry

Laundry/dry cleaning

Lawn/garden supplies

Maid services

Maintenance services

Optical aids/services

Package preparation/shipment

Painting services

Pest-control services

Pet sales/supplies

Photography and supplies

Printing services

Publications

Radon detection

Real estate sales

Recreation equipment

Recreation services

Recycling services

Rental services

Retail merchandising

Security systems

Sign products/services

Tailoring

Tax services

Telecommunications

Tools/hardware

Transportation services

Travel agencies

Video rentals

Vitamins/nutritional supplements

Water conditioning

Weight control

START NARROWING YOUR FRANCHISE OPTIONS

Now look at the list again and ask yourself the following questions. Jot down your responses in your notebook.

WOULD I ENJOY WORKING IN THIS INDUSTRY?

Look at the service or product you'd be selling. Is it something you'd be content to deal with every day?

DOES IT FIT MY LIFESTYLE?

Check off which industries would accommodate the lifestyle and work environment you want for yourself in your golden years, and cross the others right off the list.

WOULD MY TALENTS, SKILLS AND PREVIOUS EXPERIENCE BE OF ANY USE IN THIS INDUSTRY?

Experience in a certain field or business certainly helps, but life experience and maturity can somewhat make up for a lack of experience.

CHECK OUT POSSIBLE CANDIDATES

Once you've chosen your industry or industries, select a list of franchise candidates. If you need help coming up with your candidates, here are some good places to look.

THE FRANCHISE OPPORTUNITIES GUIDE

Published annually by the International Franchise Association (IFA), the *Franchise Opportunities Guide* is an excellent resource. The guide provides general information on franchising, including some of the legal questions you should ask before you buy, the self-evaluations you need to undergo, and a list of lending sources that might be able to help you finance your franchise purchase.

For the potential franchisee, however, the most useful part of the guide is its comprehensive listing of more than 2,500 franchise companies in seventy industries.

The *Franchise Opportunities Guide* sells for $15 and is available at more than 7,500 bookstores and newsstands throughout the United States. You can also order it as well as all other IFA publications—by calling the IFA at 1-800-543-1038 or faxing 412-772-5281.

THE FRANCHISE ANNUAL

A handbook and directory of nearly 5,000 franchise companies around the world. Its most complete listings are for the United States and Canada. It also includes the franchise disclosure rule required by the Federal Trade Commission, preparation of a disclosure statement, franchisee profiles, and state regulations. The publication costs $39.95, including shipping and handling, and can be ordered from Info Franchise News, 728 Center Street, Box 550, Lewiston, NY 14092-0550. Or call 716-754-4669.

THE SOURCEBOOK OF FRANCHISE OPPORTUNITIES

An annual publication that provides one of the most reliable and up-to-date compilations of available franchises. The cost is

$35, and it can be ordered from Business One Irwin, 1818 Ridge Road, Homewood, IL 60430. Or call 1-800-634-3966.

Once you've compiled a list of possible franchises you need to start investigating your candidates.

The relationship you're about to embark on will be very important to your future success, so you need to thoroughly investigate the franchisors on your list. Be sure you and your franchisor are compatible. Start a new section of your Gray Wave notebook, and keep detailed notes on the research you're going to be conducting. Here's what you need to do.

RESEARCH THE FRANCHISOR

Is the Franchisor Someone You Like and Trust?

Follow your instincts. Also check out the franchisor's reputation with other franchisees and with people who deal with the franchisor.

Is the Franchisor in Good Financial Shape?

Ask for audited records of the company's profit and loss statements, annual reports, and other financial documents.

Do You Share the Franchisor's Business Philosophy?

Ask for the company's mission statement or a statement of philosophy. Be sure you agree with the way customers should be treated and business conducted.

Is the Franchisor Involved in Any Litigation?

Is the franchisor being sued or suing anyone? If so, you might want to be cautious.

How Long Has the Franchisor Been in Business?

Remember, you're looking for a track record, established and tried business procedures, and name recognition, so you want a franchisor that has at least one or more of those. Longevity means the franchisor is doing something right.

DO YOU HAVE CONFIDENCE IN THE FRANCHISOR'S ABILITY TO DEVELOP NEW PRODUCTS OR SERVICES?

The parent company will be responsible for coming up with new products, so a good research-and-development unit is important for your future. Make sure your franchisor is open to new ideas.

DOES THE FRANCHISOR HAVE A GOOD TRACK RECORD FOR SUPPORTING FRANCHISEES, OR IS IT MORE INTERESTED IN SELLING NEW FRANCHISES?

DOES THE FRANCHISOR HAVE A GOOD REPUTATION IN THE INDUSTRY AND IN THE BUSINESS COMMUNITY?

Ask around. Talk to the customers, bankers, and suppliers. Check with the Better Business Bureau and the Chamber of Commerce. (Call the National Council of Better Business Bureaus at 703-276-0100 and the U.S. Chamber of Commerce at 202-659-6000 for specific area numbers.)

INVESTIGATE THE FRANCHISE SYSTEM

Your franchisor has developed a system that has worked for others. If you buy into it, it will guide your day-to-day operations, too. You need to check it out thoroughly and be sure that you can work within that system.

HOW LONG DOES THE FRANCHISOR REQUIRE A FRANCHISEE TO CONTRACT FOR?

At your age, this is extremely important. You want to be sure you can live happily with the length of the franchise contract. If you're not certain, see if your franchisor is willing to negotiate a shorter term or an easy buyout clause.

How Can You Get Out of the Business?

The franchise agreement will spell out the conditions under which both you and your franchisor can terminate the franchise contract. Make sure you understand what your options are. In addition, most states have laws governing when a franchisor can terminate a contract. Those laws override anything in your contract, so ask your lawyer about them.

How Many Hours a Week Will You Have to Devote to the Business?

You need to know exactly what this business will require of you and to weigh that against what you already have determined you want for your semiretirement lifestyle. It could be a terrible mistake now to say, "What the hell, I can do that," if it contradicts your earlier inclinations. You're in the heat of battle now, and that can be energizing, but keep the long haul in view.

Are the Company and Its Franchisees Members of Reputable Franchise Associations?

If the company is a member of the IFA it means the owner has, at least in theory, demonstrated a responsible commitment to good business practices. Also find out if the company's franchises are affiliated with the American Association of Franchisees and Dealers or the American Franchise Association. These organizations act as advocates for franchise owners.

Have the Company's Franchisees Formed an Association or Advisory Committee?

That would be a healthy sign that they're concerned about each other's best interests and are willing and able to work together for the common good.

How Many Other Franchises Already Exist and How Many Are Company-Owned?

Most franchise companies operate their own units as well as selling them to franchisees. If most of your franchisor's units are company-owned, are the franchised ones getting fair treatment?

DO YOU KNOW THE BACKGROUNDS OF THE EXECUTIVES IN THE PARENT COMPANY AND FEEL A RAPPORT WITH THEM?

You aren't going to be happy having to work with people you dislike or don't trust. Try to get to know the executives and others you'll be dealing with in the parent company to be sure the relationship will work. Check into their backgrounds.

DOES THE PARENT COMPANY PROVIDE INITIAL AND ONGOING TRAINING?

The franchise offering circular should tell you what to expect in terms of training, but it's not a contract. Some franchisees have found to their dismay that the training they actually received was not what they had been led to expect. So be sure your contract spells out the training program clearly.

DO YOU HAVE TO BUY YOUR SUPPLIES FROM THE FRANCHISOR?

Make sure you have the option to use your own vendors. Some dishonest franchisors will make you buy exclusively from them at a huge markup.

DOES THE COMPANY PURCHASE IN BULK AND PASS THE SAVINGS ON TO ITS FRANCHISEES?

This is one of the advantages of buying a franchise in a large company: You can save a lot of money through the parent company's bulk purchases, provided some of the savings are passed along to you.

DO YOU HAVE ANY CHOICE IN THE SERVICES YOU OFFER OR THE PRODUCTS YOU SELL?

Of course, you'll have to conform to the basic company pattern in your products and services—that's why you were interested in the franchise to begin with. But consumer tastes vary from place to place, and you want to be sure you can take advantage of market trends.

Are There Opportunities for Expansion?

If there's any chance you might decide to go wild with your new career and open additional franchises, let your franchisor know early. Find out if there are other multiunit franchisees and whether you get first crack at new franchises.

What Are the Terms for Renewal or Termination of the Franchise Contract?

Most franchise contracts are for a fixed period of time. Find out under what terms it can be renewed or cut short.

How Many Franchisees Have Failed or Left the Company and Why?

Part of the answer will be in the franchise disclosure form the franchisor must give you. If the Uniform Franchise Offering Circular format is used, it will tell you exactly how many franchisees left the company, whether voluntarily or involuntarily, during the previous three years. If the Federal Trade Commission format is used, it will provide figures from only the previous year.

If You're Buying an Existing Franchise, Find Out Why It's for Sale.

Are there any hidden problems?

What Are Your Options If You Want to Sell the Franchise?

Most franchisors put strict restrictions on how their franchises can change hands. Many will stipulate that they get first crack at it—for the same price and under the same conditions you would sell it to anyone else. Or you may need to get the franchisor to approve any buyer you find.

TALK WITH OTHER FRANCHISEES IN THE COMPANY.

This is just common sense, but so are most good business practices. Take the time to seek out and interview other franchisees about their relationship with the franchisor and whether they have found it helpful or problematic.

EXAMINE THE COSTS

HOW MUCH IS THE FRANCHISE FEE?

This is a onetime fee that gives you the right to do business using the franchisor's name, business system, trademark, and products or service. Find out how the fee is determined and what expenses are included.

WHAT ARE THE START-UP COSTS AND WORKING CAPITAL REQUIREMENTS?

Start-up costs are all the expenses related to opening the business except the franchise fee. They include deposits and rent for your location, inventory and equipment, fees and licenses, and even the invitations to your opening day reception. Working capital is the amount of cash your franchisor expects you to keep on hand for running the business. That varies greatly from business to business, but at a minimum is several thousand dollars.

WHAT ARE THE ROYALTY FEES?

Most franchisors charge from 3 to 9 percent of gross sales per month, and you should consider it just one more business expense, like your rent. Check that the fee your franchisor charges is in line with others in the industry. And if your franchisor wants to tack on another percentage point or two for advertising, make sure it's not for a campaign elsewhere in the country.

ESTIMATE HOW MUCH MONEY YOU CAN MAKE

This won't be easy, because while federal law requires the franchisor to give you a detailed disclosure document at the start, there's no requirement that the franchisor tell you how much you can expect to make. In fact, only about 15 percent of franchisors volunteer that information.

LOOK AT THE DISCLOSURE DOCUMENT.

The franchisor must include audited financial statements in the disclosure document. Those figures will include income from the royalties received from franchisees. You can use that figure to get a rough idea of what the average franchise earns. Divide the royalty income by the percentage charged as a royalty rate. This gives you the combined gross sales of all the franchises. Then divide the gross sales by the number of franchised units in the company to get the average sales per unit.

If you've figured your operational costs, you can subtract that from the gross sales per unit to get a rough estimate of what your gross (before-tax) profit will be.

VISIT OTHER FRANCHISES IN THE COMPANY

You need to check out several other franchises before signing up. Watch the traffic through the business. Talk with the franchisees. Talk with customers and employees, even if you have to be something of a detective to do it.

PUT TOGETHER YOUR OWN TEAM

Before you go any further you need to build a team of people who will help guide you through the process of buying a franchise business. You'll need a lawyer (preferably, an experienced franchise attorney), an accountant, and a banker. If you don't have such professionals lined up, do it now.

As a mature, experienced adult who already has completed at least one career, you may not have to go far to find good professionals. First look to those you know well from your past career and whose skills you have come to respect. Or, if you're settling in a new retirement area, ask your neighbors for suggestions.

Don't make the age-old mistake of hiring your wife's brother's best friend who's just getting started, just to be accommodating. That's a prescription for disaster.

Check with professional associations and with friends and associates in other businesses for candidates. Ask for a free initial meeting, and if it is declined, cross that person off your list. Ask candidates for the names of three recent clients whose circumstances are similar to yours, then contact them and ask about the candidates' professional skills and services.

Be smart about this process. Your team will be important to your future, so check their credentials, their references, and their business premises carefully. Call the Better Business Bureau and the state Division of Consumer Affairs before you sign up anyone to represent you in your new business.

EXAMINE THE FRANCHISE OFFERING CIRCULAR

Now that you have your team prepped and ready, you and they need to examine the franchise disclosure documents required in your state. One is the Uniform Franchise Offering Circular (UFOC), which I mentioned earlier; the other is called the FTC form because it was established by the Federal Trade Commission. These documents are designed to protect you by providing critical information about the franchisor.

As a further protection, the law stipulates that the franchisor cannot accept any money from you, or have you sign a franchise agreement, for ten business days after you receive the disclosure document. This gives you time to go over the document in detail with your team.

You don't have to pay for this document; it should be pro-

vided for free. And if the disclosure documents aren't provided
on time or contain false or misleading information, the franchisor may have broken the law. Any violation should be reported
to the FTC in Washington, D.C., and to state authorities.

As you and your team analyze the disclosure documents, keep
in mind that they're designed for one specific goal: to sell you
on that franchise as the opportunity of a lifetime. Your job is
to pierce that sales assault to determine whether the company
is a viable one that you can work with.

During your examination of the offering circular you'll probably talk often with the franchisor or its representatives. Keep
written records of these conversations, the questions you ask
and any promises that are made, in your Gray Wave notebook.

Then, with your attorney, examine the document for the following things.

IDENTIFICATION OF THE FRANCHISOR AND PREDECESSORS

This can give you an idea of the company's affiliations and
past businesses run by the franchisor.

PERSONS ASSOCIATED WITH THE FRANCHISOR

This section includes the names of all principals in the company, including short biographies of each describing background, position, and business experience for the previous five
years.

LITIGATION HISTORY OF THE FRANCHISOR

If the franchisor or any of the principals mentioned above has
been involved in any criminal or civil litigation for fraud, em-
bezzlement, unfair business practices, or violation of any franchise laws, that information must be included.

BANKRUPTCY HISTORY OF THE FRANCHISOR

Here the franchisor must inform you of any bankruptcy claims
filed by him or her or by the company, its affiliated companies,
and its officers and directors.

Description of the Franchise

This section provides a complete description of the business the franchisor is selling you. It includes detailed descriptions of the product, the way the business is structured, and the market for the product or service.

Initial Fees Required of the Franchisee

This section discloses the franchise fee. It reveals the amount of the fee, how the amount is determined, when and how it has to be paid, and conditions for refund of the fee. Examine this section closely to avoid unpleasant surprises.

Other Fees Required of the Franchisee

These are all the other payments to the franchisor for which you're responsible. They may include monthly royalty payments, advertising fees, training expenses, fees for outside consultants, and any costs for purchasing, renting, or leasing equipment or real estate from the franchisor. All payments, whether they are to be paid on a regular basis or irregularly, must be included.

Initial Investment

The franchisor must disclose your total initial investment item by item, indicating when and to whom payment is due for each item.

Obligations of the Franchisee to Purchase or Lease from Designated Sources

Here the franchisor must disclose all products, supplies, equipment, or real estate you are required to purchase or lease, and the vendors from whom you must obtain it all. The franchisor's financial relationship with those vendors must also be disclosed.

Availability of Financing

The franchisor will indicate whether the company or its affiliates offer financing and what the terms are.

Obligations of the Franchisor

The franchisor will describe all the services it promises to provide while you own your franchise. Also included here will be the length of time it will take from the signing of the franchise agreement to select a site and then to open for business.

Territory and Sales Restrictions

This section will tell you where you can sell your goods and services and whether you'll be the only franchise in that area. It will also tell you whether the franchisor can market the service or product in your area by any other means.

Trademarks, Service Marks, Symbols and Other Identifications

The franchisor must describe what it has done to protect the trademarks, symbols, and name of the franchise. It must list and describe all logos, slogans, or other symbols unique to the franchise.

Patents and Copyrights

The UFOC requires the franchisor to list any patents or copyrights that are part of the value of the franchise. The FTC does not require this.

Personal Obligations of the Franchisee

This section defines the degree to which you must be involved in the operation of the franchise. If your presence is required on a full-time basis, that will be indicated. Gray Wave entrepreneurs who have visions of semiretirement should read this section carefully.

Renewal, Termination, Repurchase, and Assignment of the Franchise

Statistical Information on the Number of Franchises and Company-Owned Units

RESTRICTIONS ON GOODS AND SERVICES

This will tell you exactly *what* you can and cannot sell. Read it carefully if you have any plans for creativity.

INVOLVEMENT OF PUBLIC FIGURES

If the franchisor uses the name or image of a public figure as part of its marketing strategy, the terms of the arrangement with the person must be disclosed here.

FINANCIAL INFORMATION

The franchisor must include a current audited financial statement for each of the previous three fiscal years. It must include balance sheets, income statements, and a statement of changes in financial position. This statement must be prepared by an independent accountant and audited by a certified public accountant whose official stamp must appear on the statement.

CONTRACT (FRANCHISE AGREEMENT)

The franchisor must include a copy of the franchise agreement and any other related contractual documents, such as leases.

ACKNOWLEDGMENT OF RECEIPT

The final page is an acknowledgment by you that you received the offering circular. You sign it, date it, and give it to the franchisor.

NOW, EXAMINE THE FRANCHISE AGREEMENT

If you sign the franchise agreement you're entering into a contract for a new career. You're making an investment in your future lifestyle and in your retirement future. So before you put your pen to paper, you, your attorney, and your accountant need to examine the franchise agreement carefully.

The franchise agreement is a contract between you and the franchisor that spells out exactly how the franchise is to be run, the responsibilities you have to each other, the financial obligations you each have, and how renewal and transfer of the franchise will be handled.

Franchise agreements come in many forms, depending on the type of business that's being sold. But there are a number of elements that are standard. Here are the most common points covered in franchise agreements.

Grant of Franchise

This is sometimes referred to as "recitals," giving an overview of the transaction. It names the franchisor and franchisee, defines the goals and legal status of each, and describes the franchise system.

Use of Trademarks and Identity

Here the agreement names the owner of the franchise company's trade name, trademarks, logos, and other distinguishing identification, and grants the franchisee the right to use them.

Relationship of the Parties

This section is designed to legally separate your business from that of the franchisor. It defines the franchisee as an independent business owner who contracts with the franchisor to use its business system and other services outlined in the agreement. It states that neither party is affiliated with the other or a subsidiary of the other, and that each is responsible for its own debts, taxes, and other liabilities.

Franchise Fees and Other Payments

Here the franchisee agrees to pay the franchise fee, the specified monthly royalty payment, and any advertising fees that are required. The agreement should spell out exactly what you are receiving in return for the franchise fee.

The terms of payment also will be included. For example, the entire franchise fee may be due upon signing the agreement or it may be payable in installments. There will also be a provision that defines any payments, penalties, or interest you may incur if the payments are late.

TRAINING AND CONSULTATION

In this section the franchisor will describe any training it agrees to provide you before you open for business and after. It will state the duration of the training, who is to receive the training (the franchisor may agree to train a manager as well as you), and where the training will be given. If you've little or no experience in this business or industry, study this section carefully.

OPERATING PROCEDURES

Here you will agree to operate your business following the procedures outlined by the franchisor. The franchisor may include rules dictating the hours the business must be open, the way food is prepared, minimum staffing requirements, decor, furnishings, equipment, dress codes (including uniforms), signage, floor plans, and all other factors it considers critical to operating the business uniformly with the rest of the franchises.

BUSINESS SITE SELECTION AND PREPARATION

When you sign the franchise agreement, you'll still face the tasks of securing a location for your business, purchasing equipment and inventory and hiring employees. This section will define the length of time you'll be given by the franchisor to get things up and running. It may also include provisions about ownership of equipment and furnishings.

IMAGE AND CONDUCT

When a franchisor sells you a franchise, you become a representative of the company. For this reason, you are expected to conduct yourself in a certain manner and to maintain a certain appearance, both personally and in the physical appearance of the business site. This section will describe such regulations.

ADVERTISING AND PROMOTION

This section will describe the type of advertising the franchisor will buy, where the advertising will appear, and the frequency with which it will appear. Even though you may be paying a monthly fee for advertising support, you might not have any control over it. Find out if you or your franchisor will decide where and how your business will advertise locally.

Products and Services to Be Purchased by the Franchisee

If your franchisor requires you to purchase any equipment, inventory, supplies, or services from it, it will list them here. It will also list any vendors, suppliers, or distributors you are required to deal with, as well as specifications for the inventory you'll be carrying.

There's no reason the franchisor can't make a profit on the supplies and equipment it sells you. However, if its prices are higher than those of other suppliers, it'll soon have problems. Problems will also arise if the company's franchisees begin to feel the franchisor's standards are too restrictive and are keeping them from being competitive or profitable.

Financial Reports and Audits

Your franchisor will require you to keep records of all your sales and expenses, determine your tax liability, and calculate your royalty payments. You'll probably be required to submit periodic financial reports to the franchisor, including your books, accounts receivable and accounts payable, and bank statements. The franchisor will also reserve the right to conduct audits without warning.

Assignment of the Franchise

This section will describe your options, or lack of options, in selling, or "assigning," the franchise to someone else. Most franchisors place severe restrictions on how a franchise can change hands. If they allow it at all, they usually reserve final approval of any potential purchasers.

The fate of the franchise in the event of your death or disability will also be included here. If you'd like the business to go to your heirs if you die or become disabled, the franchisor will again reserve final approval.

RENEWAL OF THE FRANCHISE AGREEMENT

This section is of special interest to Gray Wave entrepreneurs. It will include the starting date and duration of the franchise agreement and the terms under which the agreement can be renewed. Almost all franchise agreements are for a specified length of time. About half are for ten years, others may be for fifteen, twenty, or even twenty-five years. Depending on your age, you may want to negotiate the minimum time commitment.

TERMINATION OF THE FRANCHISE AGREEMENT

As in all business arrangements, franchisors and franchisees sometimes reach the point where they want to get out of the deal. This section outlines the rights of both parties to terminate the contract. If the franchisor fails to meet its obligations as outlined in the franchise agreement—perhaps it fails to provide training, for example—you usually can terminate the contract. But if you should abandon the franchise, be convicted of a felony, fail to pass the franchisor's training program, or fail to open the business once the agreement is signed, then the franchisor can usually terminate the contract. The laws governing termination vary from state to state. Regardless of the specific terms of your contract, state law or local statute overrules them.

OBLIGATIONS OF THE FRANCHISEE UPON TERMINATION OR EXPIRATION

When a franchise agreement expires or is terminated, the franchisee usually has a number of responsibilities, and this section will list them. They can include paying all the monies you still owe the franchisor, returning all manuals and other operations materials, selling the business's assets to the franchisor, and changing the appearance of the business so that it no longer resembles other franchises.

What next? You're familiar with the franchise offering circular and the franchise agreement has passed muster by you, your attorney and your accountant. You're ready to sign, right? Wrong! Don't sign anything until you get your finances worked out.

WHAT ABOUT YOUR FINANCING?

Before you sign your way into franchise entrepreneurship you need to arrange your financing. You already know exactly how much it's going to cost because that's detailed in the franchise agreement. But don't forget to include a cushion in case your franchise gets off to a slow start. The last thing you need is to feel pinched when you're trying to get your new business off and running.

Lenders will expect you to provide a significant portion of the start-up costs of the business, from 25 to 50 percent. But you still have to live. Many business experts recommend you have from six months' to a year's worth of income set aside to live on until your business is in full gear.

How much will you need? Obviously, that depends on your monthly living costs and other factors. To get a rough idea of how much you'll need to get by for a year, fill in your monthly costs in this chart and then figure your annual total.

Rent/mortgage payment	_____ x 12 =	_____
Gas and electric	_____ x 12 =	_____
Telephone	_____ x 12 =	_____
Food	_____ x 12 =	_____
Clothing	_____ x 12 =	_____
Car payment(s)	_____ x 12 =	_____
Insurance	_____ x 12 =	_____
Gasoline	_____ x 12 =	_____
Entertainment	_____ x 12 =	_____
Taxes	_____ x 12 =	_____
Debt payment	_____ x 12 =	_____
Medical	_____ x 12 =	_____
Other	_____ x 12 =	_____
	TOTAL	_____

This will give you a rough idea of what you'll need to survive for the first year you're in business. Here again, a little extra cushion wouldn't hurt—be generous with yourself.

Basically, you have three options for financing: the franchisor, your own funds, or lending institutions.

THE FRANCHISOR

For many franchisees, the franchisor may be the best bet. About a third of franchisors provide direct or third-party financing to their franchisees. Some will help you in your search for financing. Find out early in your quest if your franchisor offers financing. If so, there are several advantages. First, the franchisor knows you by now and wouldn't be selling you a franchise if you were a poor risk. Second, it will definitely cut the amount of time before you can open the business. And third, since the franchisor is lending you the money, it increases the company's stake in the business and provides extra stimulus for seeing that you succeed.

The downside is it gives the franchisor another leg up in your relationship. In addition to the monthly royalty check, you'll be sending a check to pay off the loan.

YOUR OWN FUNDS

Some of us are lucky enough to have a substantial amount of cash lying around, or assets we can convert to cash for purchasing a business. Victims of the corporate downsizing in vogue today may have a secret weapon—their severance package—they can put to work as a down payment on their franchise future.

And many graying baby boomers are likely to inherit a nice nest egg. That, too, can be an excellent source of financing for your franchise.

INSTITUTIONAL SOURCES

Forget a business loan. Banks don't lend money to start-ups. Your best bet is a home equity or personal loan.

A home equity loan, or second mortgage, is now a very popular form of financing for all sorts of things, including franchises. Banks like home equity loans because there's little risk involved. This is a bit of a simplification, but if your home is worth $175,000 and your mortgage balance is $75,000, you have $100,000 worth of equity in your home. Generally speaking you can borrow against that equity—usually up to 70 percent of its value—to finance your franchise.

You should search for a home equity loan or a personal loan exactly as you did for your first mortgage. Shop around for the best interest rates at banks, credit unions, and savings and loans.

HERE'S WHAT MY FRIEND AARON DID

Five years ago a friend of mine, Aaron Frankfurt, did exactly what Rosie Cordera decided *not* to do in chapter 5. He bought a Pak Mail franchise. He now says it's the best decision he ever made. Aaron will laugh and tell you candidly that he's not the most sophisticated or best-educated guy in the world. But he's pretty street smart, and by trial and error he and his franchise ended up just fine.

Aaron didn't take any of the tests you've taken in this book to guide your choices, or answer any questions like the ones in this chapter. But he knew himself pretty well and did a lot of soul-searching before he started down his entrepreneurial path.

Aaron was fifty-three at the time, a machinist foreman at a small manufacturing company that makes jet turbine engines. He'd gone to community college for a year after high school and decided he'd rather just get to work with his hands, so he started as an apprentice machinist. By age fifty-three he had a good deal of responsibility and was making decent money. That's when he had his first heart attack. It was a mild one, and he was back on his feet and on the job within three months. That's when the second one hit. It wasn't so mild, and he got scared.

Aaron decided to take an early retirement option. But he was too young and his work ethic was too strong to allow him to play golf all day, however much he loved the game. He figured he'd buy a business. His wife, Marcie, also was ready to retire from her job as a secretary at one of the local colleges. She didn't want to work full-time anymore, but she knew she'd go crazy if she didn't get out regularly, keep busy, and have people to talk to. They decided that if Aaron found the right business, she'd work there, too.

Aaron and Marcie had money saved up. They also had the equity in their home, which they'd paid off. Aaron thought carefully about what kind of business he should start. He felt he wasn't creative enough to start one on his own so he'd have to buy one. And frankly, he wanted it to be relatively easy.

"Look, I'm no Bill Gates. I wish I'd been as smart as the guy who started McDonald's, but I'm not. I realized that long ago, when I had trouble learning to read. But if you tell me what to do I can do it. And, dammit, I can do it well; I'm something of a perfectionist." Aaron wanted someone to say "Here's your business and here's how it runs." He wanted a prepackaged deal, like a franchise.

He also knew he wanted to work with his hands and not have to think a lot. He would probably have to deal with people, and that was okay as long as he didn't have to really push himself on them or try to be someone he wasn't.

When he and Marcie took a weekend golfing vacation with a group of friends at St. Michael's, on the Chesapeake Bay, they stopped at a town in Delaware so one couple could mail a birthday package to their granddaughter. They stopped at a Pak Mail packaging and mailing franchise, and Aaron couldn't help nosing around. He was intrigued. He sensed he had found his future.

Aaron spent two hours talking to the owner of that Pak Mail franchise. His friends and Marcie went off to a café for lunch and left him gabbing away. When he rejoined them an hour and a half later he had the name and telephone number of the Pak Mail rep in his pocket.

He ran the idea of starting a Pak Mail franchise in his town— which didn't have anything like it—by his friends. In fact, he talked so much to his friends about the business and its possibilities during that trip that they threatened never to play golf with him again. And when he got home three days later he talked with more friends and neighbors about the pros and cons. Then he called the company rep and got more information.

Aaron knew he liked working with his hands. In fact, he decided he would get great satisfaction from the precision and repetition of carefully packaging each customer's treasure. There were similarities, he felt, with the precision required of a skilled machinist.

After talking to the rep, Aaron sat down with a pad, much like your Gray Wave notebook, and a pencil, and made some lists. At the top of the page he wrote "CUSTOMERS" in capital letters and underlined it twice. Then he started listing. Right off the bat he realized he had a great captive customer base in the students at two private colleges in the area who needed to ship their belongings back and forth across the country several times a year with as little bother as possible. And often with little concern for the cost.

Then there were shoppers from the nearby mall, which had no shipping or wrapping service. And everyone complained about the long lines at the old post office, which the town had long outgrown. There were two upscale neighborhoods near the mall. He was willing to bet that the people who lived there would pay a bit extra to use his convenient mail service rather than trudge downtown to the crowded post office. All he had to do was advertise in the yellow pages and on the two campuses, Aaron figured. The packaging business definitely seemed like a go.

But Aaron is cautious by nature. He knew he'd better have someone with more business experience look at the paperwork. He didn't have to look far for his team. His longtime banker knew Aaron was a man who paid his bills and paid off his debts. One of his golf buddies was a lawyer who specialized in business purchases. Aaron had never used an accountant, but the banker and lawyer both recommended another semiretiree who was working part-time for a select group of referrals— friends of friends.

Pak Mail told Aaron he'd need $50,000 to $80,000 to get started. That included a $17,500 franchise fee, site selection, lease negotiation assistance, building and design assistance, training, on-site opening support, and one year's worth of operating capital. The higher estimate turned out to be pretty close. To be on the safe side, Aaron's accountant suggested he should have an additional cushion, and he based his planning on a $100,000 first-year cost.

Aaron and Marcie had about $40,000 in the bank. In addition, Aaron had his pension payments. Marcie's salary was modest, but she decided to keep her job for a while to help with daily living expenses. Their home was valued at $150,000. Aaron was willing to invest their savings, all $40,000, because of these other financial resources.

He also applied for a $60,000 home equity loan from his banker. He lucked out: Interest rates were at a low point, and he got his loan for just 8.75 percent.

Aaron said that from the day he got his loan to his grand opening, time seemed to fly. The process worked like one of his own well-oiled machines. Within four months he was standing in the middle of his shop in a small strip mall near the big indoor shopping mall north of town, wondering when he would wake from this dream. It was opening day, and he was a nervous wreck.

Telling his story four years later, he still gets tears in his eyes when he describes the small brass desk sign Marcie had made for the grand opening. It read AARON FRANKFURT, PROPRIETOR.

"It was so simple, but so perfect. It meant so much to me, you see," Aaron said. "I never would have thought I could have my own business. But now I do."

SO WHERE DO YOU GO FROM HERE?

It's time to consider whether you want to buy a franchise business or take another path to becoming a Gray Wave entrepreneur. Franchises are a great opportunity for someone who wants a fast, easy, "noncreative" route to business ownership. You're buying an established name, a strong partner in the franchisor, and a well-tried and tested business operation.

On the other hand, most franchises must operate full-time and at full steam to meet the franchisor's financial demands. There's also that ten- or fifteen-year contract commitment most franchisors require. A franchise simply may not meet your semi-retired lifestyle preferences.

If you can negotiate your way to a franchise agreement and

work schedule that you can live with happily for the next ten years of your life, go for it. You can get additional help in your venture from the franchise resource and reference guide below.

If you have some doubts, don't worry. There are plenty of other routes to business ownership; we'll outline them in the next four chapters. So hang in there and you'll come up with just the right, unique business recipe for you.

FRANCHISE RESOURCE AND REFERENCE GUIDE

Here's a list of sources you can use to get information on franchising and on various franchise companies.

- *American Association of Franchisees and Dealers*—The AAFD is a nonprofit trade association representing the rights and interests of franchisees and independent dealers throughout the United States. The organization has members representing more than 100 franchise companies and is steadily growing towards its goal of 50,000 members by 1997. The AAFD offers a franchise search service and can provide you with a list of contractual agreements you should have to protect yourself. You can contact the AAFD by writing to P.O. Box 81887, San Diego, CA 92138-1887, or calling 619-235-2556.

- *Evaluating Franchise Opportunities* (SBA Publications, Denver, Colo., 1989).

- *Franchise Bible,* by Erwin J. Keup (Oasis Press, 1994).

- *Franchise Buyer's Handbook,* by Timothy T. Redden (Scott Foresman & Co., 1990).

- *Franchise Handbook*—A quarterly magazine directed specifically at the potential franchisee. You can order a subscription by writing to Enterprise Magazines, Inc., 1020 North Broadway, Suite 111, Milwaukee, WI 53202; calling 414-272-9977; or faxing 414-272-9973. Each issue costs

$5.99 ($6.99 in Canada) and can also be found at news-stands and bookstores.

- *Franchises: Dollars and Cents: A Guide for Evaluating Franchises and Projecting Earnings,* by Warren Lewis (Kendall/Hunt, 1991).

- *Franchising World Magazine*—Published by the International Franchising Association, *Franchising World* can provide you with insights into franchising and help you learn a bit more about what's available. A one-year subscription is $12 ($20 in Canada and $39 for all other countries) and can be ordered by sending a check to *Franchising World*, IFA Publications, P.O. Box 1060, Evans City, PA 16033, or calling 1-800-543-1038.

- *FRANDATA* is a research and consulting group that publishes a study with complete profiles and ratings of companies in the franchising industry. You can obtain information on specific companies for between $75 and $100 per company. Write to FRANDATA at 1155 Connecticut Avenue, Washington, DC 20036, or call 202-659-8640.

- *How to Open a Franchise Business,* by Mike Powers (Avon Books, 1995).

- *International Franchise Association*—Founded in 1960, the IFA serves as a resource to both franchisors and franchisees, as well as to the government and the media. It has more than 800 member franchise companies representing more than sixty different industries, 2,400 franchisee members, and is the largest and oldest franchise organization in the world. You can contact the IFA by writing to 1350 New York Avenue, N.W., Suite 900, Washington, DC 20005-4709; calling 202-628-8000; or faxing 202-628-0812.

❧ 7 ❧

HOW TO START A GYPSY
RETAIL BUSINESS

Retailing is a time-honored American profession originally plied by independent-minded men and women who crisscrossed the desolate country in its infancy, braving the wilds and bouts of loneliness to bring pockets of settlers essential goods. These early retailers had insight, foresight, and common sense. They needed those traits to survive and thrive.

Retailers today and into the twenty-first century need the same traits: insight, foresight, and common sense. They need to be strong, energetic, and independent-minded—mavericks in the true sense of the word.

What they don't need, however, is youth, or the boundless, frenetic energy of youth that long has been considered a prerequisite for a retailer. If that sounds like heresy, listen up. As the coming Gray Wave washes over the nation, the definitions of *work* and *retailing* will change to suit your needs. You can have your retail business and a pleasurable, semiretired lifestyle.

THE ADVANTAGES OF GYPSY RETAILING

You're beyond the stage in your life when you want to spend the relentless hours a traditional retail business requires. But you want the financial and psychological rewards of owning your own retail business. So why not toss out three-hundred years of retailing and retrace the steps of our retail pioneers— but with a contemporary Gray Wave twist. How about a nontraditional, modified, gypsy retail business without the traditional store setting and with modified hours? And perhaps with out-of-the-ordinary inventory?

What we're talking about here is providing consumers with a product they want or need as simply, directly, and efficiently as possible. Maybe something they can't find in a standard store. No big storefronts or high overhead. The gypsy part means you can pick up your business and move it in a flash to follow the flow of your customers and your own inclinations.

As a gypsy retailer you take the product to your customers in mobile carts or the back seat of your car; you set up a booth at farmer's markets, craft or antiques shows, and malls; or you offer a mail-order product. You set up a stand or cart by the road or on the beach, in a business or church parking lot, or in front of the train station. Your options and locations are limited only by your imagination and by the demands of the marketplace.

Remember, as a gypsy retailer you won't have the high cost, immobility, and limited access of the traditional retailer. So you can provide customers with better service, more convenient access, and lower prices.

And you can deliver your product with a personal touch. You'll be bringing your goods right to the customers, where they need them and want them. You can get to know your customers and ask about a granddaughter's hockey game or a son's applications to college. You can provide the warmth and personal contact, the smile and handshake all too often missing in today's fast-paced, impersonal world.

A gypsy retail business also can be an outlet for your creativity. Use your imagination and creativity to decorate your cart or booth with eye-catching appeal, and your business will bloom. And the more creativity you apply to your stock, the more your cash register will ring.

Finally, as a gypsy retailer you can set your own hours by the day or the week or the season. You decide how many hours you want to work and check that against how much money you want to make. Voilà. You work as little or as long as you need to produce the desired income and work schedule. As you'll have other sources of income—Social Security and pension, most likely—you simply don't need to put in the backbreaking hours a traditional retailer would. You can have your business and enjoy your retirement, too.

THE DISADVANTAGES OF GYPSY RETAILING

Yes, there are downsides to operating a gypsy retail business. After all, a gypsy retail business is still retailing. And that means offering a selection of products a sufficient number of consumers want, in the right location, and backed with outstanding personal service. So you have to be sure you're selling a product people want. And you have to be sure you're offering it at a convenient location. Remember, *convenience* and *service* are two bywords for any successful twenty-first-century entrepreneur.

IT'S HARD WORK

You'll have to put in significant hours of hard work. Gypsy retailing is still sales, remember, and if you're not out there selling you're not making money. Somebody has to be working that cart or booth. It may be you or it may be an employee, but somebody has to put in the hours, or you're not doing business.

It may be a good idea to hire an employee to work the cart or booth at least part of the time. But bear in mind, that'll cut into your profit. You'll also have to watch closely to be sure your stand-in is providing the kind of service that will make your business a success. And chances are that while your employee is busy selling, you'll be doing the books or checking or purchasing inventory. Even a gypsy retail business, if you're serious about making money and serving customers, will require a substantial investment of your time and hard work, as well as your money.

THERE'S A RISK

Yes, your money. Gypsy or no, you still need to invest in inventory or you've nothing to sell. And that investment is a risk. If you put all your savings into Teenage Mutant Ninja

Turtles this Christmas season and every kid in America wants a Power Ranger, you're going to be frying Happy Meals next summer.

You need to know your product, and you need to know your market. If you know your market as well as you should, the investment risk can be minimized.

THE TRAVEL

There's also the travel. Depending on the nature of the product you decide to sell, you may have to travel from sales opportunity to sales opportunity. If you decide to buy handcrafted quilts and knitted goods from Appalachian women and sell them in cities in the Northeast, you're going to have to travel from craft show to craft show or from site to site, and that can entail spending a good portion of your time away from home. That kind of travel schedule may not be conducive to a semiretired lifestyle. On the other hand, you may be able to limit your geographic sales territory or limit your selling season to between September and Christmas, and still make the kind of money you'd like to make. Then you can play golf the rest of the year.

MOTHER NATURE

As a gypsy retailer, you and your mobile cart may be at the mercy of Mother Nature. If you decide to sell burritos on a busy street corner or near a school parking lot, bad weather can take a big bite out of your profits. You may be willing to withstand a drizzle, but chances are your customers may decide to buy a cup of soup or cardboard sandwich from a vending machine rather than get drenched. So your sales can be as unreliable as the weather.

A GYPSY RETAIL BUSINESS COULD BE JUST RIGHT FOR YOU

Clearly, there are pros and cons in starting a gypsy retail business. Now, take out your Gray Wave notebook, turn to a fresh page, head it "Gypsy Retail Business," and list the pros and cons of this kind of retail operation. Then go back to chapter 3 and review the "Questions to Ask Yourself." Check your notebook for the answers to those questions about how you want to spend the next decade or so. Do the gypsy retail pros and cons match with your answers to those questions? Does it look as though the two might be compatible?

This is a time for honesty about yourself, because you do need certain character traits to be a good gypsy retailer. Think people skills first. You need to really like people and like working with people, because gypsy retailing is sales. And sales depends to a large extent on personality. Your customer isn't buying just your product. Your customer also is buying a piece of you—or is not buying because of you.

Gypsy retailing also depends on service, so you have to be the kind of person who's willing to go that extra mile for a customer, even when you're tired, hungry, or just not feeling up to snuff.

And creativity is just as important. You certainly can sell a good product from a good location at a good price with a somewhat ordinary presentation. But you'll definitely sell more products, even at a slightly steeper price, if you knock 'em dead with a sensational display or advertising and marketing campaign. That's where your creativity, if you've got it, can flow.

If you fit the general outline above, chances are a gypsy retail business is just right for you. The next step is to decide what you're going to sell and who you're going to sell it to. After that we'll get to the gypsy part of your business, or how and where you're going to sell your product.

DECIDE WHAT YOU WANT TO SELL

This decision may mean the difference between success and failure for your entrepreneurial career, so you'll want to choose wisely. The first rule of thumb is to sell what you know and like. Remember, this is supposed to be fun, too. If you have a keen interest in art, you might think about searching out original watercolors from art students or other Gray Wavers or wherever you can find good work, and selling those. Maybe you've been building hand-tooled birdhouses as a hobby for the past twenty years and giving them away to family and friends. Think about selling those, and add small handmade items from other crafts-people as well.

Of course, in assessing what product you might sell, you'll have to keep in mind that it must be something you can sell from a small, movable, or temporary location—not from a large, fixed, traditional store. Not to worry. That leaves a huge array of choices.

Start out by making a list in your Gray Wave notebook of the kinds of products you use, or that interest you or your friends. The list might look something like this:

Antiques and collectibles	Hand-knitted items, quilts
Baked goods	Handmade dolls, toys
Books	Hand-sewn kids'/babies' clothes
Breakfasts	Herbs
Candy, cookies, pretzels	Imported gifts, housewares
Canned goods	Jewelry
Ceramic bowls	Knitting and needlework
Coffees, teas	Lunches, snack foods
Cosmetics	Music and musical instruments
Costumes	Paintings, small sculpture
Crocheted goods	Stuffed animals
Dinners, prepared foods	Used antique clothing
Dried flower arrangements	Vinegars, jellies, and jams
Flowers, floral arrangements	Vitamins, health products
Games	Wooden birdhouses, boxes
Greeting cards, notepaper	

Almost anything people buy that's of reasonable size can be sold from a temporary cart, booth, or shed. Use your imagina-tion in making this list and consult with your friends and rela-tives. Ask them what they buy regularly, what they'd like to be able to buy more easily and conveniently, what specialty items they'd like a better selection of. Do an informal mini-survey of their consumer spending habits. This list should be as all-encompassing as you can make it.

START NARROWING YOUR OPTIONS

Now you need to begin to narrow your candidates. Check off those items that interest you particularly for one reason or another—say, you're an avid artist, you love to read, or you're crazy about needlework. With these candidates in mind, ask yourself the following questions and jot down your answers in your Gray Wave notebook.

- Can I purchase this product locally?
- Is the local purchase point convenient for many people?
- When was the last time I tried to purchase this product?
- How often would a typical person who uses this product need or want to replace it?
- Are customers unhappy with the local store that sells this product, and why?

HERE'S HOW TO GET STARTED

Your answers to the questions above will give you some insight into whether there's a potential market for any of these products. Now, pick your clear favorite, then define your target market. That will tell you whether your future gypsy retail business has a chance to prosper, or whether you need to examine the market more closely with some other product or products in mind. In addition to helping you decide on your specialty product, this market analysis will help you later when you put together your marketing plan.

DEFINE YOUR TARGET MARKET

First, define your ideal customer. You need to decide exactly who is interested in buying your specialty product. Then decide whether there are enough of them within your area to support your business. Later you'll want to know where and how you can find them, as your future marketing will be targeted toward areas where those customers can be found.

Envision your future customers. List everything you can find out about them. Are they male or female, young, middle-aged, or Gray Wavers like yourself? What's their income, where do they live, where do they shop, and what are their hobbies? Check out places that sell your type of product and jot down the characteristics of their customers. Also contact industry and trade groups to see what market research they might have. Then create a portrait of that typical customer.

For example, say you decide you want to sell original art, watercolors and small oils or lithographs. For the sake of argument, let's also say you have a ready supply of work from local high schools, colleges, art classes, and senior centers. Common sense tells you your customers are young married or single professionals just decorating their first homes and apartments, with some discretionary income. Or perhaps they're Gray Wavers moving into a new, upscale retirement home just being built on the edge of town. They don't want or can't afford investment-quality art, but they want inexpensive originals rather than overused prints. Check out the customer flow of local frame shops, small galleries, small decorator and housewares shops, and local museums, if there are any.

LOCATE YOUR TARGETED CUSTOMERS

Now decide where your targeted customers can be found. Do you live in a booming area with a lot of suburban developments filled with young families? Or is yours a dying community where everyone under age fifty moves away? If it's the latter, don't despair. You can still try to market your original art, but you'll probably have to take your show on the road—to craft fairs, flea markets, community festivals, and maybe even motel shows. Or maybe you could couple that with a mail-order sales effort.

If yours is a young and thriving community, you should rent a booth at the mall or downtown, and go for it. You could spend part of the year selling the paintings you've collected and part of the year traveling and replenishing your stock.

You'll be able to market your artwork to the owners of that new, upscale retirement village being constructed on the edge of town and to the owners of the big, new custom homes being built for the successful young professionals in the area.

Later, when we talk more about a specific marketing plan, we'll take the carefully defined portrait of your customers that we settled on earlier and decide where they can be found. That's where you'll target your future marketing. But for now, you just need to determine that there are sufficient consumers within reach who will buy your product.

CHECK RETAILING TRENDS

Before you finalize your product selection, even if it's an unusual one that doesn't quite fit the standard store inventory, check out national retailing trends and the failure and success rates of specific types of stores. The Department of Commerce produces detailed statistical analyses of all aspects of American business, including retailing. Dun & Bradstreet also tracks small business success and failure rates by retail store type. You can call the Department of Commerce at 202-377-2000, and Dun & Bradstreet at 201-605-6000. Any information you can get on national and regional retailing trends, even if it doesn't apply directly to your gypsy retail product or business format, can help guide the choices you make.

Also, now that you've chosen your retail specialty, start reading everything you can find on that specialty. Read trade magazines and newspapers. Many of these publications track the business from the retailer's perspective, covering such issues as business trends and marketing strategies. Check the *Reader's Guide to Periodical Literature* and the business index listing for recent articles about the retail market you plan to enter.

And don't forget trade organizations and associations as valuable sources of information. Gale Research publishes the *Encyclopedia of Associations,* and the *Directory of Business, Trade and Public Policy Organizations* is available from the Small Business Administration.

TALK WITH OTHERS WHO SELL THE SAME OR SIMILAR PRODUCTS

By now you should be pretty well settled on your retail specialty, but as a final safeguard be sure to talk with other business owners in your general field. Pick their brains for do's and don'ts, successes and failures. To get the kind of honest answers and details you need, you'll probably have to go out of town for these chats, so you can assure the other business owners that you won't be a competitor. That way they'll open up more.

If you plan to sell cosmetics from a booth in the mall, talk with Mary Kay Cosmetics representatives, chat with the salespeople at department store cosmetics counters and anyone else selling cosmetics. If you're selling that original art we talked about earlier, talk with gallery owners, interior decorators, frame shop owners, and gift and import shop owners.

DISCUSS YOUR PLAN WITH POTENTIAL CUSTOMERS

Be sure to test your idea with the consumers who would be your potential customers. Talk to your friends, neighbors, and family. Ask them if they are interested in buying a product like yours, and if so, what are the key things they are looking for when they buy such a product. Ask them how much they would be willing to pay and what they would consider convenient locations for making their purchases.

Then conduct an informal survey of those you don't know. Go door-to-door and street-to-street in different neighborhoods, asking the same questions. Try random cold-calling on the telephone, but be brief, polite, and don't be upset if people are gruff at the interruption. Remember how you hate those calls? The key is to quickly establish yourself as a neighbor and a real person, not an indifferent voice calling for an anonymous mega chain. This is your first crack at establishing a customer base, so keep that in mind.

You also can bounce your idea off an independent observer by contacting the local office of the Small Business Administration. SBA sponsors a mentor's program called SCORE (Service Corps of Retired Executives), which brings together retired executives and people who are trying to launch a business. The advice is free, impartial, and rooted in experience.

Touch Base with Potential Suppliers

You now need to contact suppliers to be sure you'll have sufficient access to the products you want to sell at a workable price. As a gypsy retailer, you're likely to be selling an unusual kind of product—something homemade, handcrafted or old, refurbished or imported. You probably know where to find your product. But if it's not all lined up, start making lists in your Gray Wave notebook and begin calling and visiting the producers of your handcrafted products. Be sure to nail down prices and production schedules. But be prepared for glitches when you work with individual craftspeople rather than with strictly assembly-line, profit-centered businesses. Have a backup supply source ready.

But you may not be selling a gypsy-type product. You can sell ready-made stuffed animals, watches, or sweaters from a mobile cart as well. If you intend to sell a regular retail product, call corporate headquarters and ask for the person responsible for sales in your state or region. He or she may be on staff, working as an independent rep, or working out of a distributor's office.

Ask for a few minutes of the salesperson's time to discuss the company's products and sales policy. Find out what kind of year the company and its dealers are having. Is the market for the company's products flat, declining, or growing? What does the company do to support its dealers? Does it control distribution? Do larger accounts get preferential treatment?

Don't forget that you're talking to a salesperson who is eager to gain another account. Don't take the answers to your questions at face value. Ask for the company's past five years' financial records. If the salesperson is being honest and the company is proud of its record, there should be no problem with such a request.

PUT TOGETHER YOUR OWN TEAM

Now is the time—before you go any further—to put together the team of professionals who will help guide you through the process of starting your gypsy retail business. You'll need an accountant and a banker. You'll also need a lawyer to check out any contracts you may need to enter into with suppliers, or mall or flea market owners. In addition, a good lawyer will be helpful in researching any licenses and permits you may need for peddling or mail-order efforts. If you don't have such professionals lined up, do it now.

As an experienced Gray Waver who already has completed at least one career, you may not have to go far to find accomplished professionals. First look to those you know well from your past career and whose skills you have come to respect. Or, if you're settling in a new retirement area, ask your neighbors for suggestions.

Don't make a mercy-hire just to be a nice guy and sign on your cousin Harold's daughter's boyfriend who just got his CPA. This should be a business decision like any other, and you need the wisdom and experience of seasoned professionals. In fact, why not look for other Gray Wave semiretirees to direct your business to?

Check with SCORE again for possible candidates, and contact the American Association of Retired Persons (AARP). Also check with professional associations and with friends and associates in other businesses for candidates. Ask for a free initial meeting, and if a candidate declines, cross him or her off your list. Ask candidates for the names of three recent clients whose circumstances are similar to yours, then contact them and ask about the candidates' professional skills and services.

You need to be smart about this process. Your team will be important to your future, so check their credentials, their references, and their business premises carefully. Call the Better Business Bureau and the state Division of Consumer Affairs before you sign up anyone to represent you in your new business.

DECIDE ON YOUR GYPSY FORMAT

Okay, you're a gypsy retailer. The time has come to decide exactly what that means for you. Of course, being a gypsy means that you can always change things around if your decision no longer suits you or your customers, but to get started you need to decide where and from what you'll sell your product.

You have a number of options.

SET UP A BOOTH AT A FLEA MARKET

Flea markets aren't what they used to be in Grandma's day, when Grandma and her sewing circle used them for getting rid of their old junk and hand-tatted doilies. Flea markets today are the MTV of the retail world: big, freewheeling entertainment where you can find a vast array of everything at a big range of prices and varying quality. Consumers come to be entertained, for a weekend happening as much as to shop. But once they're there, chances are they'll shop till they drop, and your opportunities will be great.

The rental prices at flea markets vary, too, so do some comparison shopping. Obviously, those markets that draw the biggest crowds, whether because of their locations or their selections, also command the biggest rents. But they're probably worth the price.

Some gypsy retailers go from flea market to flea market, traveling the circuit. Others park themselves in a spot and stay there for years, content with their level of sales success. You may have to scout around for the best spot for your particular product.

Don't give up if the first flea market you try isn't right for you. As with any sales location, it may take a while for your customers to find you and others to start to seek you out. Or it may be that your target customer just isn't drawn to the flea market you picked. If that's the case, you can try drawing them with a targeted marketing campaign, or you can move.

And depending on your level of energy and ambition as a gypsy retailer, the best thing about flea markets may be that most of them are open only on weekends. You can still have a semiretired life.

SET UP A KIOSK OR BOOTH IN A MALL

It used to be that malls had stores—big or little, but clearly defined—that just happened to be housed under one roof to spare shoppers from having to brave the elements when going from store to store. Then they added food courts to centralize and cater to the ever-popular American shopper's pastime of noshing. Entertainment came with movie theaters and video game arcades. But there was still wasted space—space that wasn't earning income for mall owners. After all, shoppers take up only so much traveling space, right?

Have you tried to walk through your local mall lately without running into a booth or kiosk? I mean physically stumbling into one? They're hard to miss, and that's what makes them so attractive to you as an entrepreneur.

The downside, of course, is the price. With the kind of traffic most malls get, they can demand a hefty price, even for a booth in the corridor. Booth spots rent by the month, and they're in demand. The major mall in my own upstate New York community of about 90,000 county residents had one booth spot available a month before Christmas, and the mall manager said he expected to have that spot filled by the end of the week. Rental costs in the mall ranged, depending on the location, from $750 to $1,500—except during Christmas, when they jumped to $3,500 to $5,000 a month.

The mall booth probably would not pay for itself with strictly weekend work. You might be able to make money working just peak hours, however, rather than a full day every day as you would have to with a regular shop.

SELL FROM A PEDDLER'S WAGON

For this you'll probably need a peddler's license. Such mobile carts are becoming more and more popular on city streets and in parks and recreation areas, and in some communities competition for the best spots is fierce. You also need to investigate your obligations under the license agreement. Contact your City Hall and the local Chamber of Commerce, as well as your state's small business assistance agency, to determine what licenses and permits are required.

The trick here, as with any retail venture, is finding the right spot for your product. And don't forget you'll have to deal with the vagaries of Mother Nature. If you try to sell frozen yogurt on a street corner in New York State in December, you'll not only go broke, you'll wish you were selling hot chocolate and roasted chestnuts—which, of course, you could do.

Start a Mail-order Business

The beauty of a small mail-order business is that it's inexpensive to operate, can be run from home, can easily be handled part-time, and is a great way to sell things you or your friends make.

To do this successfully you need an effective way to reach potential customers—like a good, but not necessarily elaborate, catalog or an eye-catching ad or flyers you design and print yourself with a computer and the proper software. If you have access to the Internet through a commercial on-line service, you can reach potential customers via cyberspace. And you can handle your sales transactions and maintain your business records electronically as well.

Again, you'll need to check into local regulations, licenses, and tax laws. For more information on the mail-order option, check out the list of resources at the end of this chapter.

DRAW UP YOUR BUSINESS AND MARKETING PLANS

Now that you've decided what you're going to sell and how and where you're going to sell it, you need to draw up a business plan and a separate marketing plan to guide you every step of the way. Planning is the key to success as an entrepreneur, even as a gypsy retailer.

Just as you wouldn't think of starting a long journey without a map, you shouldn't consider starting your retail business without either a business plan or a marketing plan. Such plans will help you map out the route you'll follow to meet your business goals. You'll also need to check your progress regularly against your plans and fine-tune them as experience suggests.

THE BUSINESS PLAN

This should be part of your Gray Wave notebook and need not be elaborate, since you won't be submitting it to a commercial lender in the hope of obtaining a business loan. (More about that later, but commercial lenders do not finance small business start-ups. If you need financing, you'll get it elsewhere.) The plan should address your business's mission, your goals and objectives, your retail strategy, and finances.

Here's a general outline you can follow:

- *General information*—List the name of your business; your name and address; and telephone, fax, and E-mail numbers.

- *Mission statement*—This should be a general statement of one or two paragraphs explaining your philosophy and motivation in starting this business.

- *Objectives*—List your specific goals and objectives for the business.

- *The business*—Describe the business: What will you sell and to whom; where will you get your products; where and how will you reach your customers; where will your business be located; who's your primary competition; will you need to hire employees?

- *Finances*—We'll discuss finances in more detail later in this chapter, but include realistic income and expense projections. Allow some cushion for unexpected start-up costs and setbacks, and for a slower than expected growth in sales. Remember, it takes time for customers to get to know you and your products and services, and to get into the habit of seeking you out.

THE MARKETING PLAN

Although you will touch on marketing in your business plan, you need to develop a separate marketing plan to outline exactly how you'll promote your gypsy retail business for at least a year. If you want your business to thrive, you have to market yourself.

The biggest mistake most small businesses make is to rely on advertising alone. Yet advertising often is the most expensive and least productive way to reach customers. Instead, you'll want to spread your efforts among a variety of marketing opportunities, including flyers, media publicity, and promotions.

As you draw up your marketing plan, focus on the portrait of your target customer that we drew earlier in this chapter. Think about ways and places to reach that target customer, then decide:

- What mix of marketing you will do on a weekly, monthly, or seasonal basis.
- How much money you will budget for each marketing effort in that period.
- How and by whom that marketing effort will be carried out.
- How you will assess the effectiveness of your marketing plan.

WHAT ABOUT YOUR FINANCING?

Before you go any further you need to fill in the financing details in your business plan. To do that you need to determine what your business start-up costs will be. Start-up costs for a gypsy retail business will be minimal, compared with the cost of buying a franchise or an existing business, or opening a traditional store.

You also need money to live on while the business gets rolling, but I'm assuming here that what you're starting is truly a gypsy retail business, designed be operated part-time to bring in extra income, rather than your future livelihood. So living expenses should not be a concern. Your Social Security and pension payments, plus any savings, should be sufficient for living expenses.

Start a new worksheet in your Gray Wave notebook for your start-up costs. Basically, here's what you'll need:

START-UP COSTS WORKSHEET

Enter the appropriate amounts to determine your start-up cost. I've listed some typical items, but be sure to include all the specific start-up costs you'll be incurring.

Booth or kiosk rent	$_____
Telephone line	$_____
Insurance	$_____
Attorney	$_____
Accountant	$_____
Marketing / advertising firm	$_____
Displays, signs, fixtures	$_____
Computer system and software	$_____
Telephone and fax machine	$_____
Cash register	$_____
File cabinet	$_____
Copy machine	$_____
Office supplies	$_____
Start-up advertising	$_____
Inventory	$_____
TOTAL START-UP COSTS	$_____

Now that you've figured out your start-up costs, you need to arrange your financing. Basically, you have three options: your own funds, a loan from a lending institution, or a loan from family or friends.

YOUR OWN FUNDS

You may be lucky enough to have a substantial amount of cash lying around, or assets you can convert to cash. Even a gypsy retail business requires an investment in basic equipment and office supplies, as well as inventory. You have to keep records and pay bills, right?

If you're a casualty of corporate downsizing, you may have a secret weapon—a severance package—you can invest in starting up your new gypsy retail business. Or, you may be one of those lucky, graying baby boomers who just inherited a nice nest egg from Mom and Dad, or from Granny. That, too, can be an excellent source of financing for your business start-up.

INSTITUTIONAL SOURCES

Forget a business loan. Banks just don't lend money to start-ups because it's too risky. They want a proven track record of success before they'll consider a business loan. Your best bet is a home equity or personal loan.

A home equity loan, or second mortgage, is now a very popular form of financing for all sorts of things, including basic business equipment and inventory. Banks like home equity loans because there's little risk involved. It's a bit of a simplification, but if your home is worth $175,000 and your mortgage balance is $75,000, you have $100,000 worth of equity in your home. Generally speaking, you can borrow against that equity— usually up to 70 percent of its value—to finance your new business.

You should search for a home equity loan or a personal loan exactly as you did for your first mortgage. Shop around for the best interest rates at banks, credit unions, and savings and loans.

FAMILY AND FRIENDS

Family and friends can be excellent sources of financing because it can be a win-win deal for both of you. And that's because there's a gap between current lending rates and the interest rates institutions are offering on savings accounts, certificates of deposit, and other savings instruments.

Say your brother is a pretty successful pharmacist who makes enough money that he's always on the lookout for a good investment—a safe, steady place to stash his cash. Right now he has $40,000 to invest, and by sheer coincidence, that's exactly how much you've decided you need to borrow to start up your new gypsy retail business.

He doesn't want to fool around with mutual funds and other more risky forms of investment. He's done his research and knows that fixed-rate investments earn around 4.5 percent with a conventional savings account and about 6 percent with most CDs.

You, on the other hand, have discovered that a personal loan will cost you about 10 percent. So there's roughly a 4 percent window of opportunity for you and your brother to make a deal that benefits you both. If he lends you his $40,000 at 8 percent, he'll be getting a better return on his investment than he would otherwise, and you'll be getting a loan 2 percent below what's available in the marketplace. You both win.

LOOK AT THE TRANSFORMATION OF SHASHAWNA FRYE

Shashawna Frye was sixty and an accountant in the business office of the local community college when she began making her "retirement" plans five years ago. Her husband, Ron, was sixty-two and a tenured professor of comparative literature at the small private college that dominated the town in which they had lived for all forty of their married years. Retirement wasn't a word in Ron Frye's vocabulary in any language.

Shashawna's friends teased her about being the prototypical accountant—as neat and organized in her mind and in her life as she was in her accounting practices. Ron joked that if accountants still wrote out their calculations by hand in long columns in ledger books, Shashawna wouldn't need an eraser on her pencil.

So when Shashawna decided she was ready to retire and try something new, she went about it in a typically organized and rational fashion. But what few people besides Ron, her closest friends, and her daughter, Sarah, knew was that in Shashawna the steel-trap mind of the accountant harbored the soul of an artist. Actually, while not yet an artist, she was a keen lover of the art of beautiful handcrafts, particularly creative pottery. And she was determined that at the right moment—when she could free her mind of the rigors imposed by strict accounting principles—she would try her own hand at the pottery wheel.

Meanwhile, however, she also was determined to make careful decisions about her retirement career and make equally careful preparations for it well before she signed her retirement papers.

Two things happened eight years ago, when Shashawna was fifty-seven, that led her to her retirement decisions. First, Sarah began taking a ceramics class in high school and then joined the pottery club at the college where Ron worked. Her high school art teacher became a mentor and friend, and taught her the basics of throwing a pot as well as creative use of color, glazes, and design.

Second, the state started cutting funding for higher education, and within a year or two the cuts were so deep that the community college started offering early retirement incentives. Not much, but enough to get Shashawna thinking. She was ready for a change, she just wasn't sure what that change should be.

"Everyone thought they knew me. Even Ron had categorized me to some extent as AN ACCOUNTANT, in capital letters," Shashawna now says. "I was a very successful accountant and happy at it for many years, but there was more to me than that, and I was ready for it to burst out."

Over the next couple of years she figured out certain parameters for her postretirement life. She knew she wanted to work, but she didn't want to work full-time. She was ready for a total change of pace—no more sixteen-hour days, and no more columns of numbers. Well, maybe a few, if they related to her own business and weren't her only business.

Frankly, she wanted some creativity in her new life. And she thought she had figured out a way to provide herself with extra income, a creative outlet, and to do some good for struggling artists as well. She knew that Sarah and her friends in the pottery club, and people in other clubs and amateur art classes throughout the region, did some quality work as well as schlock and created far more than they could give away to friends and relatives at Christmas and for birthdays.

They had no real outlet for their work, aside from the annual county arts festival. Most had no idea that anyone actually would pay them for their work—some with justification. But Shashawna had filled her office with pieces of Sarah's pottery, a vase and a bowl and several mugs, and many people had commented and, in fact, asked if Sarah sold her work. The interest had stuck in Shashawna's mind, buried behind the accounting standards.

Shashawna thought she had detected a real consumer interest in inexpensive handmade pottery—and an answering need in potential suppliers: amateur artists and craftspeople of all ages who had no retail outlet and no business sense but who wanted to sell their work, if only to pay for more materials for more work.

She started talking to Ron, Sarah, and her own friends and neighbors, to check on whether her initial instincts were right. She learned there was real consumer interest in good-quality handmade, but inexpensive, pottery—and even in paintings and small sculpture.

''It seemed that people were really sick of buying the same slick, boring stuff from the same slick, boring catalogs and big merchandisers,'' she said. ''It was almost like a mini-revolution. Everyone I talked to said they'd really like to have a convenient way to buy something original for themselves and for gifts. They just didn't know how or where to do it.''

Then she felt she needed to research the inventory end of what she already was thinking of as her ''retirement'' business. So she dropped into all the local arts and crafts clubs and schools she could find, and put notices up on dormitory bulletin boards at the two colleges and even at her health club, asking craftspeople who wanted to sell their work to call her. She was inundated. And she was excited, truly excited and energized for the first time in several years.

"I didn't realize how bored I'd gotten until I started making those calls and handling that pottery. I knew it was a world of creativity that I wanted to enter," Shashawna said.

Of course, not all of the work she subsequently reviewed was of the quality she wanted, but she thought there was enough to get started. And she intended to take a few classes herself, and hoped someday to add her own work to the mix.

With Ron still working, money wasn't a problem in getting started. Shashawna felt she could comfortably help the college in its necessary downsizing efforts by retiring a bit early. And they still had enough savings and discretionary income for sufficient inventory and to rent a kiosk at the mall until the business took off. They didn't even need to take out any loans.

Three years ago, at age sixty-two, Shashawna opened the Artful Codger at the mall, two weeks before Thanksgiving. She had to close the day before Christmas Eve because she had run out of the stock she had thought would last her through February, when she and Ron had a trip to the Caribbean planned. The trip, incidentally, was mostly paid for by the Artful Codger.

Shashawna was so successful that she and Ron now take carefully planned in advance shopping vacations around the country. Shashawna's advance planning includes setting appointments at local arts clubs and schools, and running a week's worth of ads in local papers, soliciting interviews with potential artists. Right now she's planning a treasure-hunting as well as pleasure-hunting trip to Japan, where she'll stick to her successful formula of seeking out amateur artists.

A year ago Shashawna expanded with a peddler's wagon that Sarah operates during the summer at the beach. But she's decided against the temptation to move into a fixed store at the mall or perhaps into the renovated downtown shopping district.

"I really like the feeling of freedom I have now," she said. "With my month-to-month, relatively low-cost rent, I can close down whenever I want and go on a traveling and shopping spree, all in the name of good business, or even just for fun.

"Not that I do it all that spontaneously," she added. "After all, the artist is still warring with the accountant in me, and now the entrepreneur seems to have a firm hand on both."

SO WHERE DO YOU GO FROM HERE?

It's time to decide whether you want to start a gypsy retail business or take another route to becoming a Gray Wave entrepreneur. A gypsy retail business is a gamble, like any retail business, but it can be the perfect opportunity for the right person. You minimize your risk because your investment is relatively small—you have very low overhead because you have no fixed storefront to pay for and you can start with a limited amount of stock.

On the other hand, no matter how small you start, you will need a healthy amount of energy and enthusiasm, because selling is plain hard work, and that's what retail—even gypsy retail—is all about. You also need to be good with people—selling is all about having good people skills and putting a premium on customer service.

A gypsy retail business can be the perfect outlet for your creativity. The more creative and exciting you are with your displays, your marketing, and your inventory, the more chance you have of keeping your cash register ringing. On the other hand, if you offer the right inventory at the right price and in the right location, creativity can be the icing on the cake—nice, but not essential.

It's up to you now. If you're not really sure sales is your thing, or if you just can't get charged up about selling any particular item, relax. There are other routes to entrepreneurship that we'll outline in the next three chapters.

GYPSY RETAIL RESOURCE AND REFERENCE GUIDE

Here's a list of sources you can use to get information on retailing and mail-order businesses:

- *Consignment Boutique Primer: Entrepreneurship for the Lady Who Loves Apparel and People,* by Nimi Wanek and Ken Meyer (Meyer-Man Books, 1992).

- *From Dogs to Riches: A Step-by-Step Guide to Start and Operate Your Own Mobile Cart Vending Business. Includes Merchandise and Food Carts,* by Vera D. Clark-Rugley (MCC Publishing, 1993).

- *How to Be Successful in the Antique Business: A Survival Handbook,* by Ronald S. Barlow (Windmill Publishing, 1980).

- *How to Develop the Restaurant Business: Promotion of the Chinese Restaurant Take-Out Order Business* by Chau Liang (Gold Town Sales, 1993).

- *How to Make Twenty Thousand Dollars a Year in Antiques,* by Bruce E. Johnson (Ballantine Books, 1987).

- *How to Open Your Own Store,* by Michael Antoniak (Avon Books, 1994).

- *How to Own and Operate a Card and Gift Shop,* by Patti Brickman (Greeting Card Association, 1988).

- *How to Start a Mail-Order Business (for Under $10,000),* by Mike Powers (Avon Books, 1996).

- *How to Start and Operate a Mail-order Business,* by Julian L. Simon (McGraw-Hill, 1993).

- *How to Start and Run Your Own Retail Business,* by Irving Burstiner (Carol Publishing Group, 1994).

- *Is There a Product Inside You? How to Successfully Develop and Market Any Product,* by Reece A. Franklin (AAJA Publishing Company, 1990).

- *Mail Order Legal Guide,* by Edwin J. Keup (Oasis, 1993).

- *Mail Order Riches Success Kit,* by Tyler G. Hicks (International Wealth, 1994).

- *Mail Order Selling: How to Market Almost Anything by Mail,* by Irving Burstiner (Prentice-Hall, 1989).

- *Money in Your Mailbox: How to Start and Operate a Successful Mail-order Business,* by Perry L. Wilbur (Wiley, 1992).

- *One Thousand One Ideas to Create Retail Excitement,* by Edgar A. Falk (Prentice-Hall, 1994).

- *Selling What You Make: Profit from Your Handcrafts,* by James E. Seitz (McGraw-Hill, 1992).
- *Start and Run a Profitable Craft Business: Your Step-by-Step Business Plan,* by William Hynes (Self-Counsel Press, 1993).
- *Start and Run a Profitable Retail Business: Your Step-by-Step Business Plan,* by Michael M. Coltman (Self-Counsel Press, 1993).
- *Start Your Own Coffee and Tea Store* (Pfeiffer & Company, 1994).
- *Start Your Own Gift Basket Business* (Pfeiffer & Company, 1994).
- *Start Your Own Mail-order Business* (Pfeiffer & Company, 1994).
- *Starting a Business to Sell Your Artwork* (Business Of Your Own, 1988).
- *Starting a Business to Sell Your Craft Items* (Business of Your Own, 1988).
- *Starting a Clothing Boutique* (Business of Your Own, 1988).
- *Starting a Flower Shop* (Business of Your Own, 1988).
- *Starting a Gift Shop* (Business of Your Own, 1988).
- *Starting a Mail-order Business* (Business of Your Own, 1988).
- *Starting an Antique Shop* (Business of Your Own, 1988).
- *Successful Retailing,* by Paula Wardell (Upstart Publishing, 1993).
- *Upstart Guide to Owning and Managing a Florist Service,* by Dan Ramsey (Upstart Publishing, 1994).
- *Upstart Guide to Owning and Managing an Antiques Business,* by Lisa Angowski Rogak (Upstart Publishing, 1994).
- *Your Own Shop: How to Open and Operate a Successful Retail Business,* by Ruth Jacobson (McGraw-Hill, 1991).

8

HOW TO START A MOBILE SERVICE BUSINESS

Service industries are the brightest stars in the nation's economic firmament, and a mobile service business, modified to meet the special needs of a semiretired Gray Wave entrepreneur, could brighten your future as well.

Service firms provide more than a third of all jobs in the United States today. Service industries fueled U.S. economic growth between 1987 and 1992. During that time total sales of service industries increased by more than 26 percent in inflation-adjusted dollars, compared with a smaller 2.8 percent increase for retailers, according to a November 1995 article in *American Demographics* magazine. Service employment expanded by more than 20 percent, compared with 3.5 percent for retailers. And the number of service businesses increased more than 12 percent, compared with 1.5 percent for retailers.

In the twenty-first century, experts say, almost 90 percent of all jobs will be service-based. Why the service industry success story? Because service businesses sell time and expertise, not a product. As we enter the twenty-first century, people are either too busy to run their own errands and do their own chores or simply have better things to do with their time and can afford to pay for those services from others.

And don't forget—people are living longer. Many of those older people no longer can do all the things for themselves they once could, so they hire someone else to cut the grass, rake the leaves, and maintain the garden. Or chop their firewood. Or buy their groceries. Or polish their silver. Or perform a million and

141

one other chores. All those chores that people can't do, or choose not to do, for themselves spell opportunity for the owner of a mobile service business.

THE ADVANTAGES OF MOBILE SERVICE BUSINESSES

The sheer beauty of starting a mobile service business is that it's so easy and inexpensive, and there are many—in fact, countless—opportunities. Anyone can do it, provided he or she has the right entrepreneurial backbone. You don't need a special skill or talent, although that doesn't hurt. You don't need to be extremely smart or particularly prescient. You don't need to be a whiz at picking the next big product or have a small fortune to invest in inventory.

All you need is the ability to do a job—even a simple, basic task—that a few people are willing to pay someone to do for them. You need to be able to look around you and say, "Hey, I can do this particular thing well for myself. I bet other people might be more than willing to pay me to take the job off their hands." Your opportunities are limitless. You can turn any job, any simple task, into a mobile service business. And with little investment.

The key here is to keep in mind who you are right now, at this stage of your life, and what you want and need out of your mobile service business. If you were deciding to start your own service business at a younger age—say, in your twenties or thirties—you'd probably come up with a bigger idea, requiring a bigger investment and a bigger commitment of time and energy than you need to make now. That's because this business would have to bring in enough bucks to support you and your growing family.

It would take a lot of clients and more hours than you have in a given week to make enough money doing people's laundry in their homes or washing their cars in their driveways to support a growing family. You simply couldn't make that pay. To make a laundry business or a car wash earn enough to support a growing family, you'd have to give up the mobile nature of the business at the very least. And that would mean a bigger investment of time, energy, and money—in equipment and a fixed business establishment—than you're probably interested in making as a Gray Wave entrepreneur.

So if service businesses spell growth and success for the future—and they do—stick to a mobile service business. That will allow you to minimize your investment. And you can decide just how much of a commitment you want to make to your business.

Think about it. If you can throw your tools or lawn mower or shopping baskets into the trunk of your car and take your service to your customer, you minimize your overhead by eliminating the need for rent on a storefront or shop. And you have the option of limiting the number of customers you service and the hours, number of days, and even the seasons you work. You can work as little or as much as you like, to provide the income and activity level you desire. I'm assuming you'll have other sources of income—Social Security and probably a pension—so you don't need to work those long, hard, wearying hours the owner of a traditional service business would. You'll be able to lead whatever kind of semiretired lifestyle you choose. If you want afternoons free for sailing on the lake in spring and summer, that's your choice.

Perhaps the biggest plus for a service business, though, is the interaction with people. No matter what kind of service you choose to perform, from organizing closets to installing audio and video equipment, service businesses are people-oriented businesses. They touch people's lives by performing essential tasks. And the better service you provide—in the specific work itself, but also in your manner with your clients—the more rewarding and satisfying your business will be. For you *and* your clients.

THERE ARE DOWNSIDES TO STARTING A MOBILE SERVICE BUSINESS

Although the future shines bright indeed for the service industry, there are some downsides you should consider before you decide to grab some of that luster for yourself.

Remember, a mobile service business sells a service. So you need to be sure you can offer a service—a skill or area of expertise—that people need and want. And to be a successful entrepreneur in the twenty-first century you'll need to sell convenience as well, because that's what consumers will be looking for in the future. For the owner of a mobile service business, convenience won't be a problem—you'll be taking your service right to your client's door. But consider these potential negatives:

THE MONEY

If you're primarily interested in making a lot of money, you'd better look elsewhere. Generally, the kind of semiretired mobile service businesses we're talking about here—with little investment in equipment and overhead—won't make you a fortune. But you can make sufficient income to provide some of the little luxuries you otherwise couldn't afford on your pension and Social Security alone.

Of course, the amount of money you can make depends on the kind of service you provide and the number of hours you're prepared to work. If you decide to start a housecleaning service, you can charge anywhere from $15 to $40 an hour, depending on your location. That kind of hourly rate can add up if you put in three or four half days a week.

But if you decide to do laundry for busy professional couples with young children or wash cars or provide regular shopping services for elderly shut-ins, it's unlikely you can charge more than $10 an hour and find enough clients to make it pay.

THE (HARD) WORK

Most mobile service jobs involve physical labor, although they vary greatly in how physical that work may be. Cleaning houses can be exhausting. So can mowing lawns and chopping wood and washing cars. Running errands and grocery shopping and sitting for the elderly won't be as physically demanding, although we're still not talking desk jobs here. You need to decide how much energy you've got and how much you're willing to expend on your new business.

Your future income will be directly related to how much time and energy you put into the business. If you're not performing a service, if you're not working, you won't be earning money. If your housecleaning service takes off and you decide to hire help, you'll certainly expand your profit potential, minus what you pay that help.

But when you take the step of hiring employees to provide the service for you, you need to insure that they meet your quality control and customer service standards. You're the one the client will be contracting with for that service, and you're the one who will be responsible for making sure the job is done properly.

THE UNCERTAIN SCHEDULES

Clients can be very fickle, as changeable as Mother Nature. And your carefully worked out work schedule can be shot in a matter of minutes at the whim of a whimsical client or two. Say you do facials in your clients' homes. You've got your workweek carefully mapped out, with facial appointments at nine and eleven A.M. Tuesday through Saturday. That leaves your afternoons free for your bridge club and book group, as well as for other interests and responsibilities.

But Monday morning at eight Anna Smith calls to reschedule her nine o'clock because her daughter's baby-sitter is sick and she has to fill in. Then Nicole Graham calls on your cell phone—she's got the flu and needs to reschedule for next week, but she wants to do it the afternoon your bridge club meets because it's the only open time she's got—and her mornings are all tied up.

Next, Mr. Hooks calls with his usual crisis. He needs to move up his appointment to nine tonight because he's got to fly to the West Coast on the red-eye for an early meeting and he needs to look his best. And so on.

You get the picture. When you're operating a service business, and particularly one you pick up and carry with you, clients assume, and perhaps rightly, that your mission is to serve them and their needs, not your own. And their needs by nature are changeable. It can be extremely inconsiderate and irritating, not to mention stressful. But if you want to operate a successful mobile*service business, you'd better get used to it.

MOTHER NATURE

Depending on the nature of your mobile service business, the whims of Mother Nature may have as much impact on your future work life as the whims of your clients. And that can be costly as well as irritating. Many of the jobs people want others to do for them involve outdoor work—like house painting, gardening, and lawn mowing. Those jobs just can't be done in a downpour, so your financial expectations will have to be as flexible as the weather is changeable.

A MOBILE SERVICE BUSINESS COULD BE JUST RIGHT FOR YOU

There are definite pros and cons in starting a mobile service business, and if that's the entrepreneurial route you're thinking of taking, get a fresh page in your Gray Wave notebook and head it "Mobile Service Business." Now list the pros and cons. As you do that, glance back at chapter 3 and review the "Questions to Ask Yourself." Check your notebook for the answers to those questions about what kind of semiretired lifestyle you want to lead in coming years. Do the mobile service pros and cons seem compatible with your answers to those questions? If so, you may have found your future business type.

But first you need to double-check yourself and your own answers, and you need to be brutally honest. After all, although the financial investment in a mobile service business is relatively minimal, you still don't want to spend money on a business that isn't going to work out because of who you are and the way you are. You also don't have time and energy to waste on an enterprise that's doomed to failure because it's not right for you.

So what kind of person does the owner of a mobile service business have to be? Think service first—customer service—two bywords for businesses in the 1990s and beyond. If you set out to provide a service to clients, you need to bear in mind the cardinal rule in any business (but particularly a service business): The client is always right. You need to like people and have the people skills required for working with others on a regular basis.

And you need to be the kind of person who is eager to go that extra mile for a client, no matter how much you'd rather be doing something else at that particular moment. No matter how obnoxious or unreasonable that client may be in his or her dealings with you.

You also have to be flexible. If you're providing a mobile service, you're going to have to be willing to adjust to the whims and needs of your clients, and perhaps to Mother Nature as well.

It certainly will help if you have a real skill or expertise in a given area. But that's not necessary. There are plenty of jobs that need doing that most people can learn to do efficiently. If you find real pleasure in the task, it'll make your business seem more like fun than work. But that, too, isn't a requirement for a true entrepreneur.

What is a requirement for the owner of a mobile service business is the kind of personality that can stick to a somewhat repetitive, often not very creative, task day after day and hour after hour and get it done with ease and with a smile. These aren't idea jobs for people who want to sit around and apply their brainpower to knotty problems. And they're not for people who get bored easily and continually want to try something different.

Frankly, a mobile service business is perfect for someone who's used to and enjoys plain, simple work. The kind of work that you do, get done, then put aside and out of your mind and go on to something else.

Do you see yourself in that role? Does the idea of providing a basic service to others feel like the right fit for you? If so, the next step is to decide what kind of service you're going to provide and to whom.

DECIDE WHAT KIND OF SERVICE YOU WANT TO PROVIDE

This will be a key decision for your future happiness and well-being, financial and otherwise. And because your options are virtually limitless, you need to be smart about your decision-making process. You can take the obvious and safe approach and establish a business doing something you know well, like delivering your own home-cooked dinners to busy families. Or, if you're the adventurous type and are eager to learn something new, you can do some research about twenty-first-century trends and service needs, further analyze your own interests, and then educate yourself in a new skill. And, of course, bear in mind as you begin to narrow your options that you'll need to be able to pack your service equipment into the back of your car or truck for the added convenience the mobile aspect of your business will offer clients.

Now, let's look at some broad categories of service jobs that offer unique opportunities for ambitious Gray Wave entrepreneurs in the twenty-first century.

DOING HOUSEHOLD CHORES

One sure-bet trend expected to continue into the twenty-first century is the double-income family, in which both parents work. Americans over the years got used to a very high quality of life. After World War II they developed a taste for luxuries of all kinds, from push-button appliances to a new car every few years. Then came more exotic and pricey luxuries, like imported beers and imported automobiles, and the taste for all of them was addicting.

It wasn't a problem during the boom years after World War II, but as the recession of the 1970s and 1980s struck and prices rose, it took the income of both adults in a family to maintain a comfortable lifestyle—not to mention keeping up with the Joneses.

These two–wage-earner families had more money to spend but less time to devote to necessary household tasks. Who has the energy to scrub floors, wash and iron, or care for pets and appliances after a fourteen-hour day on the stock exchange? That created and continues to create opportunities for service businesses to flourish.

Filling Businesses' Service Gaps

Many businesses, in an effort to reduce overhead and operational costs, have either reduced products and services or sought a less expensive way of providing those products or services to their customers. This has created opportunities for smaller entrepreneurs to fill in the gaps. Instead of maintaining costly staff and equipment to provide those services, the larger business can contract with you, the independent contractor, to provide that service in its stead.

For example, the daily newspaper in my community used to have a full-time janitor/handyman on staff. But that cost salary plus fringe benefits, and the benefits added up. So a few years ago in a cost-saving measure, when the long-time janitor retired, the newspaper's publisher took the opportunity to replace a permanent staff member with a mobile cleaning service operated by a "retired" couple. That couple, in their mid-sixties and healthy as a pair of pack mules, eventually took over the cleaning of several of the main office and business buildings in town and are making a healthy income to cushion their somewhat deferred retirement.

They told me they'd rather work a little harder for a few more years than many people their age ordinarily would—but for themselves—so that when they really do feel the urge to make a full-time job of relaxation they'll be able to do it with some style.

Filling Staff Gaps

In many cases, the corporate downsizing trend that has struck American businesses has resulted in a reduction in necessary support staff, as well as in personal hardship for families. But stockholder-conscious corporate executives, faced with rising costs and decreasing profits, realized it's smart business strategy to hire temporary workers and independent contractors to perform many basic business functions rather than maintain a large payroll.

Businesses today are hiring outside workers to do temporary jobs of all kinds, including legal work, public relations, marketing, bookkeeping, and a host of other basic business tasks. That leaves greater opportunity, as well as greater flexibility, for people who can fill those gaps.

The key here is to establish yourself as an entrepreneur, the owner of a mobile service business, even if that service is more professional than physical. That way you can call more of the shots and open up more opportunities.

For example, say you were an executive secretary for a medium-sized business, supervising a staff of four secretaries, for forty years before retiring at age sixty-three. Your supervisory and secretarial skills are excellent. Now you want to work about thirty hours a week, but you want some variety and some control over your situation. So you advertise as a freelance executive secretary who specializes in "reengineering" clerical staffs for increased productivity, working on a part-time and/or temporary project basis.

You can take a single high-intensity job for six months or a year, or a couple of more routine jobs for fifteen hours each a week. If nobody needs to be reengineered at a particular time, you can always fill in with straightforward freelance secretarial work until something more challenging comes along.

REPAIRING PRODUCTS

Because of the lingering effects of the recession, job uncertainty, and ever-higher prices, many people today are opting to repair existing products rather than replace them at the first sign of a problem. At the same time, consumers are choosing to spend a little more on a better quality product. That means it suddenly makes more sense for them to maintain and repair it as long as possible before investing in a new one. Everything from lawn mowers to snow blowers to vacuum cleaners can be repaired, and a handy Gray Wave entrepreneur can establish a profitable business providing those mobile services.

Servicing Lifestyle Needs

Here's where twenty-first-century opportunities will abound. You can pick your target market and lifestyle, and choose a service that people in that market, living that lifestyle, need filled. For example, all kinds of people today are interested in entertaining. Let's face it, we all have piles of invitations to return but just can't get it together to organize a party. So why not start a party-throwing service? You could specialize in kids' birthdays or business cocktails or holiday specials, or you can do a little of everything to broaden your appeal.

Or how about organizing and doing the detail work for trips? Again, you could specialize in putting together fun tours for seniors, doing everything from planning itineraries to booking rooms to hiring tour guides and picking up tickets. Or specialize in offbeat family vacations or honeymoons or school trips or camping trips—or all of the above.

Or organize redecorating efforts. You don't have to actually be a decorator. But busy professionals often don't have the time to redecorate rooms or even replace old wallpaper or carpeting. Offer to do the dirty work for them.

You can carefully follow the taste and instructions of your client, offering advice when requested, but you're the one who races around town picking up sample fabric and wallpaper books, choosing paint and carpeting samples, and getting estimates from workmen if you don't want to do the work yourself.

Your client says, "I want to redo my eight-year-old son's bedroom. He loves hockey and skiing. I want navy blue and red, with some touches of bright green for color. I want wallpaper, carpeting, and curtains, and I want lots of shelves for toys and athletic equipment. And he needs a desk. Here's my budget, bring me some samples." You're off and running a business.

DO A LITTLE TREND-TRACKING

Before you make your final decision on what your mobile service business will be, double-check your choice against the yardstick of tomorrow's society. In other words, be a futurist—

a trend-tracker. After all, you may be missing out on a better bet because your vision just isn't broad enough.

READ PUBLICATIONS YOU DON'T USUALLY READ

Go to the library, or to the news dealer with the largest magazine selection in town, and buy all the specialty magazines you can find. Then pick up newspapers from major cities across the country and regional magazines from wherever you can find them. Read everything you wouldn't normally read. Read ethnic publications. Read the ads to see who advertisers are targeting and who is reading these publications. Be sure to pick up a few issues of *American Demographics,* the magazine that tracks demographic trends.

Look for ideas of services you could provide to these niche readers. Make notes in your Gray Wave notebook as you read.

WATCH TV SHOWS YOU DON'T NORMALLY WATCH

Be sure you have access to cable TV before you start this assignment and have your Gray Wave notebook handy, as well as *TV Guide.* Then, spend a weekend, plus one or two weekdays, watching TV around the clock. Take special notice of the commercials. You'll get a different perspective of the world and of what people's needs may be. You may get some good business ideas as well.

HIT THE MALLS, DOWNTOWN, AND LOCAL DINERS

The idea is to find out what people are thinking about, what their needs and desires are. At the mall, sit in the food court and watch as they go by. Then, watch what they're buying. Listen in on conversations.

Strike up conversations with waitresses at the diner. Buy a cup of coffee for somebody and start up a conversation about what's happening in his or her life. Think of this as research, because that's just what it is. Take notes; look for patterns, ideas, trends. All of this research will help you get a better idea of what today's consumer needs in the way of service.

START NARROWING YOUR OPTIONS

There's clearly a world of opportunity out there. All you need is some creative thinking, a desire to provide a service, mobility, and in some cases a specific skill. Now you need to begin narrowing your options and making some decisions about what service you're going to provide.

First, think about what kinds of activities interest you most. Say you're a voracious reader or love to sew or love working with little children. Jot down in your Gray Wave notebook any skills you have that you could potentially put to work in your interest area. If you love working with little children, you could baby-sit, do substitute bedtime reading, or do early-evening cooking sessions for groups of neighborhood kids.

Next, with your interest areas and skills in mind, make a short list of, say, five possible services you could base a part-time, mobile business on. Then ask yourself the following questions and note your answers in your Gray Wave notebook.

- Is this service available locally?
- Is the local service provided conveniently to clients?
- Have I ever thought about trying to hire someone to perform this service for myself? How recently?
- How often would a typical client use this service?
- Are clients unhappy with the local business that provides this service, and why?

HERE'S HOW TO GET STARTED

Look carefully at your answers to the questions above. They'll tell you whether there's a potential market for the services you're considering for your business. Now decide which of the five potential services on your list meets the criteria of being interesting to you; being doable; and being something for which your answers to the questions above indicate a market need.

That should narrow your choices to one clear, leading contender. Next, define your target market. That will tell you whether you can expect your future mobile service business to bloom, or whether you need to examine the market more closely and come up with some better ideas. This market analysis also will help you later, when you draw up your business and marketing plans.

DEFINE YOUR TARGET MARKET

First, you need to define your ideal client. Decide exactly who would be most interested in contracting for your service. Then decide whether there are enough of those clients within a reasonable geographic area to support your business. Remember, this is a mobile service business, which means you'll be taking your service to the client. This isn't the kind of business you can do by telecommuting, or by hoping to draw clients to you. So if your clients are fifty miles apart, that'll obviously cut down on the amount of business you can do and the profits you can earn.

You'll also need to pinpoint where and how you can reach these clients, because your future marketing will be targeted where those clients can be found.

Now you need to paint a profile of your future clients. Close your eyes and envision them. List everything you can about them. Are they male or female; young, middle-aged, or Gray Wavers like yourself? What's their income, where do they live, where do they shop, and what are their hobbies? Check out places that sell products or related services they might use and jot down the characteristics of their clients. If there are relevant industry or trade groups relating to your service, you might try contacting them. Then create a portrait of that typical client.

For example, say you decide to start a pet-sitting business. You can stay overnight to spare owners the need of placing their discriminating pets in an impersonal kennel, or just look in on them a couple of times a day to walk them, feed them, and generally care for them. Your clients may be away on vacation or business, or even executives who work sixteen-hour days and just need someone to look in on their pets during the regular workday.

Your clients can be anyone who owns a pet, but most of your business probably will come from someone who travels a lot. Young, single professionals or families going on vacation. Or perhaps they're Gray Wavers who now have the luxury of traveling whenever the spirit moves them. Their pets are like their children, and they want to pamper them.

Locate Your Targeted Customers

Now decide where your targeted clients can be found. Do you live in a thriving community with lots of young families? Is there a comfortable retirement community as well? Are more people moving into the area than are moving out?

You'll probably be able to market your pet-sitting service to owners of homes in that new, upscale retirement village being constructed on the edge of town and to the owners of the big, new custom homes being built for the successful young professionals in the area.

Check out new developments and old neighborhoods. Check out pet shops, pet grooming businesses, breeders, and kennels as well. Are they flourishing?

Later, when we talk more about a specific marketing plan, we'll take the carefully defined portrait of your clients that we settled on earlier and decide where they can be found. That's where you'll target your future marketing. But for now, you just need to determine that there are sufficient consumers within reach who will buy your service.

Talk with Others in the Field

This can be tricky. You definitely should talk with other business owners in your general field, but a potential competitor isn't likely to share much valuable information. And it may be difficult to find someone who provides exactly the kind of mobile service you're thinking of providing. But be as creative and as thorough here as possible.

You may need to travel to nearby communities to find people to talk with, so you can assure them you won't be a competitor. They're likely to be more forthcoming that way. As long as you can assure them you're not a competitor, most business owners love to talk about their triumphs and tragedies.

And if you're having trouble finding someone who offers exactly the same service, try talking with owners of the traditional version of your business. For example, if you're thinking of starting a mobile hairdressing business and can't find one anywhere, talk with the owner of a fixed hairdressing business. You should pick his or her brains for client likes and dislikes, do's and don'ts, and his or her own successes and failures.

DISCUSS YOUR PLAN WITH POTENTIAL CLIENTS

You also need to test your idea with people who would be your potential clients. Talk with your friends, neighbors, and family members to determine if they would be interested in buying a service like yours. Ask about their key priorities in their purchase of this service. Why do they want to buy this service? Are they primarily interested in convenience, speed and efficiency, quality, or a special skill? How much are they willing to pay for this service? How often would they need it?

Next, conduct an informal survey of potential clients you don't know or don't normally come into contact with. Go door-to-door and street-to-street in a variety of neighborhoods, asking the same questions. Try random cold-calling on the telephone, but be ready for the cold shoulder or worse, the sound of the phone slamming in your ear. Many people don't like to be bothered at home, but it's certainly worth the effort for what might be valuable insight from those more objective than your friends and neighbors or even someone answering a knock at the door.

You also can bounce your idea off an independent observer by contacting the local office of the Small Business Administration. The SBA sponsors a mentor program called SCORE (Service Corps of Retired Executives), which brings together retired executives and people who are trying to launch a business. The advice is free, impartial, and rooted in experience.

PUT TOGETHER YOUR OWN TEAM

Before you go any further you need to put together the team of professionals who will help guide you through the process of starting your mobile service business. You'll need an accountant and a banker. You'll also need a lawyer to prepare any contracts you may enter into with clients. In addition, a good lawyer will be helpful in researching any licenses and permits you may need. If you don't have such professionals lined up, do it now.

As an experienced Gray Waver who already has completed at least one career, you may not have to go far to find accomplished professionals. First look to those you know well from your past career and whose skills you have come to respect. Or, if you're settling in a new retirement area, ask your neighbors for suggestions.

Don't hire someone just to be a nice guy or fulfill a family obligation. This should be a business decision like any other, and you need the wisdom and experience of seasoned, successful professionals. And speaking of seasoned, don't overlook other Gray Wave semiretirees with part-time professional businesses of their own.

Check with SCORE again for possible candidates, and with the American Association of Retired Persons (AARP). Also check with professional associations and with friends and associates in other businesses for candidates. Ask candidates for a free initial meeting, and if they decline, cross them off your list. Ask for the names of three recent clients whose circumstances are similar to yours. Contact these references and ask about the candidates' professional skills and services.

This is a decision you need to make with care. Your team will be important to your future, so check their credentials, their references, and their business premises carefully. Call the Better Business Bureau and the state Division of Consumer Affairs before you sign up anyone to represent you in your new business.

DRAW UP YOUR BUSINESS AND MARKETING PLANS

Now that you've decided what service you're going to provide, you need to draw up a business plan and a separate marketing plan, to guide you in starting your business. Planning is the key to success for every entrepreneur, even the owner of a mobile service business.

Just as you wouldn't think of starting any journey without a map, you shouldn't consider starting your service business without a business plan and a marketing plan. They will help you map out the route you'll follow to accomplish your business goals. You'll also be able to check your progress regularly against your plans, and fine-tune them as experience suggests.

THE BUSINESS PLAN

This should be part of your Gray Wave notebook and need not be elaborate, since you won't be submitting it to a commercial lender in the hope of obtaining a business loan. (More about that later, but commercial lenders do not finance small business start-ups. If you need financing, you'll get it elsewhere.) The plan should address your business's mission, your goals and objectives, your strategy, and finances.

Here's a general outline you can follow:

- *General information*—List the name of your business; your name and address; and telephone, fax, and E-mail numbers.

- *Mission statement*—This should be a general statement of one or two paragraphs explaining your philosophy and motivation in starting this business.

- *Objectives*—List your specific goals and objectives for the business.

- *Define the business*—Describe the business: What service will you provide and to whom; how will you provide the service; where and how will you reach your clients; where will your business be based and where will you provide the service; who's your primary competition; will you need to hire employees?

- *Finances*—We'll discuss finances in more detail later in this chapter, but include realistic income and expense projections. Allow some cushion for unexpected start-up costs and setbacks, and for a slower than expected growth in clients. Remember, it takes time for people to get to know you and your business, and to get into the habit of calling on you.

The Marketing Plan

You will touch on marketing in your business plan, but you also need to develop a separate marketing plan to detail exactly how you'll promote your mobile service business for at least a year. If you want your business to be successful, you have to market yourself.

The biggest mistake most small businesses make is to rely on advertising alone. Yet advertising often is the most expensive and least productive way to reach clients. Instead, you'll want to spread your efforts among a variety of marketing opportunities, including flyers, media publicity, and promotions.

As you draw up your marketing plan, focus on the portrait of your target client that we drew earlier in this chapter. Think about ways and places to reach that target client, then decide:

- What mix of marketing you will do on a weekly, monthly, or seasonal basis.

- How much money you will budget for each marketing effort in that period.

- How and by whom that marketing effort will be carried out.

- How you will assess the effectiveness of your marketing plan.

Keep in mind that your marketing techniques, particularly at the start, don't necessarily have to be sophisticated or high-tech. For example, if you're starting that pet-sitting business, ask pet store owners and travel agents if you can place small notices of your service on their bulletin boards or counters; many will be happy to do so. Or you can target their customers with mailings.

But don't stop there. Pet owners—particularly young executives, families, Gray Wavers, and others with pampered pets—can be found in lots of other places. Put notices on health club, church, and grocery store bulletin boards, to name just a few.

WHAT ABOUT YOUR FINANCING?

By now you've researched and decided what your mobile service business will be and what professionals will help you get started. You've drawn up a business plan and a marketing plan. The next key step is to plan and secure your financing, if that's necessary. Many service businesses can be started from savings, without any real financing help. Businesses like pet-sitting, house-sitting, child care, even laundry service, don't require much more than your own time and effort and perhaps a giant-sized box of detergent.

For other businesses, however, you may need to purchase basic equipment. Some can be fairly costly, like a snow blower and tractor-mower for a lawn-care and snow-removal business.

And to put your business on a businesslike footing, you'll want an answering machine, a fax and a computer with basic business software to help with your billing and client accounts. So you need to determine what your business start-up costs will be, even though they may be minimal compared with the costs associated with starting other kinds of businesses that require extensive inventory or the high overhead of a fixed location.

You also need money to live on while the business gets rolling, but your Social Security and pension payments, plus any savings, should be sufficient for living expenses. The kinds of mobile service businesses we're talking about are intended to be part-time businesses that supplement your retirement income and lifestyle, not make up your entire livelihood. Of course, depending on how much time you want to put into it and whether you are interested in hiring employees, your business may become more successful—and more profitable—than you ever dreamed.

So start a new worksheet in your Gray Wave notebook to calculate your start-up costs. Basically, here's what you'll need:

Startup Costs Worksheet

Enter the appropriate amount to determine your overall costs. I've offered a typical list, but be sure to customize it to fit whatever type of mobile service business you're launching.

Telephone installation	$_____
Insurance	$_____
Professional services	$_____
Attorney	$_____
Accountant	$_____
Marketing/advertising firm	$_____
Computer hardware and software	$_____
Telephone and fax machine	$_____
File cabinet	$_____
Copy machine	$_____
Office supplies	$_____
Your service equipment	$_____
Total advertising	$_____
TOTAL START-UP COSTS	$_____

Now that you've figured out your start-up costs, you need to secure financing if necessary. Basically, you have three options: your own funds, a personal loan from a lending institution, or a loan from family or friends.

Your Own Funds

You may be lucky enough to have sufficient savings, or assets you can convert to cash. Even the simplest mobile service business requires an outlay for office supplies. You have to keep records and send and pay bills, right?

Maybe you have a severance package you can invest in starting up your new mobile service business. Or, better yet, perhaps you just inherited a healthy sum from Mom and Dad, or from Aunt Betty. That, too, can be an excellent source of financing for your business start-up.

INSTITUTIONAL SOURCES

Forget a business loan. Banks just don't lend money to start-ups because it's too risky. They want a proven track record of success before they'll consider a business loan. Your best bet is a home equity or personal loan.

A home equity loan, or second mortgage, is now a very popular form of financing for all sorts of things, including basic business equipment. Banks like home equity loans because there's little risk involved. It's a bit of a simplification, but if your home is worth $175,000 and your mortgage balance is $75,000, you have $100,000 worth of equity in your home. Generally speaking, you can borrow against that equity—usually up to 70 percent of its value—to finance your business needs.

You should search for a home equity loan or a personal loan exactly as you did for your first mortgage. Shop around for the best interest rates at banks, credit unions, and savings and loans.

FAMILY AND FRIENDS

If you're on good terms with your family they can be an excellent source of financing. The same is true of friends. There's no question it can be a win-win deal for both parties. That's because there's a gap between current lending rates and the interest rates institutions are offering on savings accounts, certificates of deposit, and other savings instruments.

Say your sister is a successful lawyer who makes good money and is always on the lookout for a good investment. Right now she's got $10,000 to invest, and by sheer coincidence, that's exactly how much you've decided you need to borrow to start up your new mobile service business.

She doesn't want to mess with mutual funds and other more risky forms of investment. She knows that fixed-rate investments earn around 4.5 percent with a conventional savings account and about 6 percent with most CDs.

You, on the other hand, have discovered that a personal loan will cost you about 10 percent. So there's roughly a 4 percent window of opportunity for you and your sister to make a deal that benefits you both. If she lends you her $10,000 at 8 percent she'll be getting a better return on her investment than she would otherwise and you'll be getting a loan 2 percent below what's available in the marketplace. You both win.

HERE'S WHAT HAROLD AND MAUDE DID

Harold and Maude Blumkin both worked for the city school district for thirty-some years before retiring two years ago at age sixty. Harold had been a custodian, and Maude had worked in food service.

Their total annual income had always been modest, and with four kids to raise there was never much left over for savings. There certainly was never any extra money for travel or even family vacations, except camping and fishing.

Harold and Maude had worried about what kind of retirement lifestyle they would be able to afford. They knew they would never have to eat cat food, but frankly, they were hoping they would finally be able to buy into a modest slice of the American retirement pie. They realized, however, that in order to be able to take some trips and maybe buy a boat for fishing and sunning on the lake, they were going to have do something on the side to generate extra income.

They also were tired of worrying about money, so this time they decided to do something about it and be smart. They decided to plan ahead, before they retired. Neither Harold nor Maude wanted to work for anyone else ever again. Both had their share of bad bosses, and they were determined to try something on their own—and together.

They really wanted to spend time together, even after all these years. Their children kidded them about holding hands at the movies, just like they did when they started dating at age sixteen.

"The simple truth is, we just like each other," Maude told me. "No one can make me laugh so hard I cry, like Harold does."

"Yeah, and no one laughs at my jokes the way Maude does," Harold said with a grin.

They started making lists four years ago, trying to come up with an idea for a business. They thought about retail sales, but just couldn't get excited about selling anything in particular. Besides, they said, in addition to not knowing *what* to sell, they really didn't know *how* to sell. And they wanted to be more active. They wanted to be actually doing something, preferably physical.

It struck them both one Saturday morning when Maude was mopping the bathroom floor for the second time that week, after one of their grandchildren's puppies had tracked muddy paw prints on the linoleum. Harold kidded Maude about insisting that her floor be clean enough to eat off of.

"You're a cleaning fanatic," Harold said.

"Yes, and you'd have divorced me long ago if I wasn't," Maude snapped back. "You're as fanatical as I am cleaning your garage and basement."

Then they looked at each other and started laughing. That was it, they agreed. They both prized good housekeeping and got great satisfaction out of getting the job done. Why not start a cleaning business?

They started another list—of things they did and didn't want to do in their cleaning business. First, they wanted their days free for boating and fishing. So they wanted to work mostly nights, though not every night. That generally ruled out homes, which was fine, because although cleaning is good, hard work, and they thrived on hard work, they didn't want to undertake projects that were too big to finish in a couple of hours at a time.

So they put a couple of little ads in the local shopper newspaper and got nowhere. They decided to make some telephone calls to small businesses and offices, and that got them a couple of jobs they could do on weekends and in the evenings after work. They wanted to be sure their business would bring in a decent supplemental income when they finally retired.

What really convinced them it would work and they could retire, though, was when Maude suggested they add gas station rest rooms to their repertoire.

"They're one of my pet peeves," she explained. "They're usually so dirty, probably no one ever cleans them. So I figured why not hit all the gas stations in town and make them a proposal. We could do those anytime, put them on a regular schedule. And they really don't take any time to clean, once you get past the first time or two."

Which is exactly what they did. Now gas station rest rooms, and even some gas station offices, are a good portion of their thriving business. And best of all, their business bought them the kind of four-person fishing boat they never thought they'd be able to own, short of winning the lottery. Now their problem is making sure they save enough free time in their busy weeks to hang out a "Gone fishin' " sign.

SO WHERE DO YOU GO FROM HERE?

Now it's decision time—time to decide if a mobile service business is right for you or if you want to investigate another route to Gray Wave entrepreneurship. A mobile service business is hard work and often not glamorous, but it can be an excellent opportunity for the right person. Your risk is minimal because your investment is relatively small. You have very low overhead because you have no fixed location to pay for, as you take your service to your clients in your car or truck.

And clearly, there are as many opportunities for mobile service businesses as there are things that people need to have done for their business or their personal lives every day. And in many cases, to provide these services all you need are your own skill and expertise.

On the other hand, no matter how few clients you start with, and no matter how small you decide to keep your business, you will need a good dose of energy and enthusiasm, because most service businesses entail hard work. You also need to like people and be able to work with them, because the service you will be providing is for them and dependent on your relationship with them to a certain extent. *Customer* and *service* are the two most important words for the owner of a service business.

If you're a highly creative person looking for an outlet for your creativity, a mobile service business probably won't satisfy you—unless you find doing specific regular tasks like mowing lawns or doing laundry over and over creative. But if you're the kind of person who finds deep satisfaction in performing certain tasks and seeing a job well done, a mobile service business may be perfect for you.

Now it's up to you. If you're not really sure a service business is for you, don't worry. There are other routes to entrepreneurship, which we'll outline in the next two chapters.

MOBILE SERVICE BUSINESS RESOURCE AND REFERENCE GUIDE

Here's a list of sources you can use to get more information on starting a mobile service business.

- *Be the Boss II: Running a Successful Service Business,* by Sandi Wilson (Avon Books, 1993).
- *Catering: Starting and Running a Money-Making Business,* by Judy Richards (McGraw-Hill, 1994).
- *Great Businesses You Can Start on a Shoestring in a Recession or Depression* (Gordon, 1992).
- *How to Start a Service Business,* by Ben Chant and Melissa Morgan (Avon Books, 1994).
- *How to Start a Window-Cleaning Business: A Guide to Sales, Procedures and Operations,* by Judy Suvall (Cleaning Consultants, 1988).
- *How to Start and Operate a Recycling Business,* by John P. Allison (RMC Publishing Group, 1991).
- *Mind Your Own Business: The Best Businesses You Can Start Today for Under Five Hundred Dollars,* by Stephen Wagner and the editors of *Income Opportunities* (Adams, 1992).

- *One Hundred & Eighty-Four Businesses Anyone Can Start & Make a Lot of Money,* by Chase Revel (Bantam, 1984).

- *One Hundred & One Best Businesses to Start,* by Sharon Kahn and Philip Lieff (Doubleday, 1992).

- *One Hundred & Sixty-eight More Businesses Anyone Can Start & Make a Lot of Money,* by the staff of *Entrepreneur* (Bantam, 1991).

- *Painting Contractor: Start and Run a Money-Making Business,* by Dan Ramsey (TAB Books, 1993).

- *Professional Cleaning and Building Maintenance: How to Organize a Money-Saving Business or Department for Floor and Building Care,* by Bill Clarke (Cleaning Consultants, 1965).

- *Start and Run a Profitable Catering Business: From Thyme to Timing: Your Step-by-Step Business Plan,* by George Erdosh (Self-Counsel Press, 1994).

- *Start and Run Your Own Profitable Service Business,* by Irving Burstiner (Prentice-Hall, 1992).

- *Starting and Operating a Landscape Maintenance Business,* by Laurence W. Price (Botany Books, 1989).

9

HOW TO ESTABLISH A HOME-BASED CONSULTING BUSINESS

You've been in business successfully for more than thirty years, working for someone else but accumulating knowledge, skills, experience, and contacts.

Now you're getting restive. Some of your friends are talking about retiring and some even have taken the plunge. Maybe your company is making noises about downsizing.

But you know in your gut you're just not ready for all the nonproductive leisure time retirement usually entails. You're something of a workaholic and you can't go cold turkey into retirement.

Why not put all that acquired expertise to work for yourself for a change—and share it with those who can use it—by establishing a home-based consulting business? If you're just not ready for full-time retirement, or if you feel the need for additional retirement income, consider starting a home-based consulting business.

Both consulting businesses and home-based businesses are booming and are expected to be bigger than ever into the twenty-first century and beyond. That's partly because we've come full circle. Before the industrial age, most people worked at home, and their work lives and personal lives were fully integrated. There were no huge, collective workplaces; in fact, most work was done piecemeal, by individuals working alone. The industrial age and assembly lines changed that. But now we're fully ensconced in the information age, and technology and global commerce have made it possible—even preferable, in many cases—to work efficiently and comfortably at home again.

The rush to corporate downsizing also has created opportunities for consultants, as business owners seek help in reengineering their companies to be leaner and more competitive in a tougher marketplace. In this age of increasing information, specialization, and high technology, smart managers are realizing they need help with certain aspects of their businesses.

According to a recent article in *The Wall Street Journal,* income from part-time home-based consulting businesses has exploded, from just over $6 million in 1989 to about $10.5 million in 1995. And consulting itself is a $17-billion-a-year business today.

According to a survey by the American Management Association, 56.7 percent of respondents said they spent more on consultants in 1994 than they did the previous year, and more than two thirds said their spending levels would remain the same or increase in 1995. Some experts are saying those numbers could double by the end of the century.

The biggest consulting specialties, according to the survey, were information technology, 69 percent; training, 63 percent; and strategic planning, 40 percent. But there's plenty of opportunity in other areas as well, particularly for a Gray Wave entrepreneur with a full range of experience.

So let's take a closer look at the idea of establishing a home-based consulting business.

THE ADVANTAGES OF A HOME-BASED CONSULTING BUSINESS

The beauty of a home-based consulting business is the ease with which you can launch it. Your den can quickly be converted to an office, and you can print up your own business cards on your home computer. Voilà; you're in business as a consultant.

Obviously, it's not quite that simple, but it's pretty straightforward nonetheless. A consultant is someone who is paid to give advice to someone else. You don't have to be an expert in every field, but you do have to know how to find the information or skills your clients need.

One of the great benefits of establishing a home-based consulting business is the low cost. You don't have to buy inventory, and your overhead is minimal.

And if you're not feeling as young as you once did, or quite as energetic, don't worry. You can work as little or as much as you like as a home-based consultant. You can decide how many clients you want and how demanding your daily and weekly schedules should be. If you want to factor in a couple of regular weekly golf leagues, no problem. You'll have the freedom to do just that.

Certainly, working at home has unique advantages. First, it's cheaper. Your start-up costs are minimal, and so is your overhead. Obviously, you save on office rental by working at home. You'll need appropriate office and computer equipment, but beyond that, most of what you need is carried compactly on your shoulders.

There's also the freedom and pleasure you'll feel at working in an environment you have chosen and designed, and in which you feel most comfortable. At home you'll be able to open a real window and breathe fresh air instead of stale, recirculated, institutional carbon dioxide.

Aesthetically, this surely will be more pleasing than other options. After all, you decorated your home to suit your needs, tastes, and style. Contrast that to large impersonal office buildings or small, sterile strip mall offices, and already your creative and problem-solving juices will be flowing more freely.

You also can be as accessible to your friends and/or clients as you choose. You can decide to set strict working hours and specific visiting or playing hours, or you can go with the flow. Again, it's your choice, and you can do what works best for you. Now you can actually heed the call of your own biorhythms, rather than contorting yourself to the dictates of a boss's decisions for a mass of employees. And if you want to work with your favorite music playing in the background, that's fine, too.

Don't forget to keep a strict accounting of the space in your home devoted to your business, including telephone, perhaps cleaning service, and even lawn maintenance. Your accountant will be on top of this, but with a home-based business you'll be able to write off a portion of your household expenses when figuring your taxes.

Perhaps best of all, you'll never again confront that nerve-racking, gut-wrenching, twice-daily grind called commuting. When your business is in your home, you're already there when other frenzied businesspeople—commuters—are tearing their hair out on the expressway or fighting their way to a seat on the high-speed line. You can even turn over and go back to bed for another hour or so, if that's what you feel like doing. After all, it's your business and you're already there.

THERE ARE DOWNSIDES TO STARTING A HOME-BASED CONSULTING BUSINESS

A home-based consulting business sounds heavenly so far, doesn't it? But there are some downsides, too. Let's take a look:

THE SPACE PROBLEM

Maybe your house really doesn't have an extra room that's ready to be converted into your new office. It would be a bit inconvenient to have to use your bedroom as an office, and move stacks of files and computer disks every time you're getting ready for bed.

THE PHONE CRISES

Then there are the telephone snafus. If your telephone rings constantly it's a sign your business is healthy. On the other hand, that could drive your family crazy. Your family's personal calls could be a stumbling block if a client repeatedly has trouble reaching you. Of course, there are solutions to phone problems: answering machines, call waiting, and even a second phone line.

STAYING ON TOP

This is key—perhaps the most critical factor you'll need to analyze. If you're selling yourself as an expert in your field, you need to be on top of the latest developments in that and related fields. Magazines, newspapers, and newsletters will help, but you also need contact with your peers, and especially with leaders in the field. Attending seminars, conferences, and trade association meetings will be essential.

You'll also need to make special efforts to have regular contact with your peers, clients, and potential clients, as those contacts no longer will come as naturally. The old adage "out of sight, out of mind" can prove all too true, so you'll have to seek out new business contacts aggressively.

THE LONELINESS

Even for people who essentially are loners, the enforced aloneness of working at home can become a problem. You'll have to make an effort to get out of the house and meet people not connected with your business. You may become so obsessed with your new business that you make little time for anything else, and that can begin to be confining and limit your outlook on life—and eventually your business perspective.

So be sure to make plans to socialize regularly and then actually do it. Make regular dates to work out at the health club or play tennis or ride horses—whatever gets you out and about with friends and family, not just business acquaintances. Loneliness can be a subtle, slowly debilitating disease that you need to stave off aggressively.

WHERE TO MEET

It may not be convenient or appropriate to invite clients to your at-home office for business meetings, so you'll have to find a comfortable, reliable, quiet alternative. You may want to join a health club with a café, and kill two birds with one stone—exercise and a meeting space. Or talk with the owner of a local restaurant about taking a little extra time over lunch once or twice a week. He'll probably be happy for the regular business, and won't object as long as he knows what you're planning ahead of time.

THE DISTRACTIONS

This, too, can be a major stumbling block to working at home. You'd better be disciplined if you decide to go for it, because all your favorite toys and your favorite playmates will be there to lure you from your appointed task: the stereo, the TV, your spouse, your friends, that new novel you just started and don't want to put down, or a new recipe you're dying to try out.

As a semiretired, part-time, Gray Wave entrepreneur this won't be quite such a problem, but there definitely will be times when your home surroundings will call out to you when you should be buckling down to business, and you'd better be ready to be firm with yourself or risk losing a good client.

A HOME-BASED CONSULTING BUSINESS COULD BE JUST RIGHT FOR YOU

If a home-based consulting business sounds enticing to you, open your Gray Wave notebook to a clean page and head it "Home-Based Consulting Business." Then list the pros and cons of that kind of business. Next, take a look back at chapter 3 and review the "Questions to Ask Yourself." Check your notebook for the answers to those questions about the kind of life you want to lead in the future. Do the home-based consulting pros and cons seem to fit with your answers to those questions? If so, you're probably on the right track.

But before you go much further we need to do a little reality check. After all, you want to be sure you've got the right character traits to work at home and be a consultant. There's no point in starting something that sounds attractive but really isn't quite right for you. Although the financial investment in a home-based consulting business is relatively minor, you still don't want to spend money on a business that isn't going to work out because you're not being honest with yourself.

So what kind of person should the owner of a home-based consulting business be? You need to be two things: the kind of person who can work happily and productively at home, and the kind of person who can be a consultant. Let's analyze both kinds of people.

To work successfully at home you need to be self-sufficient, a self-starter, and something of a loner. You're probably going to be spending a lot of time by yourself, so you'd better be able to find satisfaction in your work and in your own company.

You also need to be disciplined enough to avoid the temptations and distractions associated with working in your home. When friends knock at the door, will you be able to gently send them on their way, explaining that you're working on an important deadline project? Will you have the strength to pass by the TV when the closing arguments in something as gripping as the O. J. Simpson trial are being broadcast live? What about those nagging chores that'll intrude on your thoughts and lure you away from your desk? Chores like throwing in a load of laundry or emptying the dishwasher. Before you know it, a whole morning's worth of work can go down the drain, literally, when you work at home.

The good news about working at home is that you can give yourself a well-earned break in front of the TV every now and then. Or take a quick catnap on the sofa.

You also have to be aggressive enough and determined enough to make special efforts to make and keep contacts and seek out clients, because they won't be drawn magically to your front door.

What about the other half of this equation—the consultant part? To be a successful consultant you need to know your business—your area of expertise—well enough to convince others you can teach them something they need to know, or show them how to make their own businesses more efficient and more profitable. Or both.

You have to be able to find answers, solve problems, and do research to give your clients what they need.

You have to be enough of a people person to make the contacts and get to first base with a potential client. And when you're just starting out, and don't have a briefcase full of testimonials from satisfied former clients to pull out, you have to be persuasive enough to turn first base into a home run by getting the job. It'll be a grand slam when you successfully complete that project and get your testimonial.

Remember, as a home-based consultant you won't have inventory you can show potential customers or a straightforward service you can demonstrate. Your service will be more cerebral, so you'll need to be able to convince them with sound thinking and good ideas that you can help them achieve their goals. In short, you and your expertise are the product in this business, and you're going to have to sell yourself to get ahead.

Do you have the qualities I just outlined? Can you close your eyes and visualize yourself in this kind of role? If so, the next step is to decide exactly what kinds of skills and expertise you'll sell.

DECIDE WHAT KIND OF CONSULTANT YOU'RE GOING TO BE

If you're starting a gypsy retail business you can decide to sell just about anything. If you're starting a mobile service business, your options also are almost unlimited, because most people can perform numerous tasks that others are willing to pay them to do.

But if you're establishing a home-based consulting business your choices will be more limited. Basically, there are two general kinds of consultants: those who do consumer consulting and those who advise businesses.

If you want to be a consumer consultant, your options are more open. You can start building marketable consulting skills in areas that interested you in the past but weren't part of your business portfolio, or in totally new areas.

If you're going to be a business consultant, you'll want to build your consulting business on your areas of experience and training. The trick will be to pull from your years of business experience just the right set of skills and expertise to market to the right clients.

Essentially, all consultants are problem solvers. As a consultant you engage in a four-step process to advise your clients and solve your clients' problems. First, you diagnose the problem. Then you devise a plan to solve the problem. Next you help implement the plan. Finally, in stage four, you determine the effectiveness of the plan and whether it needs modifications. Consumer consultants as well as business consultants basically follow that broad outline in carrying out the process of their consulting businesses.

CONSUMER CONSULTING

There's no question that consumers today need help making all kinds of personal decisions. The marketplace can be confusing, with fads and fashions changing by the minute and advertising bombarding us and even our children from dawn to dusk with a bewildering array of personal choices. Consumers need help with everything from fashion makeovers to spiritual guidance to retirement planning and dealing with death.

Here's a list of broad areas you can choose from for consumer consulting:

Beauty and fashion	Job hunting
Career planning	Meditation and relaxation
College shopping	Pet selection and care
Death and aging	Social and wedding planning
Financial planning	Spirituality and astrology
Health and fitness	Study skills and achievement
Home and family	Time management
Image improvement	Writing and speaking skills

BUSINESS CONSULTING

As a business consultant you'll want to build your business on your years of experience and training, and your specific skills. Businesses hire consultants to advise them in almost every area of business management and operations, from marketing to efficiency and time management. For example, businesses need help with:

Accounting	Executive searches
Advertising and marketing	Food services
Communications	Government relations
Data processing	Insurance

International markets	Quality control
Investments	Real estate
Management	Records management
Payroll and benefits	Research and development
Personnel	Retail sales
Printing and graphics	Telecommunications
Production	Training and education
Public relations	Transportation
Purchasing and inventory	Travel

There are more than eighty thousand consultants in business in the United States today. The joke is that anyone carrying a briefcase and coming from out of town is a consultant. So you need to find a consulting niche, a specialty, to set you apart. You also need to be able to clearly spell out for potential clients what your specialty is, what you can do for them.

In this age of intense competition and specialization, you need to be able to communicate very clearly the reasons why a potential client needs your services. It won't be effective to promote yourself simply as a general business consultant. Instead, you need to figure out what you do best and what you can learn to do effectively, and then focus on and promote those specific skills.

START NARROWING YOUR OPTIONS

It's time to begin sharpening the focus on exactly what consulting services you'll offer. First, carefully analyze what you do best and what your interests are. Then analyze what potential clients might need. You can specialize in several kinds of related tasks, but if your focus is too broad you'll lose the edge that specialization brings.

Make notes on your analyses in your Gray Wave notebook. Now, ask yourself the following questions and write your answers in the notebook.

- What kinds of business experience have I had?
- What specific skills and accomplishments can I point to?
- What training, formal and informal, have I completed?
- What knowledge and skills will I need to become an effective consultant in the areas I'm considering?
- What do I enjoy doing for others?
- Do I prefer working directly or indirectly with others?
- What are my main interests and hobbies?
- Do many consultants offer these services in this region?
- Am I willing to seek and service clients beyond the region, electronically and through travel?

HERE'S HOW TO GET STARTED

Carefully review your answers to the questions above. They'll help you determine what consulting services you are best suited to offer and whether there's a potential market for those services.

That should help you begin to sketch the outlines of your home-based consulting business. Now you need to define your target market. That will tell you whether you can expect your future business to succeed, or whether you need to go back to the drawing board and further sharpen your focus. This market analysis also will help you later, when you map out your business and marketing plans.

DEFINE YOUR TARGET MARKET

First, define your ideal client. You need to figure out exactly who would be most interested in contracting for your services. Then decide whether there are enough of those clients within your reach—whether that means close to home or around the globe—to support your business.

Just remember, although your business will be based at home and much consulting work is information-based and can be handled electronically, most clients still won't hire someone to perform an important task without spending time with that person.

They also want to be sure you have a feel for their business. So although the whole world can idealistically be your target market, be sure you understand and accept that realistically you'll need to aim narrower.

You'll also need to pinpoint where and how you can reach potential clients, because your future marketing will be targeted to where those clients can be found.

Now, close your eyes and envision your future clients. List everything you can about them. If you're going to be a business consultant, try to establish a portrait of both the businesses that might need your services and the people who run those businesses. If you're going to do consumer consulting, picture the consumers who'll be your clients. Are they male or female, young, middle-aged, or Gray Wavers like yourself? What's their income, where do they live, where do they shop, and what are their hobbies?

In the case of consumer consulting, check out places that sell products or related services they might use and jot down the characteristics of their clients. Contact relevant industry or trade groups relating to your target clients for possible demographic information. Then create a portrait of your typical client.

For example, say you're a consumer consultant who advises clients on image makeovers—specializing in the "total look," from makeup to hairdo to wardrobe. Your potential clients may be young professionals with a few years in business under their belts, looking to get a leg up on the career ladder. Or maybe they're smart young college grads having trouble landing that first job. They're smart enough to know they need some help settling on the right professional look. Or perhaps they're middle-aged, blue-collar workers who want to start their own mobile service business and realize they need a more polished appearance to inspire confidence in potential clients.

Your clients can be anyone who wants to look better or different than they already do, for whatever reason. The possibilities are endless, and it'll be up to you to decide exactly who you want to target specifically and go after them. The shotgun strategy will land some clients, but a more targeted, focused approach will continue to reap rewards when the shotgun runs out of ammunition.

But what if you're planning on being a business consultant? Let's say you're going to specialize in formulating strategic plans. Every business, large and small—but particularly stale ones—can get a jump start from an effective strategic plan. To start out, as a Gray Wave entrepreneur, you may want to look at small- to moderate-sized local and regional businesses that appear moderately but not hugely successful and that haven't changed much in recent years. Look for signs that the businesses could use a makeover, then target the owners.

You'll need to "credentialize" yourself as an expert in strategic planning. You do that by writing articles and books, and making speeches at seminars, conventions, and local business groups. Then you network. And not just by joining the Kiwanis or Rotary and handing out your business card. You need to create an image of yourself as a respected leader in the field, so that when there's a need for someone who does what you do, your name will roll off businesspeople's tongues.

LOCATE YOUR TARGETED CUSTOMERS

Now that you know who your target clients are, you need to decide how big the potential market for your services is and where future clients can be found. Whether you're a business consultant or a consumer consultant, the process is much the same. You need to analyze your market. For a Gray Wave entrepreneur, that, most likely (at least at the start), will be your local and regional community. Depending on the nature of your consulting business, you'll need to ask yourself some of the following questions:

Do you live in a thriving community with a sufficient number of small- and moderate-sized businesses? Is your downtown business section vital? Is there a thriving business and technology park? Are there good opportunities for young professionals or new service businesses? Are there colleges or technical schools with enthusiastic graduates? Are more people moving into the area than are moving out? Or should you market your consulting services to a wider market via the Internet or through national business publications?

As a consumer consultant, you'll probably be able to market

your image makeover service to those young college grads we identified earlier and to the owners of the suburban tract houses that serve as starter homes for young professionals in the area. Or even to middle-aged, new singles eager to bring fresh romance and excitement to their lives.

As a business consultant specializing in strategic planning, you'll need to target business owners, and you'll find them at Rotary and Kiwanis, the downtown businesspersons' association, and the Chamber of Commerce. Or they'll be keeping in shape while making their own contacts at health clubs and on golf courses, or relaxing at the symphony.

Later, when we talk more about a specific marketing plan, we'll take the carefully defined portrait of your clients that we settled on earlier and decide exactly where they can be found. That's where you'll target your future marketing. But for now, you just need to determine that there are sufficient potential clients within reach who would be willing and able to purchase your service.

Talk with Other Consultants

You need to touch base with others in the field, but this can be problematic. So you have to assure the consultants you contact that you'll be specializing in services quite different from theirs and therefore won't be a competitor. Obviously, potential competitors aren't going to be eager to share much useful information. Find out how they got started, how they advertise and market themselves, what they would do differently if they were starting out today. Ask about their successes and their failures, their client likes and dislikes, their do's and don'ts. You'd be surprised at how willing business owners are to talk about their businesses if they can feel assured that you won't be trying to steal their clients.

You might actually consider hiring your own consultant, both to see how such a business is operated and for genuine help getting started. Rhonda Abrams, a small business consultant who writes a syndicated newspaper column, just celebrated her tenth year as a consulting entrepreneur. When she was starting out, she said, she hired an established consultant to help her narrow her focus and find her own consulting niche.

DISCUSS YOUR PLAN WITH POTENTIAL CLIENTS

You also need to test your idea with potential clients. Consumer consultants should talk with friends, neighbors, and family members to determine if they would consider hiring the services of such a consultant. Business consultants need to check with friends and neighbors who are business executives on their need for such a service.

Both kinds of consultants need to ask potential clients about their goals and key priorities in their purchase of this service. Why do they want or need this service? Do they want you to solve their problems or teach them how to solve their own problems? How much are they willing to pay for this service? How often would they use it?

Then conduct an informal survey of potential clients you don't know or don't normally come into contact with. Consumer consultants can go door-to-door and street-to-street in a variety of neighborhoods, asking the same questions. Try random cold-calling on the telephone, but be ready for the cold shoulder— or worse, the sound of the phone slamming in your ear. Many people don't like to be bothered at home, but it's certainly worth the effort for what might be valuable insight from those more objective than your friends and neighbors.

Business consultants should target the yellow pages, area business directories, Chamber of Commerce listings, and new business openings listed in newspapers.

You also can bounce your idea off an independent observer by contacting the local office of the Small Business Administration. The SBA sponsors a mentor program called SCORE (Service Corps of Retired Executives), which brings together retired executives and people who are trying to launch a business. The advice is free, impartial, and rooted in experience.

PUT TOGETHER YOUR OWN TEAM

Up to now you've been in the research and analysis mode, finalizing your choice of a future business. Before you go further you need to put together the team of professionals who will help guide you through the process of starting your consulting business. You'll need an accountant and a banker. You'll also need a lawyer to prepare any contracts you may enter into with clients and to research any licenses and permits you may need. If you don't have such professionals lined up, do it now.

As an experienced Gray Waver who already has completed at least one career, you may not have to go far to find skilled, responsible professionals. Consider those you know well from your past career and whose skills you have come to respect. Or, if you're settling in a new retirement area, ask your neighbors for suggestions.

But don't make the classic mistake of hiring someone just to be a nice guy or to fulfill a family or friendship obligation. This should be a business decision like any other, and you need the wisdom and experience of seasoned, successful professionals. Speaking of seasoned, don't overlook other Gray Wave semiretirees with part-time professional businesses of their own.

Check with SCORE again for possible candidates, and with the American Association of Retired Persons (AARP). Also check with professional associations and with friends and associates in other businesses for candidates. Ask candidates for a free initial meeting, and if they decline, cross them off your list. Ask for the names of three recent clients whose circumstances are similar to yours. Contact these references and ask their opinion of the candidates' professional skills and services.

These are key decisions and you need to make them carefully and thoughtfully. Your team will help guide your future, so check their credentials, their references, and their business premises carefully. Call the Better Business Bureau and the state Division of Consumer Affairs before you sign up anyone to represent you in your new business.

DRAW UP YOUR BUSINESS AND MARKETING PLANS

Now that you've identified what services your consulting firm will offer, you need to draw up a business plan and a separate marketing plan to provide you with a road map in starting your business. Planning is the key to success for every entrepreneur, including the owner of a consulting service.

Just as you wouldn't think of starting a long trip to an unknown destination without a map, you shouldn't consider starting your consulting business without a business plan and a marketing plan. They will help you map out the route you'll follow to meet your business goals. You'll also be able to check your progress regularly against your plans and fine-tune them as experience suggests.

THE BUSINESS PLAN

This should be part of your Gray Wave notebook and need not be elaborate, since you won't be submitting it to a commercial lender in the hope of obtaining a business loan. (More about that later, but commercial lenders do not finance small business start-ups. If you need financing, you'll get it elsewhere.) The plan should address your business's mission, your goals and objectives, your strategy, and finances.

Here's a general outline you can follow:

- *General information*—List the name of your business; your name and address; telephone, fax, and E-mail numbers.

- *Mission statement*—This should be a general statement of one or two paragraphs explaining your philosophy and motivation in starting this business.

- *Objectives*—List your specific goals and objectives for the business.

- *Define the business*—Describe the business: What consulting services will you provide and to whom; how will you provide those services; where and how will you reach your clients; who's your primary competition; will you need to hire employees?

- *Finances*—We'll discuss finances in more detail later in this chapter, but include realistic income and expense projections. Allow some cushion for unexpected start-up costs and setbacks, and for a slower than expected growth. Remember, it will take time for people to get to know you and your business and to get into the habit of calling on you.

The Marketing Plan

You will touch on marketing in your business plan, but you also need to develop a separate marketing plan to detail exactly how you'll promote your home-based consulting business for at least a year. If you want your business to be successful, you have to market yourself.

The biggest mistake most small businesses make is to rely on advertising alone. Advertising often is the most expensive and least productive way to reach clients. Instead, you'll want to spread your efforts among a variety of marketing opportunities, including flyers and media publicity.

As you draw up your marketing plan, focus on the portrait of your target client that we drew earlier in this chapter. Think about ways and places to reach that target customer, then decide:

- What mix of marketing you will do on a weekly, monthly, or seasonal basis.
- How much money you will budget for each marketing effort in that period.
- How and by whom that marketing effort will be carried out.
- How you will assess the effectiveness of your marketing plan.

Keep in mind that for consumer consultants particularly, marketing techniques don't have to be sophisticated or high-tech in the beginning. For example, if you're starting that image makeover business, ask beauticians and health clubs if you can place small notices of your service on their bulletin boards or counters; many will be happy to let you do so.

Or you can target their customers with mailings and place notices in college newspapers, dormitory lounges, and student union bulletin boards. Think about where your clients spend their time and find ways to reach them at those places.

WHAT ABOUT YOUR FINANCING?

Now that you've decided what your home-based consulting business will be and what professionals will make up your core team, and you've drawn up your business and marketing plans, it's time to look at your financing. As I pointed out at the start of this chapter, the beauty of establishing a home-based consulting business is its low cost. You have almost no overhead and you don't have to buy inventory. You're carrying your inventory and your equipment on your shoulders.

So you may not need financing help. Instead, you may be able to launch your business with savings or even with credit cards. On the other hand, in today's technological age, communications equipment can be costly. You may not want to dip into your savings or your stream of income.

You'll probably have to purchase basic office equipment. You'll need an answering machine, copier, fax machine and computer with word processing, database, and accounting and billing software. If you intend to produce your own promotional materials you should invest in a laser printer and desktop publishing software.

If you buy a modem and telecommunications software, you can tap into on-line information systems that allow you to communicate with clients and other consultants. You can also monitor industry trends and solicit clients in the business and financial areas of the commercial on-line services such as CompuServe, Prodigy, and America Online.

So you need to determine what your business start-up costs will be, even though they may be minimal compared with the costs associated with businesses that require extensive inventory or a nonhome location.

You also need money to live on while the business gets rolling, but for Gray Wavers that shouldn't be a problem. Your Social Security and pension payments, plus any savings, should be sufficient for living expenses. Your home-based consulting business is intended to be merely a part-time business that supplements your retirement income and lifestyle, not your entire livelihood. If your business really takes off and you decide it's more fun working for yourself than bowling and playing bridge, you may decide to forget about being even semiretired. But that's down the road a bit.

For now, start a new worksheet in your Gray Wave notebook to calculate your start-up costs. Basically, here's what you'll need:

Start-up Costs Worksheet

Enter the appropriate amounts to determine your overall costs. I've listed some typical expenses, but you should make sure your list is specific for the particular kind of home-based consulting business you're going to start.

Telephone installation	$_____
Insurance	$_____
Professional services	$_____
Attorney	$_____
Accountant	$_____
Marketing/advertising firm	$_____
Computer	$_____
Modem	$_____
Printer	$_____
Software	$_____
Commercial on-line service	$_____
Fax machine	$_____
Telephone	$_____
Beeper	$_____
Answering machine	$_____
Furniture	$_____
Copy machine	$_____
File cabinet	$_____
Office supplies	$_____
Stationery	$_____
Total advertising	$_____
TOTAL START-UP COSTS	$_____

Now that you've figured out your start-up costs, you need to arrange financing, if necessary. Basically, you have three options: your own funds, a personal loan from a lending institution, or a loan from family or friends.

YOUR OWN FUNDS

If you're a dedicated saver, you may have sufficient savings. Or you may have assets you can convert to cash. Even the simplest consulting business requires an outlay for office supplies. You have to keep records and send out bills, right?

While getting downsized isn't pleasant, you may be lucky enough to have come away with a severance package you can invest in starting up your new business. Or maybe you've inherited a little nest egg. That, too, can be an excellent source of financing for your business start-up.

INSTITUTIONAL SOURCES

Forget a business loan. Banks don't lend to start-ups because it's too risky. They want a proven track record of success before they'll consider a business loan. Your best bets are credit cards, a home equity loan, or a personal loan. Base your choice on how much you need to borrow. If you need only a little, use credit cards; a bit more, take out a personal loan; if you need to borrow a lot, better get a home equity loan.

Provided your credit cards aren't maxed out, they can be an easy, convenient way to finance your start-up purchases. But they'll cost you. While you might get lucky and hit a special, low introductory interest rate on a new card, be sure to read the fine print to find out when the rate zooms up to the general, out-of-sight level of most credit cards. And there's a limit to how much you can charge on a credit card.

Like credit cards, a personal loan can be easy and convenient. You can borrow more, too, than usually is the case with credit cards. And if you shop around, you should be able to do much better on the interest rate.

A home equity loan, or second mortgage, is now a very popular form of financing for all sorts of things, including basic business equipment. Banks like home equity loans because there's little risk involved.

This is a simplification, but if your home is worth $175,000 and your mortgage balance is $75,000, you have $100,000 worth of equity in your home. Generally speaking, you can borrow against that equity—usually up to 70 percent of its value—to finance your business needs. Even better, the interest on a home equity loan usually is tax deductible, effectively lowering the cost of the loan.

You should search for a home equity loan or a personal loan exactly as you did for your first mortgage. Comparison-shop for the best interest rates at banks, credit unions, and savings and loans.

FAMILY AND FRIENDS

If you're on good terms with your family, they can be an excellent source of financing. The same is true of friends. It can be a win-win deal for both parties, because there's a gap between current lending rates and the interest rates institutions are offering on savings accounts, certificates of deposit, and other savings instruments.

Say your cousin is a successful novelist who's rolling in money and is always on the lookout for a good investment. Right now she's got $15,000 to invest, and by sheer coincidence, that's exactly how much you've decided you need to borrow to start up your new home-based consulting business.

She doesn't want to deal with mutual funds and other more risky investment instruments. She knows that fixed-rate investments earn around 4.5 percent with a conventional savings account and about 6 percent with most CDs.

Meanwhile, you've discovered that a personal loan will cost you about 10 percent. So there's roughly a 4 percent window of opportunity for you and your cousin to make a deal that benefits you both. If she lends you her $15,000 at 8 percent, she'll be getting a better return on her investment than she would otherwise, and you'll be getting a loan 2 percent below what's available in the marketplace. You both win.

LOOK AT WHAT TINA WALTON
HAS UP HER SLEEVE

Tina Walton's just forty-nine; too young to think about retiring, right? She's got a good job in the financial aid office of an excellent university in the Northeast, and her job is secure. She's good at her job, she's worked at the university for fifteen years, and she's in no danger of being laid off.

Nonetheless, Tina is deep into retirement planning. But with a twist. Tina isn't gathering cruise brochures or sending for information on hiking trips in the Himalayas. And she's not investigating retirement villages in Florida, although she has started taking golf lessons. Instead, Tina has begun taking steps to plan and develop her own retirement business. She wants to be ready when the time comes, and she wants to be able to call the shots.

A divorce three years ago literally knocked her off her feet and started her thinking about retirement. The divorce caught her totally by surprise, she says, although now she admits she should have seen the signs. Her husband, a research scientist at the university, started working longer and longer hours at the lab. For relaxation he joined the health club and started playing squash with his lab partner, a young female teaching assistant.

Tina doesn't really like to sweat. Exercise to her is a sedate walk to the local coffee shop, where she can sit and read poetry, her true love, or work on her own writing over cappuccino. Or it's a stroll across campus to the music school for practice with the chorus. After the divorce, Tina realized that she and Norm hadn't really shared much in the past few years, aside from brief catch-up conversations over dinner—if they both managed to make the meal. And even that was unlikely.

But shocked she was, and devastated. She really thought she loved Norm and had expected to spend her life, into retirement, with him. When he moved out she couldn't eat or sleep for a while, and eventually she got pneumonia. She was in the hospital for six weeks, and that's when she finally shook herself mentally by the shoulders and gave herself a stern talking-to.

"I said to myself, 'Listen, you can either sit in a corner and whimper the rest of your life, and worry about all the things you're not going to be able to have, and all the things you're not going to be able to do, because you're single, or you can get your act together and make your own future. It's up to you.' "

Tina says she realized then that she had been expecting Norm to take the lead in planning for their retirement, and that he had. She hadn't a clue about what kind of savings plans they had or where their pension money was invested, or any of the details she should know in order to assure the financial security of her own senior years. She panicked a bit, but decided to set about learning what she needed to know to plan her own retirement finances and future, just as she had set about learning during her years in graduate school. She was, figuratively, back in school—the school of life.

So she took several workshops on retirement planning and made some decisions to shift where her pension monies were being invested. And she discovered that while her retirement income looked okay, Social Security was shaky and she didn't feel comfortable relying on it. And without her ex-husband's pension bolstering her own, she wasn't sure she would be able to finance the quality of retirement life she'd been looking forward to. More important, she realized she didn't want to just retire alone in her Northeast college community and "vegetate."

So she started planning further. Being analytical by nature, she analyzed what kind of life she did want to live and where. She decided she wanted to be in a more temperate climate, like the Southwest. And in a university community, for the cultural advantages, like the chorus and symphony, she'd grown accustomed to. Now she's taking vacation trips throughout the Southwest, scouting specific communities in preparation for a move.

More important, she decided she likes what she's doing and wants to translate that into a consumer consulting business of her own. She knows that colleges and universities, like businesses everywhere, are downsizing and are unlikely to hire an almost-retiree. But she figured that with the way student financial aid is dwindling as federal and state budget appropriations for higher education decrease, more and more families will need help competing for money to put their children through college. And she's betting they'll be willing to pay an expert consultant to help them find their way through the maze of options, forms, and red tape.

So Tina not only is scoping out her future semiretirement community. She's also started drawing up a business plan for her consulting business, and has taken on a few clients already. Basically, she's testing the waters, to see if she can bring in clients and serve their needs. She knows that satisfied clients and word of mouth are her best advertising. She's working weekends and nights while she's still employed at the university—sort of a moonlighting consultant.

She's not ready to make her move yet, but she's beginning to think it might come sooner than she had expected. She's getting impatient to go out on her own and get on with the next stage of her life in a fresh environment. And the best thing is, Tina says, she'll be able to do this consulting business from her home, which, she hopes, will overlook rugged Southwestern mountains.

"And I'll be able to do it forever, or at least as long as I like," she said. "I've only got two clients, but I haven't even advertised. They're friends of friends," she said. "And I haven't even thought up a name for this business, or any of the other details. But I've grown so excited about being on my own that I may move quicker than I expected. It's a challenge that's really given me a new lease on life."

SO WHERE DO YOU GO FROM HERE?

Now is the time to decide whether a home-based consulting business is right for you or if you'd rather look elsewhere for a Gray Wave business enterprise. A home-based consulting business can be the perfect option for the right person. There's no overhead and very little investment for your start-up, so the risk is minimal.

But it isn't for someone who wants to be physically active on the job or who wants to be out and about. And you do need to have certain skills and expertise valuable to others—or you need the ability to learn quickly a new area of expertise. You need to be able to solve problems and find answers to difficult questions.

You also need to be something of a loner. You need to be able to work happily at home, despite the lack of companionship of an office and despite the distractions of home. You also must be highly motivated, a self-starter, and have plenty of self-discipline. And you need self-confidence, because you're not selling a product or an easily visible, cut-and-dried service; you're selling what's in your head.

You definitely need good people skills. For no matter how highly regarded you are in your field, no matter how good your reputation, you'll still have to compete for and win clients, and that means constantly selling your biggest asset—yourself.

It's all up to you now. If you're not really sure you've got the right set of skills and attributes to be a home-based consultant, or if you just want something a little more straightforward, don't worry. You can think more carefully about the options I've outlined in earlier chapters or read on to chapter 10.

HOME-BASED CONSULTING BUSINESS RESOURCE AND REFERENCE GUIDE

Here's a list of sources you can use to get information on home-based consulting:

- *Complete Marketing Handbook for Consultants,* by Don M. Schrello (University Associates, 1990).
- *Consultant's Calling: Bringing Who You Are to What You Do,* by Geoffrey M. Bellman (Jossey-Bass, 1990).
- *Consultant's Guide to Winning Clients,* by Herman Holtz (Wiley, 1989).
- *Consultant's Manual: A Complete Guide to Building a Successful Consulting Practice,* by Thomas L. Greenbaum (Wiley, 1994).
- *Entrepreneurial PC: The Complete Guide to Starting a PC-Based Business,* by Bernard J. David (McGraw-Hill, 1994).

- *Growing Your Home-Based Business: A Complete Guide to Proven Sales and Marketing Communications Strategies,* by Kim T. Gordon (Prentice-Hall, 1992).

- *Home Business Desk Reference: Everything You Need to Know to Start and Run Your Home-Based Business,* by David R. Eyler (Wiley, 1994).

- *Home Office Book,* by Mark Alvarez (Goodwood, 1990).

- *Home-Based Entrepreneur,* by Linda Pinson and Jerry Jinnett (Upstart Publishing, 1993).

- *How to Start a Home Business,* by Mike Antoniak (Avon Books, 1995).

- *How to Start a Word Processing–Secretarial Business: Be Your Own Boss And Never Fetch Coffee Again!,* by Louise Hagan (Whyte Rose, 1994).

- *How to Start and Build a Successful Manufacturers' Agency,* by James Gibbons (Prentice-Hall, 1988).

- *How to Start and Run a Writing and Editing Business,* by Herman Holtz (Wiley, 1992).

- *How to Turn Your FAX Machine into a Money Machine,* by Marcia J. Hootman (New Wave, 1993).

- *How to Start a Service Business,* by Ben Chant and Melissa Morgan (Avon Books, 1994).

- *How to Succeed As an Independent Consultant,* by Herman Holtz (Wiley, 1993).

- *Information for Sale,* by John H. Everet (McGraw-Hill, 1994).

- *Insider Home Business Riches,* by John Collins (Lion, 1989).

- *Mailing List Services on Your Home-Based PC,* by Linda Rohrbough (TAB Books, 1993).

- *Management Consulting: A Game Without Chips,* by Thomas G. Cody (Kennedy Publications, 1986).

- *Marketing Your Consulting and Professional Services,* by Richard Connor and Jeff Davidson (Wiley, 1990).

- *One Thousand One Hundred One Businesses You Can Start from Home,* by Daryl A. Hall (Wiley, 1995).
- *Overnight Consultant,* by Marsha D. Lewin (Wiley, 1995).
- *Personal Selling Strategies for Consultants and Professionals: The Perfect Sales Equation,* by Richard K. Carlson (Wiley, 1993).
- *Start and Run a Profitable Consulting Business: Your Step-by-Step Business Plan,* by Douglas Gray (Self-Counsel Press, 1990).
- *Start and Run a Profitable Freelance Writing Business: Your Step-by-Step Business Plan,* by Christine Adamec (Self-Counsel Press, 1994).
- *Start and Run a Profitable Home-Based Business: Your Step-by-Step First Year Guide,* by Edna Sheedy (Self-Counsel Press, 1990).
- *Start and Run a Profitable Travel Agency: Your Step-by-Step Business Plan,* by Richard Cropp and Barbara Braidwood (Self-Counsel Press, 1993).
- *Start Your Own Desktop Publishing Business* (Pfeiffer & Company, 1994).
- *Start Your Own Money Making Computer Business* (Pfeiffer & Company, 1994).
- *Start Your Own Resume Writing Business* (Pfeiffer & Company, 1994).
- *Start Your Own Secretarial Service Business* (Pfeiffer & Company, 1994).
- *Start Your Own Temporary Help Agency,* by JoAnn Padgett (Pfeiffer & Company, 1994).
- *Start, Run and Profit from Your Own Home-Based Business,* by Gregory F. Kishel and Patricia G. Kishel (Wiley, 1991).
- *Starting & Operating a Home-Based Business,* by David R. Eyler (Wiley, 1990).
- *Starting a Business in Your Home,* by Tonya Bolden (Longmeadow, 1993).

- *Starting a Home-Based Business (Full or Part-Time),* by Irene Korn and Bill Zanker (Carol Publishing Group, 1992).
- *Starting a Public Relations Firm* (Business of Your Own, 1988).
- *Starting a Secretarial Service* (Business of Your Own, 1988).
- *Starting and Building Your Own Accounting Business,* by Jack Fox (Wiley, 1991).
- *Stealing Home: How to Leave Your Job and Become a Successful Consultant,* by Peter C. Brown (Crown Publishing Group, 1994).
- *Upstart Guide to Owning and Managing a Consulting Service,* by Dan Ramsey (Upstart, 1994).
- *Upstart Guide to Owning and Managing a Desktop Publishing Business,* by Dan Ramsey (Upstart, 1994).
- *Upstart Guide to Owning and Managing a Newsletter Business,* by Lisa Angowski Rogak (Upstart, 1994).
- *Upstart Guide to Owning and Managing a Résumé Service,* by Dan Ramsey (Upstart, 1994).
- *Upstart Guide to Owning and Managing a Travel Service,* by Dan Ramsey (Upstart, 1994).
- *Upstart Guide to Owning and Managing a Consulting Service,* by Dan Ramsey (Upstart Publishing, 1995).
- *Working from Home,* by Paul and Sarah Edwards (St. .Martin's, 1985).
- *Your Home Business Can Make Dollars and Sense,* by Jo Frohbieter-Mueller (Chilton, 1990).

10

HOW TO BUY AN EXISTING BUSINESS

After reading the last several chapters, starting a new business may seem like an awful lot of plain hard work. Even a part-time, semiretired, Gray Wave business. You're probably asking yourself, why not just take a shortcut and buy an existing business? Why not save yourself a few steps and a lot of headaches and buy a business someone else already took the trouble to establish? Good questions. If you can afford to, why not?

You can save yourself a good deal of time and energy by buying an existing business. On the other hand, you also may be buying additional headaches—and even heartache—by buying someone else's mistake.

THE ADVANTAGES OF BUYING AN EXISTING BUSINESS

There's no question that starting a business from scratch is the truest form of entrepreneurship. However, many people become quite successful by buying existing businesses. Let's look at the pros and cons.

Although it doesn't fit the classic definition of becoming an entrepreneur, buying an existing business has definite advantages. It's less risky than starting a business from scratch. And it's a lot faster—potentially, you can start ringing up sales or bringing in clients as soon as you sign the purchase agreement. And the quicker you take over the operation, the faster profits can start piling up. You'll get a faster return on your initial investments of time and money. With one financial transaction you can become an entrepreneur, and if you have enough working capital you won't have to keep digging into your pockets or seek additional financing.

An existing business also has a track record, a customer base, inventory, location, equipment, name recognition, and staff. And if you're looking to enter an industry in which you have no experience, buying an existing business has the added advantage of providing a built-in teacher: the previous owner. If her or his continued presence and assistance are made part of the deal, you'll theoretically be able to profit from the business while you're learning it.

You may not want to retain all those theoretical assets, but they're a beginning. All you have to do is sign that purchase agreement, hand over a bank check, and you're in business. Just think—your ideal business might be on the market right now, waiting for you to make your move. On the other hand, don't move too quickly.

THERE ARE DOWNSIDES TO BUYING AN EXISTING BUSINESS

The biggest drawback is the cost. Remember all those pros I mentioned above? You'll be paying for them, paying for a ready-made business to step into. Not only that—those assets also could prove to be fool's gold that ends up in the debit column of your Gray Wave notebook after you take a closer look at a prospective business.

The business's track record may be a minefield, ready to explode. Such name recognition you don't need. The inventory and equipment may be outdated and worthless, the location too expensive or on the road to nowhere. The current staff may be incompetent or unmanageable. Finally, it's possible that your built-in teacher is a burned-out ignoramus who couldn't care less whether you or the business lasts one day longer than it takes to cash your check.

And depending on your personality, buying a business may not provide enough of a creative outlet. You won't be starting a business from scratch. But in order to maximize the advantages and minimize the potential pitfalls, you're going to have to work just as hard as if you were starting your own business from scratch. You'll have to work hard to come up with ways to make your new business prosper and grow, to find new clients or customers, and to find new ways to serve them better.

Finally, keep in mind that to find the right business to buy, you may have to relocate. Good business opportunities aren't a dime a dozen. If you're not willing to move, you may not be able to find just the right business for you.

BUYING AN EXISTING BUSINESS COULD BE JUST RIGHT FOR YOU

If you can afford it or can find sufficient financing, buying a business may be the way for you to go. If you're not consumed with an overwhelming creative urge but do have a strong desire to own and operate your own business, you may want to think about buying one. You still need to have a strong entrepreneurial personality, but you can be a little more flexible—willing to take over and improve on someone else's project rather than being single-minded about pursuing your own individual vision.

If you're eager to get started quickly and impatient with some of the steps required when starting your own business—such as researching twenty-first-century trends and testing your basic concept—you're the right kind of person to take a shortcut and buy an existing business.

DECIDE WHAT KIND OF BUSINESS YOU WANT TO BUY

The first step, and often the most difficult one, is to decide what kind of business you want to buy. This decision may mean the difference between success and failure for your entrepreneurial career, so you'll want to choose wisely. Your choice should depend on four things: your interests, your skills, what's available, and what kind of financial resources you can marshal. The last thing you should do is buy a business just because it's for sale, because it appears successful, or because the price is right.

Keep in mind that it will be advantageous to have some experience and expertise in the kind of business you decide to buy. When you're starting your own business you generally can learn as you take the long, exploratory steps to start-up. But when you buy a business you have to step right in as the owner and operator, and there's little time to learn on the job.

Besides, how will you be able to evaluate the business you're thinking of buying if you don't know anything at all about it?

Remember, too, that this is a retirement business for you. As a Gray Wave entrepreneur your goal is to combine a productive, exciting business career with a satisfying, "semiretired" lifestyle. You're looking for supplemental income, perhaps even substantial supplemental income, but not a business that will supply your only source of income. That means you're probably looking for a nontraditional business, or any business you can operate on a flexible or part-time basis.

Before we explore some specific options, turn back to chapter 3 and review the "Questions to Ask Yourself." Check your Gray Wave notebook for the answers to those questions about how you want to spend the next decade or so.

Obviously, you can purchase just about any business. However, I'd suggest you look most carefully at two kinds of businesses I've previously encouraged your fellow Gray Wavers to start: gypsy retail businesses and mobile service businesses. Both fit the lifestyle needs of Gray Wavers very well.

One other thing—I'm not suggesting you buy an existing consulting business, the third major starting-from-scratch option I've covered in this book. That's because when you buy a consulting business you're really buying nothing more than the files and Rolodex of the previous owner. Unless you have a personal link to all those clients they're not likely to stick with you. It makes more sense to start your own consulting business than it does to buy someone else's.

What About Buying a Gypsy Retail Business?

If you're interested in retailing, you should consider buying a gypsy retail business, one without a traditional store setting and with modified hours. The last thing you want at this time of your life is the grueling hours and high overhead of a traditional retail business.

A gypsy retailer provides consumers with a product as simply, directly, and efficiently as possible; maybe the product is something they can't find in a standard store. There are no big storefronts and high overhead; the gypsy part means you can pick up your business and move it to follow the flow of your customers and your own inclinations.

As a gypsy retailer you take the product to your customers in mobile carts or the back seat of your car; at farmer's markets, craft or antiques shows and malls; or you offer a mail-order product. You set up a stand or cart anyplace you see identifiable customers—by the road or on the beach, in a business or church parking lot, or in front of the train station. Your options and locations are limited only by your imagination and by the demands of the marketplace.

When you buy an existing gypsy retail business you're buying the track record, inventory, goodwill and name recognition, customer base, and cart or location, just as in a traditional retail business. It's just more portable should you decide a change in location would be desirable.

Almost anything people buy that's of reasonable size is being sold from a temporary cart, booth, or shed. Ask friends, relatives, and other acquaintances what they buy regularly, what they'd like to be able to buy more easily and conveniently, what specialty items they'd like a better selection of. Do an informal mini-survey of their consumer spending habits. This list should be as all-encompassing as you can make it.

Then, based on their answers and your interests, single out a couple of items that appear to have the most sales potential, and you'll be ready to hunt for a business to buy.

(For more information, take a look at the chapter on starting your own gypsy retail business—much of that material applies here as well.)

HOW ABOUT BUYING A MOBILE SERVICE BUSINESS?

You don't need a special skill or talent to own and operate a mobile service business, although that wouldn't hurt. What you do need is the ability to do a job—even a simple, basic task—that people are willing to pay someone to do for them. It can be something you already know how to do, like lawn care, or something you can learn quickly, like basic home repairs. Your opportunities are limitless. Any job, any simple task, can form the basis for a mobile service business.

The key to a mobile service business is the mobility—you take your service and whatever equipment you need to the client in the trunk of your car. And that means the cost of buying an existing mobile service business is relatively inexpensive. After all, just as is the case with a gypsy retail business, you're not buying or leasing a fixed location with high overhead. You're buying the track record, equipment, goodwill and name recognition, customer base, and, if necessary, a truck or van to provide your mobility.

Here are some broad categories of service jobs that offer unique opportunities for ambitious Gray Wave entrepreneurs in the twenty-first century.

- *Household chores*—Two–wage earner families have more money to spend but less time to devote to necessary household tasks.

- *Businesses' service gaps*—To reduce costs, many businesses have either reduced products and services or sought less expensive ways of providing that product or service to their customers.

- *Staff gaps*—Corporate downsizing, perhaps necessary to streamline American business and make it more competitive, has resulted in many cases in a reduction in necessary support staff.

- *Repairing products*—People today are repairing existing products rather than replacing them at the first sign of a problem.

- *Lifestyle needs*—You can pick your target market and lifestyle, and buy a service business that people in that market, living that lifestyle, need filled.

(For more information, take a look at the chapter on starting your own mobile service business—much of that material applies here as well.)

START NARROWING YOUR OPTIONS

It's time to carefully examine the businesses-for-sale ads in your local and regional newspapers. In your Gray Wave notebook, make a list of anything that catches your eye as a possible prospect. Generally, the more details an ad offers, the more serious is the attempt to sell the business.

Also, check around to see what businesses are about to come on the market. Many businesses that are for sale never make it to the classifieds because they're snapped up before that by smart, aggressive entrepreneurs. Check with your local business organizations and the Chamber of Commerce. Check with friends, neighbors, and other professionals you know. Some of the best business deals are hatched as a result of word of mouth, rather than advertising—somebody knows somebody who's thinking about selling a business.

Then, too, some business owners think about listing their businesses but never quite get around to it. Some never even pass the word around—it's just a seed in the back of their minds. And some aren't even considering selling out. All they need is a good push—and the right price—and they'll sell in a minute.

Everyone has a price. Telling business owners you want to take care of them for the rest of their lives is an attractive offer—especially for someone who has struggled for years to make a business work and who may have little or nothing in the bank for retirement. If you present the purchase of the business as the opportunity for a lifelong income, even the most contented business owner may sit up and take notice. So if you see a business you like but it isn't on the market, don't hesitate to approach the owner directly. The worst she or he can do is say no.

Obviously, your chances of finding the perfect business to buy are much greater if you have an idea of what you want and if you are willing to relocate to find it. If you can't bring yourself to think about moving, you may not be the right kind of person to buy an existing business.

PUT TOGETHER YOUR PROFESSIONAL TEAM

Before you go any further you need to put together the team of professionals who will help guide you through the process of analyzing a business prospect and buying a business. This is too complex a process to do on your own. You'll need a lawyer, preferably one who specializes in business purchases, and possibly a business appraiser. You'll also need an accountant and a banker. If you don't have such professionals lined up, do it now.

Look for professional credentials, experience in the kinds of businesses you're looking into, and objectivity. You'll need objective professionals to balance the natural enthusiasm and eagerness you'll be bringing to the bargaining table.

At this stage of your life, you may not have to go far to find accomplished professionals you can rely on. First, look to those you know well from your past career and whose skills you have come to respect. Or, if you're settling in a new retirement area, ask your neighbors for suggestions.

Don't hire someone just to be a nice guy or to fulfill a family obligation. This should be a business decision like any other, and you need the wisdom and experience of seasoned, successful professionals. And speaking of seasoned, don't overlook other Gray Wave semiretirees with part-time professional businesses of their own.

Check with SCORE (Service Corps of Retired Executives) for possible candidates, and with the American Association of Retired Persons (AARP). Also check with professional associations and with friends and associates in other businesses for candidates. Ask candidates for a free initial meeting, and if they decline, cross them off your list. Ask for the names of three recent clients whose circumstances are similar to yours. Contact their references and ask about the candidates' professional skills and services.

This is a decision you should make with care. Your team will be important to your future, so check their credentials, their references, and their business premises carefully. Call the Better Business Bureau and the state Division of Consumer Affairs before you sign up anyone to represent you in your business purchase.

ANALYZE YOUR OPPORTUNITIES

Once you've got your list of possible purchase opportunities and your team of professionals, you need to do a thorough analysis of each business. At least you'll want to examine the top two or three, if you should be lucky enough to have a longer list. This study should be as detailed as if you were starting the business from scratch.

The first question to resolve, if the business isn't a mobile or gypsy one, is whether the location is a good one. Look at pedestrian and street traffic and traffic patterns, the character of the area, nearby construction, and parking. Once you've determined that the location's viable, look at the details of the business.

Here are some basic questions to ask as you begin your analysis:

How Long Has the Business Existed; Who Founded It, and How Many Owners Have There Been?

A high turnover in ownership spells trouble, any way you look at it. Owners don't get rid of a business quickly if it's successful. And a business that has existed in the same spot for some time is more likely to have built up a sound customer base and goodwill than one that's new to a spot.

Is the Business Profitable? Are Profits Increasing or Decreasing and Why? Can the Profit Picture Be

IMPROVED OR DO CIRCUMSTANCES BEYOND YOUR CONTROL MAKE THAT UNLIKELY?

You'll need to examine the business's financial records for at least the last five years, including balance sheets, income statements, tax returns (both federal and state), and other financial statements. Ideally, these should be prepared by a CPA and organized for easy analysis. Your accountant should examine the financial records while your attorney performs a lien and judgment search on the owner and the hard assets of the business.

Keep in mind that tax returns may not tell the whole story about a business's profitability. Many small businesses try to hide some of their profits to avoid paying tax on them. But you can't rely on figures from a "second set" of books. You can't just take an owner's word, or hand-scribbled notes, as proof of such "hidden" profits. If the owner intends to base the selling price on a certain level of profitability, he or she will have to be able to back up that profit picture with something tangible.

Ask to see records of bank deposits and bills paid to suppliers. Reconcile those with sales records. Also, try to compare the business's operating expenses and profits with those of similar businesses. You can get some average figures from trade associations to use as a benchmark.

WHAT'S THE TRACK RECORD FOR WRITING OFF BAD DEBTS? ARE FIXED ASSETS, SUCH AS EQUIPMENT, PROPERLY DEPRECIATED? DOES ACTUAL INVENTORY ON HAND MATCH WITH RECORDS?

You and your accountant will need to draw up a detailed annual income and operating expense statement, including your salary and personal expenses, to determine the future profit potential of the business. Look at current profitability based on your numbers and the actual expenses. Then, estimate if you can cut expenses and/or increase income to improve the profitability picture.

Examine the Business Licenses, Contracts, and Lease, If There Is One.

What are the conditions, terms, and lengths of these agreements? Are they assignable? Can they be renewed? Are increases in rents and fees spelled out?

Look Closely at the Tangible Assets You'd Be Buying.

Is the inventory fresh or obsolete? Is the equipment in good repair and up-to-date? Who owns what? Are there any liens against these assets? Has the business joined the information age?

What About That So-called Goodwill?

Ask suppliers, customers, and trade associations about their view of the business. Ask your friends and neighbors as well. Is there really goodwill, or does the business have a reputation for less-than-stellar service?

Study the Sources of Supply.

Are they adequate, and will you be able to continue to do business with them at a reasonable rate?

Investigate the Competition.

This is key. How many competitors are there, and how well do they serve their customers? Is the competition a threat to the business you're thinking of buying or is there room for you both? Is a major mass-merchandiser getting ready to open down the street and put you out of business? Check with the Chamber of Commerce and local business groups to see what new businesses may be coming to the area.

Figure Out Why the Owner Wants to Sell.

Is there a problem that's not immediately obvious? There could be a million reasons that won't impact your future success. On the other hand, if there are real problems, the owner isn't likely to volunteer them. Never take the seller's word for why he or she is selling the business. You and your professional team will have to do some detecting to get to the truth. You'll need to have a clear idea of the motivation for selling to aid you when you're negotiating the purchase price.

After this careful analysis of the prospects, you should have narrowed your options and you should be ready to start on the logistics of negotiating the deal.

DECIDE HOW MUCH THE BUSINESS IS WORTH

Forget what the seller is asking. You have to decide what the business is worth to you. And that will depend on the ability of the business to make a profit for you. Generally, there are four ways to determine the value of a business: by liquidation value, by book value, by market value, and by formula value.

LIQUIDATION VALUE

Liquidation value is determined by calculating what the tangible assets of the business would bring at auction. It is the lowest value you can assign to a business and the cheapest way to buy. But chances are you're not looking at a business on the auction block.

BOOK VALUE

Book value is, simply enough, the value listed in the books of the business.

MARKET VALUE

A better way to estimate the price is to look at the market value of a business, which reflects an accepted expert estimate—often made by a business broker or accountant. It is based on rules of thumb acquired through years of experience and can be useful in establishing a general price range for a business you're interested in.

Sellers will object to these three methods of determining value because they don't account for what's called "goodwill." The best way to think of goodwill is as the payment you make to the original entrepreneur for all the hassles and hardships she or he had while growing the business to its present level. Unfortunately, it's very difficult to quantify how much this is worth to you.

Formula Value

The best way to set a price on a business that includes fair valuation of goodwill is to determine the business's formula value. This is a fairly complex process. You'll probably have your accountant help you, but it's important for you to understand how it works, so I'll use round numbers as examples.

You'll probably need to read these paragraphs several times before you understand the concept. Valuing businesses is a very esoteric art, rather than a science, and has been the subject of massive studies and voluminous works. What really counts is that your accountant knows what he or she is doing.

First, establish the adjusted value of the business's tangible assets by subtracting the total liabilities from the total assets. But rather than using the numbers from the seller's balance sheet, make judgments based on the research you've done. Let's say you determine this is $100,000.

Next, estimate how much you could earn annually by placing that amount in some other type of investment. Let's say you figure out that you could earn $10,000 by investing that same $100,000 in a Treasury Bill.

Now, add that potential earnings to the current salary you're making. If you aren't currently drawing a salary, use the salary you plan to draw as owner of the business. Let's say you're currently earning $50,000. Add that to the potential earnings of $10,000 and you come up with $60,000.

Determine the average annual net earnings of the business for the past three to five years. (Net earnings is the net profit the business made before the owner took out a salary.) Let's say that in 1993 the business had an annual net earnings of $69,000. In 1994 the figure was $71,000. And in 1995 it dropped down to $70,000. The average of these three numbers is $70,000.

Subtract the total of earnings power and current salary (in our example, $60,000) from the average annual net earnings of the business ($70,000 in our example). The resulting number ($10,000) is called the extra earnings power of the business.

You can use this extra earnings power figure to determine the value of the business's goodwill.

You do this by multiplying the earnings power number by a "certainty" figure. This certainty figure comes from estimating:

- how unique and powerful the goodwill seems to be;
- how long it would take to bring a new business up to this performance; and
- how well-established the business is.

The more certain it is that the business will continue in the manner it has, the higher a certainty figure you should choose. Work with a range from 1 to 5. A business that's been around for twenty years, is well-known, and has been consistently profitable gets a certainty figure of 5. A business started a year ago, with no track record of profitability, gets a certainty figure of 1.

Let's say the business you're valuing has been around for ten years, is fairly well-known, has achieved a moderate amount of goodwill, and has had steady profits for more than five years. A certainty figure of 3 would seem justified.

Multiply the extra earnings power ($10,000) by the certainty figure (3), and you'll come up with an estimate of the value of the business's goodwill ($30,000).

The final step in determining formula value is to go back to the business's adjusted tangible net worth ($100,000) and add it to the value you've assigned to the business's goodwill ($30,000). The total ($130,000) is the formula value of the business.

The formula value offers objectivity. But as a future Gray Wave entrepreneur, you should look at the issue subjectively as well. What is this business worth to you and what will it mean to you?

Don't forget what kind of lifestyle you want to lead in the next third of your life. You still may want to be semiretired and not make this a sixty-hour-a-week job. It probably won't be your sole income. You'll still have Social Security and perhaps pension and whatever savings you don't use to help finance your purchase.

The objective value of the business is one thing; its subjective value to you may be quite another. And only you can decide what that is.

WHAT ABOUT YOUR FINANCING?

There are more options for financing the purchase of a business than there are for starting one. That's because the current owner can serve as a source of financing. But before you go looking for money, you have to have a purchase strategy and a price in mind.

There are two ways to buy a business: buy the balance sheet or purchase the assets. Buying the balance sheet means assuming both the assets and the liabilities of the business. Most sellers prefer this option. But buyers generally do better if they purchase the assets and let the current owner dissolve the company and take care of the liabilities.

To a certain extent, your financing options depend on the price of the business you're buying. But chances are, for a suitable Gray Wave, semiretirement business, we're not talking about a lot of money. At least not enough money to interest a commercial lender, who's looking for big-money loans with big paybacks and little risk. A good bet is a home equity or personal loan. Loans from family and friends can work, too. And Small Business Administration loans are available for the purchase of existing businesses. But your best bet is seller-assisted financing.

YOUR OWN FUNDS

Maybe you've been a saver all your life. Or maybe you're lucky enough to have a substantial amount of cash lying around, or assets you can convert to cash for purchasing a business. Victims of the corporate downsizing in vogue today may have a secret weapon—their severance packages—they can use to purchase a business.

And many graying baby boomers are likely to have inherited a nice nest egg. That, too, can be an excellent source of financing for your business.

INSTITUTIONAL SOURCES

As I suggested earlier, forget a business loan. Your best chance is a home equity or personal loan.

A home equity loan, or second mortgage, is now a very popular form of financing for all sorts of things, including businesses. Banks like home equity loans because there's little risk involved. It's a bit of a simplification, but if your home is worth $175,000 and your mortgage balance is $75,000, you have $100,000 worth of equity in your home. Generally speaking, you can borrow against that equity—usually up to 70 percent of its value. Even better, the interest on a home equity loan might be tax deductible, effectively lowering the cost of the loan.

You should search for a home equity loan or a personal loan exactly as you did for your first mortgage. Shop around for the best interest rates at banks, credit unions, and savings and loans.

FAMILY AND FRIENDS

Some people say there's no quicker way to lose a friend than to lend him or her money. But if you get along well with a well-heeled friend, she or he can be an excellent source of financing. The same is true of family. It can be a win-win deal for both parties, because there's a gap between current lending rates and the interest rates institutions are offering on savings accounts, certificates of deposit, and other savings instruments.

Say your friend is a rocket scientist who's rolling in money and is always on the lookout for a good investment. Right now she's got $45,000 to invest, and by sheer coincidence, that's exactly how much you've decided you need to borrow to buy that gourmet coffee bar and get rolling. The other $20,000 you'll pull from your savings.

She doesn't want to deal with mutual funds and other more risky investment instruments. She knows that fixed-rate investments earn around 4.5 percent for a conventional savings account and about 6 percent with most CDs.

Meanwhile, you've discovered that a personal loan will cost you about 10 percent. So there's roughly a 4 percent window of opportunity for you and your friend to make a deal that benefits you both. If she lends you her $45,000 at 8 percent she'll be getting a better return on her investment than she would otherwise and you'll be getting a loan 2 percent below what's available in the marketplace. You both win.

The Small Business Administration

The U.S. Small Business Administration has a number of different loan programs that your local office can describe in detail. Generally, you must have been rejected by at least three other financial institutions before you can apply for an SBA loan. Various groups, such as minorities, also are targeted for SBA assistance.

There are also SBA loan guarantee programs that work with local banks to guarantee loans to small businesses. There's usually a long waiting list for SBA loans—and tons of paperwork to plow through before you can get one—but they're available.

Seller Financing

This can work as many different ways as there are buyers and sellers. But basically, if the seller wants to get a price badly enough, he or she will agree to let you pay the business off with a small sum down and the rest in monthly installments. With or without interest. Some sellers actually prefer this method of financing because it can guarantee them a steady income.

There is some risk to sellers, but because the business generates a certain amount of profit, they should be willing to take a chance.

NEGOTIATING THE DEAL

This is probably the single most negotiable transaction around. And it should be, considering all the assumptions and estimates and guesses you have to make.

That's why you should never pay all cash for an existing business. The seller should in some way guarantee the claims that have been made that you've been unable to substantiate. The only way to do that is by taking back some paper—in effect, giving you a mortgage on the business.

The terms of the deal may, in fact, be more important than the actual purchase price. Obviously, the longer the terms and the lower the interest, the better off you are. The financial arrangements you make with the seller are limited only by law and the creativity of you, your attorney, and your accountant.

One part of the package can be that the former owner serves as your teacher and in-house consultant for as long as is necessary. Obviously, you'll have to pay for this service, one way or another. But how you pay is entirely up to you and the former owner.

HERE'S WHAT JOHN AND BETH KILLIAN HAVE PLANNED

Beth and John Killian are planning ahead. They're still young by any standard. And quite well off. She's forty-four and he's forty-five. She's a homemaker and takes primary care of the couple's three children. He's a very successful options trader, part owner of a trading firm that has offices on both coasts and also owns three seats on the New York Stock Exchange.

John's been earning roughly $1 million a year for the past six or seven years. A healthy chunk of that goes back into the business. Another healthy chunk supports an extremely comfortable—by some standards, luxurious—lifestyle. That still leaves a nice sum left over to stash in their two IRAs and other accounts.

When they first got married, Beth worked at a couple of

different jobs. But she never got a career off the ground. Then John started earning big money. By the time they started having kids they could afford to have her stay home with them. It made both their lives easier—and, frankly, she liked it.

She felt satisfied pouring her time and energy into her family and her home. The kids thrived on it. So did she. She loved the basic tasks that comprise a homemaker's day: cooking meals, baking bread, shopping, schlepping kids, and picking up dry cleaning. She didn't feel the need for anything more while the children were still young. But as they started growing up she began thinking about what she wanted to do when they left the nest.

She thought about buying a business. Certainly they could afford to do that. She considered a gourmet cheese shop, a clothing boutique, a handmade jewelry shop. All seemed like good possibilities in their upscale, suburban community, but none of them really excited Beth. So she put the idea on hold.

Then John started changing. He had always loved his work—the big-stakes gambles, the gamesmanship, the daily scramble, the pit fights, even the tension and stress. The adrenaline kept his juices flowing and his competitive edge honed. But eventually the pace started taking a toll. He became irritable, quick-tempered. He started snapping at Beth and at the kids. He couldn't relax at all, not even in the evenings and on weekends.

He started making jokes about hating everyone and arming himself with an Uzi. And although he didn't have a mean bone in his body and wouldn't deliberately hurt anyone, these cracks led him to realize he was hurting himself and that he had better do something about it.

He and Beth talked it over and decided to start planning for a simpler life. They realized they wanted a lifestyle that allowed them to live where they liked and do the things they enjoy doing. For years they had regularly visited Beth's mother and stepfather at their vacation home in Vermont, skiing in the winter and swimming and hiking in the summer. They loved the outdoor, woodsy flavor of that life.

Beth's mother's best Vermont friends—a former New York City couple now in their late-sixties—owned and operated a four-guest room bed-and-breakfast, the Moose's Muse, just down the road. Whenever they visited Vermont, Beth and John would stop at the Moose's Muse for the afternoon high tea that was a specialty of the place. And during each visit, John and Beth would revel in the absolute peace and stillness of the place and the beautiful view of the pond and mountains out the back door—even though they never actually saw a moose.

When John realized he was no longer happy duking it out every day on the options exchange, and Beth began thinking about an eventually child-free future, they decided to do more than worry.

"We knew John was a walking time bomb, and that if he didn't make a change soon, the stress might really hurt him. All the money just wasn't worth it if we didn't get to enjoy it in the end."

They gave themselves five years. First, they talked to the couple who owned the bed-and-breakfast. The McArthurs hadn't seriously considered cashing it in and moving south, but they thought about it and conceded they were getting tired and the winters were starting to wear on them.

So when John and Beth approached the McArthurs about buying them out in five years, they agreed to consider it seriously. They thought five years might be just right.

When the time comes, John says, he doesn't want to have to start from scratch. He wants to just put his money down and buy a going business. He wants the transition from the high-stress options exchange to the relaxed, country B&B to be relatively easy and stress-free.

Although they don't have an ironclad contract or purchase agreement, they do have the beginnings of a win-win deal for both couples. Besides, John says, if that deal falls through, he'll find another nice B&B to buy. In preparation for their retirement future, Beth has started a hotel-management course at a local university, and they've both begun scouring the countryside for good antiques.

"Hey," John says, "I'll always be a type-A personality, even when I retire to Vermont. The first thing I want to do is put on an addition and maybe start a weekend dinner and jazz club in the barn. I certainly intend to make some money at this, in addition to enjoying myself and getting ready for my own style of 'retirement.' "

SO WHERE DO YOU GO FROM HERE?

Now is the time to decide whether you want to buy a business or if you'd rather review the other options for Gray Wave entrepreneurs covered in earlier chapters. Buying an existing business can be a quicker and safer route to entrepreneurial success than starting a business from scratch. But it's also possible to get taken. So be sure you know what you're doing, what you're buying and how to negotiate the right deal. And put your expert advisers to work.

Remember, buying the business is just the first step. As an entrepreneur—even a semiretired Gray Wave entrepreneur—you're going to have to work hard and love what you're doing to make it work. And you'll definitely need good people skills. For no matter what business you buy, and no matter how highly the business is regarded when you buy it, when you take over it's going to be you and your name on the line. You'll have to compete for and win those customers or clients, and show them that you can get the job done. And that means constantly selling your biggest asset—yourself.

RESOURCE AND REFERENCE GUIDE FOR BUYING AN EXISTING BUSINESS

For further information on buying an existing business, take a look at the following. I've included books on selling businesses, too, since it helps to understand the motivations and strategies of the other side.

- *Buying a Business: A Step-by-Step Guide to Purchasing a Business,* by Ronald J. McGregor (MI Management Group, 1990).

- *Buying and Selling a Business: A Step-by-Step Guide,* by Robert Klueger (Wiley, 1988).
- *Complete Guide to Buying a Business,* by Richard W. Snowden (AMACOM, 1993).
- *Complete Guide to Selling a Business,* by Michael K. Semanik and John H. Wade (AMACOM, 1994).
- *How to Buy a Business,* by Richard A. Joseph, Anna M. Nekoranec, and Carl H. Steffans (Dearborn Financial, 1992).
- *Small Business Valuation Book: Easy to Use Techniques for Determining Fair Price, Resolving Disputes, and Minimizing Taxes,* by Lawrence W. Tuller (Bob Adams, 1994).
- *Valuing a Business: The Analysis and Appraisal of Closely Held Companies,* by Shannon P. Pratt, Robert F. Reilly, and Robert P. Schweibs (Irwin, 1994).
- *Valuing Small Businesses and Professional Practices,* by Shannon P. Pratt, Robert F. Reilly, and Robert P. Schweibs (Irwin, 1993).

11

TEN TIPS FOR EVERY GRAY WAVE
ENTREPRENEUR

If you've gotten this far in this book you're probably raring to race down the road to Gray Wave entrepreneurial success. You've probably done your research, decided what kind of business you want to start—or buy, and maybe you've even got your business plan mapped out.

But before you hit the start switch, here are ten final tips you'll want to consider—tips on computer technology, extending credit, personal selling, and other areas of importance. These tips are applicable to all the varied kinds of entrepreneurial endeavors I've outlined in preceding chapters, and they can help insure your future success.

TIP #1: LEAP INTO THE INFORMATION AGE

Telecommunications has set new standards for small business. Your customers and contacts not only expect you to have a telephone, but a fax machine and some form of messaging service as well. The fax is a necessary convenience for the timely sharing of documents and correspondence. You'll need an answering machine or voice mail service to avoid missing calls and sales. These are the minimum requirements for today's small business.

But you should go even further. Jump into the information age, if you haven't already. The computer has become a necessary tool for small business success, not just a luxury or an expensive toy. But in order to gain the full benefit of computer technology, you must know what to choose and how to use it efficiently. And that involves much more than turning a computer on and typing a letter.

The right hardware and software can mean doing in minutes what used to take hours, or even days. It also can be an easy, efficient, direct lifeline to your customers. First, however, you'll need to identify the specific technology that will help your business. When evaluating the range of options, weigh the merits of each against these considerations:

- Will the tool or service enable you to make more productive use of your time?

- Will it enable you to do a better job of what you're already doing?

- Can you use it to broaden your reach in the marketplace?

- Does it improve customer service by reducing response time or giving clients better access to you?

- Will the technology pay for itself in cost savings, increased productivity, or expanded sales opportunities?

It's important to tailor the technology mix to your business operation. List every task your business performs during a given day, and consider whether technology can help you accomplish that task more efficiently or productively. Invest only in the tools for which you have a proven use. Then expand your capabilities as your needs evolve.

If you're not sure about whether a specific technology will help you, do some experimenting. Most reputable computer and office equipment companies will offer free demonstrations and trials.

Why invest in anything when you're not sure it offers the solutions you need? For telecommunications services such as an 800 (toll-free) number, conference calling, and E-mail, it's easy and inexpensive to experiment with your options. Sign up for these services and track the results for a couple of months. If they're effective, keep the service; if not, cancel it.

With hardware, the up-front investment is more substantial.

And there's always the likelihood that this year's breakthrough will be quickly outdated. If you're watching your budget, leasing equipment may make more sense than outright purchase at first. Try now, buy later: It's an inexpensive way to sample technology before its benefits are proven.

But if you decide to buy, do it right. Mapping out your expectations will simplify your job. Then just match software and hardware to your needs, watch out for a few common pitfalls, and you'll be fine.

The Biggest Mistake

People often buy hardware, then try to decide what to do with it. This is definitely the wrong way to go. It's more important to decide which software meets your needs, then choose hardware that will run it.

Cost Versus Price

When comparing systems, make sure it's apples to apples. The price of one system often seems higher, but when the cost of its extra features are considered, it may be a better deal. Also consider future expansion—can you add peripherals with ease, or do you need costly expansion cards to control them?

Beware of Software Packages

Many systems come with large software packages; that's often a good thing, but be careful. Packages are often used to make it seem like a better deal than it really is. Check the actual retail price of the programs included to determine their value. More important, is it software you'll use?

Monitor Myths

Don't fall for the rainbow effect. Millions of colors sound great, but most users only need two: black and white. Contrast and clarity are more important. You're going to be staring at this thing for a long time. Make sure you can read the display. Consider a larger screen if you'll be doing any sort of design or page layout. The time saved in scrolling around alone will be worth the extra cost, but make sure your computer can handle it.

FINDING A CONSULTANT

Finding that correct combination of hardware and software may require specialized knowledge and expertise. Just as it often makes sense to stick to your own area of expertise—running your business—and hire legal and tax advisers, so it often makes sense to hire a technology adviser: a computer consultant.

The best way to find a computer consultant is through personal recommendations. Ask other small business owners, in the same or similar industries, for suggestions. In addition, most hardware and software companies maintain lists of consultants knowledgeable about their products. Contact companies whose products you're considering and ask for their recommendations.

Then check your industry's trade magazine. There are probably ads for computer consultants in the back. Telephone those listed and ask about their clients, services, and credentials. If you discover they're geared toward servicing larger firms, ask if they can suggest consultants who service businesses the size of yours.

When you have a list of candidates, you need to interview those who look most promising. But remember, you're in charge. Don't let the consultants intimidate you with technological jargon. A technical consultant will be responsible for one of the most important elements of your business, so she or he must be able to explain the business in language that you can understand. That's a consultant's job.

If you don't understand something, ask. If you can't understand the explanation, find another candidate. The problem isn't just going to disappear, and it is bound to get worse when equipment and software arrive.

The consultant must understand your business and work flow, so have specific scenarios in mind that you can discuss. Before the interview, outline your average workday. Then list every task your business needs to perform, so the consultant can understand the scope of your needs.

Experience in your particular business is good, but not essential. The ability to react quickly and solve problems is just as, if not more, important. In addition, broad-based experience in other businesses could bring solutions you'd never have thought of.

Make sure the person you're interviewing will be the person actually performing the work. Discuss availability and access in emergencies. Will the consultant be available on weekends? Evenings? Can he or she be paged? Are there surcharges for emergency service? Ask if you'll be billed for all telephone calls.

Independent research can save you a great deal of money. Most consultants will supply you with hardware and software, but you should know the actual consumer price of anything you're going to buy from a consultant.

You have a right to know a consultant's markup. Most will provide itemized invoices and charge a fee (based on an hourly rate) for research and the selection of equipment. If a consultant won't tell you her or his markup or won't provide itemized bills, there's a reason. Cross that person off your list.

Hourly rates usually are linked to the scope and duration of the job and generally are negotiable. The more you'll be using the consultant's services, the less you can expect to pay per hour.

Finally, make this a win-win situation. If you're pleased with the service you're receiving, offer to serve as a reference. Such a vote of confidence can result in even better service.

TIP #2: EXTEND CREDIT TO EXPAND YOUR MARKET

Today, when consumers and even businesses are increasingly buying products and services on credit, rather than with cash, smaller companies willing and able to extend credit have a distinct marketing edge over the competition. However, there's a big risk attached to extending credit: The bill may never get paid in full.

One way small companies can deal with this dilemma is to pass the risk on to someone else. For example, a credit card company. There is a catch, however. Most credit card companies charge a fee for this service, ranging from 1 to 4 percent of the sales price. Most also are surprisingly selective about which businesses they will allow to accept their cards.

Those companies either unable or unwilling to pass along the risk have another option. It's possible for even the smallest business to offer its customers or clients credit without going broke, provided it develops and implements sound policies for extending credit, monitoring collections, and enforcing payment.

CHECK OUT YOUR CUSTOMER FIRST

It's essential to, if at all possible, get information on customers and clients before extending them credit. That way, if you discover that a customer or client has a history of paying late, you can refuse to extend credit. Develop a credit application requesting name, address, telephone number, Social Security or employer identification number, and the name and location of the customer's bank. This information will help if there's trouble collecting the debt.

The application should also ask for a list of outstanding obligations, such as bank loans, mortgages, and credit card balances. This information can provide a rough estimate of how much debt the customer or client is already servicing.

There should be a section of the application asking businesses to provide at least two credit references, preferably vendors they purchase from on a regular basis. Obviously, these should be contacted and quizzed about the business's credit record.

Finally, the application should contain language authorizing you to conduct a complete credit check. Reports can be obtained on both individuals and businesses from organizations such as TRW and Dun & Bradstreet.

YOU MAY NEED TO USE A COLLECTION SERVICE

As a Gray Wave entrepreneur, you don't want to be in the business of collecting bills. In fact, you're only lending money, or extending credit, to maintain a competitive edge. Bill collecting takes time, energy, and persistence, not to mention persuasive skills. It's a job, frankly, best left to lawyers and collection agents, even though they charge hefty fees ranging from 20 to 50 percent of funds collected.

Once an account is more than thirty days past due, you should begin considering handing it over to someone else for collection. Some businesses routinely put all bills forty-five days past due in for collection, while others wait until ninety days have passed.

As an alternative to a collection agent, you may want to consider settling with a delinquent client or customer for a lesser amount, or agreeing to an extended payment schedule. Whichever way you go, be sure to think twice about extending credit to that person or business again.

TIP #3: "SELL YOURSELF" TO INSURE SUCCESS

As an entrepreneur, every time you sell your product or service you're selling yourself. To insure success, you need to be sure that your selling technique is personal—an intimate, personal exchange of goods or service between you and the customer. The only way to keep customers is to provide quality products and superior service. But you'll be even more successful if they feel that your warmth and character, your honesty and integrity, are part of the bargain.

Building trust takes time. But when you're trying to make a sale, time is short. Therefore, it's important to know shortcuts. People instinctively trust someone they believe cares for them. In demonstrating you care you'll foster that feeling of trust. Here are some keys to creating a caring environment.

APPEARANCES COUNT

You should dress appropriately for your business, but regardless of what you wear, it should be neat, clean, and simple, not fussy. Pay careful attention to your grooming. Be businesslike. Keep your workplace clean and comfortable as well.

MAKE YOUR GREETING COUNT

Getting off to the right start is crucial. Greet customers warmly. Smile, shake hands, and be sure to look them in the eye. Greet them by name if you can; if you don't know or can't remember a customer's name, introduce yourself by name.

DON'T RUSH TO BUSINESS

Engage the customer in pleasant conversation by asking questions. Try to find common ground, even if it's the weather. It's the thought that counts, not the scintillating conversation.

BE RESPONSIVE

Don't try to do two things at once when you're greeting the customer. You can't fill out an order while a customer is trying to carry on a conversation. Lean forward when customers are talking and acknowledge what they're saying by nodding your head. Be expressive.

TELEPHONES AREN'T ANONYMOUS

Treat telephone communications as you would face-to-face meetings: Be warm and cordial, be personal, engage in brief pleasantries.

BE COURTEOUS

It may save time, but it will cost you business if you forget the little courtesies in the crush of business. Don't forget to say please and thank you.

In the end, your goal is not just to make a sale but to keep a customer by building customer loyalty. So an important part of your job will be your follow-up after the sale is made. That means you need to ask the customer for feedback, both positive and negative.

You should also keep in touch after the sale by communicating regularly with customers. Let them know about upcoming sales or promotions, drop them a line (your new computer equipment will help) to check on their progress with your product or service. Your goal is to make each customer feel special. Make them feel you truly have their interests at heart. And you should—because their interests are your interests. Their continued loyalty will help your business to grow.

Dealing with Complaints

Every business owner makes mistakes. Every entrepreneur has at least one dissatisfied customer. Sometimes the fault genuinely is yours or an employee's. Other times the customer or client is wrong.

Your job, regardless of who's at fault, is to turn a no-win situation into a win-win one by responding promptly to customer complaints. Remember, the only way for you to win is to insure that the customer is never wrong. So you need to demonstrate how deeply you care about what has gone wrong and how committed you are to making things right. Do whatever it takes to resolve the situation to the customer's satisfaction. Then, follow up to make sure the customer remains satisfied. Make sure the customer is aware that you really are concerned and want her or him to remain a good customer.

Personal selling comes down to common sense. It's nothing new and it's no gimmick. But it's amazing how many otherwise savvy entrepreneurs forget the basics in the heat of the daily business grind. Don't let that happen to you.

TIP #4: SET YOUR PRICES RIGHT

Setting prices is where many new business owners are most insecure, and therefore where they make some of their worst mistakes. In short, most entrepreneurs set their prices too low. Worried about making sales, some entrepreneurs set their prices according to what their competitors are charging, some add a mere "reasonable" profit to costs, and some cut prices nearly to the bone in the hope of attracting a greater volume of sales.

None of these is a method for a new business owner to emulate. Setting prices too low may cause customers to assume your products are inferior to the competition's. In addition, you may not be able to survive long enough to compete with more established businesses that are in a position to set their prices low.

How, then, should you determine the right price for your products and services?

- First, figure out your costs.
- Second, choose a pricing strategy.
- Third, convince yourself to act with confidence, patience, and pride—and aim high, because when you set a price, you also set an image for your business.

DETERMINING COSTS

To figure out your costs, you need to tally three factors:

1. Material costs, such as parts and supplies.

2. Labor costs, which should include hourly wages plus benefits.

3. Overhead costs, or the indirect costs of everything else, such as clerical and janitorial expenses, taxes, depreciation, and so on.

PRICING STRATEGIES

You have five pricing strategies to choose from:

1. *Comparable pricing*—Setting a price close to your competitor's price works only when both firms are established. When you are the new business on the block, comparable pricing will not give your competitor's customers any reason to switch to you.

2. *Low pricing*—As was discussed above, in most cases this is a fatal mistake.

3. *High pricing*—The best option for a new small business, high pricing reflects an image of quality, distinguishes you from your competitor, and helps you recover start-up costs quickly.

4. *Good-better-best pricing*—This gives customers choices within the same product line. One offers the best price, one the best value, and one the best quality.

5. *Promotional pricing*—By setting one price below cost you can attract sales of other goods. Discounted pricing, such as "2/10, net 30"—which gives customers a 2 percent discount if they pay within ten days and otherwise requires them to pay the full amount within thirty days—also can encourage sales as well as prompt payment.

TIP #5: COLLECT ACCOUNTS RECEIVABLE FASTER

As a small business entrepreneur, it's always in your best interest to have as much cash available as possible. One way of maximizing your working capital is expediting the accounts receivable process. For example: Standard business practice requests customer payments after thirty days. But if you were to alter the payment terms to fifteen days—or less—it could substantially lessen your need to borrow money and increase cash flow. That money could be used in any way you see fit: to pay bills, or even to expand your business. Below are some other ways to help put the cash in your hands, where it belongs.

INVOICE IMMEDIATELY

Too often, businesses wait to send out their bills, virtually guaranteeing a slowdown in the payment cycle. Send out your invoices as soon as possible. Although customers may be reluctant to pay right away, you've at least gotten the billing cycle under way.

BEGIN COLLECTION EFFORTS THE DAY AFTER PAYMENTS ARE DUE

This shows you're in earnest about getting paid on time, and it will most likely result in your getting paid ahead of the rest of the pack. Don't wait until the account becomes seriously delinquent. Not only can this destroy cash flow, it increases the odds of nonpayment.

START YOUR COLLECTION EFFORT WITH A FRIENDLY REMINDER

There's no need to be hostile or threatening in the beginning. If the first reminder you send fails to yield payment, send another copy of the invoice along with a cover letter stating that you thought it important to put in writing your understanding of the situation to date. The subtext, of course, is that you're creating a paper trail should you need to bring the person to court. Close with a heartfelt hope that the situation is remedied as soon as possible. Most customers will respond to the implied threat. If this fails, consider suspending credit after ninety days.

SEE IF YOU CAN NEGOTIATE LONGER PAYMENT TERMS ON YOUR ACCOUNTS PAYABLE

Trying to slow down payment of accounts payable should be a part of your accounts receivable collection efforts. Find out if your vendors will accept payment within sixty days rather than the standard thirty. Suppliers in highly competitive industries are most likely to agree to this.

TIP #6: BECOME A SKILLED INTERVIEWER

Few of us—even those Gray Wavers who are former managers—have obtained the skills to become effective interviewers. Managers are not ordinarily taught these skills. Although it's not terribly difficult to determine a candidate's technical expertise, that's not usually why people fail at a new job. They generally fail because they can't work as part of a team, they're not flexible, or because the new employee's expectations about recognition, environment, or management style haven't been met.

Good interview skills can heighten your awareness of areas of strengths or weaknesses—or simply sound the alarm that this is not a good fit. One word of caution, however: Although you'll be asking a lot of questions, keep your mouth shut as much as possible. You'll learn more and evaluate better by simply listening.

The following questions are designed to help you make some decisions about a candidate's appropriateness.

Describe an Instance Where You Used an Unusual Solution to Solve a Common Problem

This will give you some insight into the candidate's creativity, and risk taking relative to problem solving.

What Do You Believe is the Personal Profile for Someone to Be Successful at This Job?

The answer gives you some idea of how close the candidate's ideas are to your views on what's required to be successful. It also gives you insight into what the candidate believes are the key responsibilities of the job.

Describe a Situation in Which You Were a Member of a Team but Disagreed with the Way Others Wanted to Approach a Project

This helps to give you some idea of the candidate's team work skills, the candidate's ability to communicate ideas, and how the candidate approaches conflict and resolution.

Define Cooperation

This will give you more information on the candidate's ability to work as part of a team.

Give Me an Example of a Time You Needed to Understand the Position of Another in Order to Get Your Work Done. How Did You Go About Getting that Understanding?

The answer will show whether the candidate considers the opinions of others and the effect that his decisions have on others. Is the candidate's style autocratic or participatory?

WHAT DO YOU CONSIDER A POSITIVE WORK ENVIRONMENT?

This answer shows whether the candidate will be comfortable in your environment. If the answer describes an environment unlike yours, forget it.

DESCRIBE THE BEST/WORST BOSS YOU EVER HAD

This can give you information about the candidate's expectations about how he should be managed and usually gives you an idea of how the candidate will manage others.

HOW WOULD YOUR SUBORDINATE DESCRIBE YOUR STRENGTHS AND WEAKNESSES?

This question addresses the candidate's self-awareness, confidence, honesty, and sensitivity to others.

WHAT DO YOU THINK ARE THE TRAITS OF THE IDEAL MANAGER?

This will provide you with information on the candidate's philosophy and expectations.

DESCRIBE A MISTAKE YOU MADE IN YOUR LAST POSITION AND WHAT YOU LEARNED FROM IT

This will give you some insight into the candidate's self-awareness, analytical ability, problem-solving ability and objectivity.

DESCRIBE A SITUATION IN WHICH YOU HAD TO MAKE A DIFFICULT DECISION

This will demonstrate the candidate's willingness to do the right thing even when it might result in an unpopular outcome. This, in turn, will also demonstrate the candidate's strength of convictions.

What Are You Most Passionate About?

This will speak to the candidate's motivation, intensity, and priorities.

How Would You Define Success in Life?

This will give you a view of the candidate's personal and professional priorities, values, sense of life balance, motivation, and maturity.

When You're Not Working, How Do You Spend Your Time?

The activities the candidate describes reflect personal style and mutual areas of comfort.

What Books Have You Read? How Have They Affected You?

This gives you some idea of what intellectually stimulates and challenges the candidate.

What Personal Characteristics Sometimes Interfere with the Way You Work?

This will give you insight into the candidate's self-awareness and honesty.

Could You Describe Your Ideal Job?

This will demonstrate the candidate's creativity, insight into personal and professional needs, expectations, and motivation.

How Do You Plan Your Day?

This will indicate how the candidate handles time management, "prioritization," and flexibility.

TIP #7: HIRE TEMPS WHENEVER POSSIBLE

Temporary employees are a solution for many growing businesses not ready to make long-term employment commitments. Also, if an agency is used, there are no costly benefits to absorb, no payroll taxes to pay, and no tax forms to be filed.

Finding the right temp is challenging and often daunting. There are essentially two ways: Do it yourself or hire an agency. No matter which way you choose to go, the one thing to remember is: The better you craft the job description of the position you are seeking to fill, the more likely you'll make a successful placement.

FIVE TIPS FOR DO-IT-YOURSELFERS

This can be problematic, but if it's the way you want to go, here are some essential tips to live by when finding a temp.

1. *Search your own network*—Often the best source for candidates is not a newspaper campaign but personal referrals from current employees, friends, and other business peers. An excellent source of candidates can also be local college bulletin boards.

2. *Weed out candidates*—Two immediate ways to help sift through the résumés and begin the screening process are to set aside any résumés that have unexplained chronological gaps, typographical errors, or grammatical mistakes. Although cover letters may not be an essential requirement for the job you're filling, they can often be a good indicator of the individual's accuracy and meticulousness.

3. *Make your own appointments*—Don't delegate the task—no matter how tedious—of scheduling the interview appointments for the candidates that interest you. It can be enlightening to speak directly with the candidate: the impression you receive on the telephone is the impression your clients will be receiving.

4. *Focus on their past and your needs*—The important questions to ask in the interview should focus on the candidate's

past job performance and present needs. These are three essential questions: Why do you choose to temp? Why did you leave your last permanent position? Why does this temp position appeal to you?

5. *Always ask for references, and check them*—This means actually speaking directly with previous employers and asking them pointedly whether this person is qualified. Find out about the candidate's past performance and attitude on the job. It's important that you ask the previous employer if he or she would rehire the candidate.

Five Tips for Hiring a Temp Agency

Although using an agency can be more costly, it can save you time in the long run. You'll be putting yourself in the hands of professionals who make it their business to screen candidates and find the right individual for the job you're seeking to fill.

1. *Shop agencies*—They should undergo the same scrutiny as potential employees. Ascertain how long they've been in business. Be certain the agency screens and tests skills and checks references. Try to get a guarantee. There is a range of fees—check them in advance and compare them with the fees charged by other agencies.

2. *Establish a strong rapport with the agency recruiter*—A good one-on-one relationship will help the agency fulfill your needs. Have the recruiter visit your business premises and introduce him or her to other company employees. Let the recruiter get a good sense of what a workday is like.

3. *Be explicit about your expectations for the job and the company's policies*—Accurate job descriptions are critical, as is a complete list of the technical skills required (such as familiarity with specific computer software, typing, dictation, and so on). Be clear about dress code, smoking policies, and other office regulations.

4. *Realize that you get what you pay for*—Temps are paid according to their skills. If you ask for a lesser rate, you should reduce your expectations for production.

5. *When temps arrive, be sure to acclimate them*—Tell them what you want done for the day, where to find things (coffee, rest room, supplies) and when to break for lunch. If temps are treated like semipermanent employees, they will perform best.

TIP #8: FOCUS ON PUBLIC RELATIONS

As advertising costs have continued to rise over the years, companies have turned more and more to no-cost public relations. That's because it has a proven track record for getting your message to target audiences, increasing sales, encouraging purchase and consumer satisfaction, creating and sustaining company image, and enhancing trust in you and your business.

However, not every business is ready to enter into the competitive world of public relations. There's nothing more dangerous for a company than presenting itself or a new product to the scrutiny of the public and the media before everything is absolutely ready to go.

Here are a few questions to consider before embarking on a public relations program:

- Does your company have a mission statement?
- What is the product or announcement that defines your publicity campaign?
- Have you outlined your target audience, and do you know the target media that services those consumers?
- Do you have a product image or spokesperson to represent the company and deliver its message?
- Can you pinpoint easily what makes your company stand out against its competitors?
- What, if any, are the misconceptions of your company in the marketplace, and can you rebut them?
- What is the weak point of your company, and can you respond to it?
- Do you have the right resources and the appropriate num-

ber of people to handle the requests that will result from the publicity?

- Is this the best time to embark on a public relations campaign?

If you can satisfactorily answer all of the questions above, your company should be ready to consider a public relations program. Remember, publicity works best when it's integral to the company's marketing and sales strategy and corporate culture.

CREATE A MISSION STATEMENT

All effective publicity begins with a clear understanding of the company's mission. Often overlooked, it is the most concise way a company can define its relationship with its various publics and reveals much about the company's corporate culture and marketing orientation.

CREATE PRESS MATERIALS

Develop written materials that include product or company announcements, "backgrounders" on the company and its principals (with bios), a question-and-answer sheet with the designated expert, topics of discussion for interviewers, praise sheets and/or sell sheets, positive print coverage on the company and/or its product, a bio of the spokesperson, and targeted pitch letters for the media. These press kits can be accompanied by video footage to highlight the announcement.

CONTACT TARGETED TELEVISION, RADIO, AND PRINT MEDIA

Research media and develop a database, create your targeted pitch and backup strategies; and, most important, follow up. Make yourself available to tour your target markets for greater visibility. Consider radio giveaways.

CREATE AN EVENT

This helps market your company, product, or service directly to the public and provides an angle for press coverage. Tie the function to current events or news stories, holidays, or anniversaries. Involve local or national celebrities, or feature a contest to involve your constituency.

WRITE A BYLINED ARTICLE OR OP-ED PIECE

If you can't get the media to write about your company, take matters into your own hands. Provide your trade or targeted consumer magazine with an article that will position you as an expert in the field. The op-ed piece should present a formal point of view or a debate that can platform your company's message.

SPEAK TO LOCAL BUSINESS GROUPS, CONSUMER GROUPS, AND CLUBS

Talk to any group that will have you. More groups than you would imagine are on the lookout for new faces to speak on a wide variety of issues related to their lives, not just to their specific fields of interest.

DEVELOP A CUSTOMER NEWSLETTER AND BUSINESS BROCHURE/MANUAL

These will help you communicate regularly with committed and potential clients or customers about news, products, and sales of interest to them. Create a short response questionnaire for potential customers to comment on product preferences, then add their names to your mailing list.

GAIN ENDORSEMENTS AND AWARDS FOR YOUR COMPANY

Focus attention on your company or product by getting a high-profile association, publication, or person to give it a stamp of approval.

*   *   *

Although there's no magic involved, there is an art to getting your message out effectively. Here are some general tips to help you communicate better with customers and target customers:

Make Your Position Clear

What sets your company apart in the eye of the beholder? Do you really offer a better product? More "bang per buck" in value provided? Do you have a "service edge"? Whatever it is, articulate it and communicate it, through as many avenues as you can, in brochures, sales presentations, articles, and advertising, so your customers start to remember it.

Become Known As an Expert

A little positive publicity goes a long way, especially if it's seen by prospective customers. Daily newspapers and industry trade reporters are always on the lookout for new sources for stories and comments. Get to know a few of them. Be accessible. Often, those quoted are the ones who respond the fastest to the reporters, rather than the most expert.

Don't Shoot from the Hip

Getting an opportunity to be quoted in the media is great—but you can blow it if you aren't schooled in being quotable. At minimum make sure you rehearse communicating key messages about the company. Consider working with a media consultant to construct all messages—written or oral—and to enhance your interview skills.

Increase Strength Through Numbers

Small businesses often find it too expensive to buy advertising, create big events, sponsor seminars, and undertake other publicity activities. Try getting a group of small businesses together, either through your local Chamber of Commerce or other local business groups, or informally on your own. Form your own network to make group purchases and hold mutually beneficial group events.

PLAN CHRISTMAS IN JULY

Consumer product companies know that holidays such as Mother's Day, Graduation Day, Christmas, and so forth provide guaranteed opportunities to showcase products and services—from holiday gift sections in newspapers and magazines to events at the local mall. But plan ahead—many consumer magazines start their Christmas sections in July. On a regional basis, look for opportunities to participate in well-known local events that will provide you with important visibility in the community.

A PICTURE IS WORTH MORE THAN A THOUSAND WORDS

With our shorter and shorter attention spans, people will look at a great photograph before reading a lot of words. You can expand the impact of media coverage of a particular event or product through interesting photography. It's worth the investment to use top professional photographers.

MAIL TO YOUR "FRIENDS"

Create your own mailing list of business contacts—prospects, suppliers, customers, investors, and others—and send information to them regularly. For example, inexpensive reprints of articles about your company or products, new brochures, and even letters providing an update on your business's progress are appropriate. Include a return postcard, which enhances follow-up. Mail with regularity—quarterly or even monthly. Don't stop if the initial return is not high. Images are built and many sales are made through cumulative impact.

A NOTE OF THANKS

You can create good word-of-mouth publicity through strong customer service policies—from thank-you letters to customers, to rapid response to customer inquiries and complaints, to training service personnel to be gracious no matter how trying the situation. This is a must and will go a long way to fostering those warm and fuzzy feelings that keep customers coming back. It's not the quantity of activities but the quality that counts. Select a small number of activities and commit the time to get them done; don't bite off more than you can chew. It's important to stick with the effort, year after year, for it to have an impact on your business's image.

TEN SPECIFIC TIPS

1. Support local charities by donating your products.
2. Support local charities by donating your time.
3. Obtain endorsements from product users.
4. Participate in local business initiatives and organizations.
5. Create a businesspersons' association.
6. Work with civic organizations.
7. Become active in local politics and the school board.
8. Befriend the local media.
9. Contribute to, and endorse, local political candidates.
10. Network with, and support, community religious organizations.

TIP #9: POLISH YOUR BUSINESS IMAGE

PAY ATTENTION TO YOUR TELEPHONE ANSWERING SYSTEM

The telephone is the most powerful tool a small business has. It's a lifeline to clients, customers, vendors, and professionals. And although it may be physically impossible for you to be available at the other end of the line twenty-four hours a day, you want those trying to reach you to feel that you are.

That's why the telephone answering system you choose is vital. It must convey to clients and customers that you're interested in their needs and desires. That way they'll be more likely to leave a message. "Hang-ups" are more than a nuisance, they represent lost business. Here are some suggestions:

Ideally, your telephone should be answered by a knowledgeable member of your support staff. There's nothing like a caring, competent person servicing the telephone lines to instill confidence in clients.

Answering services are generally the worst option. The operator often knows nothing about the business, and it shows. It's easier and faster for customers to leave a message on a machine than with an individual who may stumble over terminology and names.

The advances in communications technology make voice mail systems a good compromise for small companies that cannot afford support staff. However, these systems must be caller-friendly and simple to maneuver through.

The outgoing message should be in your voice. Your tone and inflection must encourage those who would otherwise hang up to leave a message.

Consider recording a new message daily that contains the day and date. This indicates that you use the system regularly.

Be informative but brief. Let callers know you're on another line or out, but that you retrieve messages on a regular basis and will respond as quickly as possible.

BUSINESS CARDS LEAVE A VISUAL IMPRINT

Your stationery and business cards are not only vital tools for conveying information about your business to customers and clients, they're also tools for demonstrating the high level of your professionalism. Here are some suggestions for making the most of them:

Logos and designs can add unnecessary cost to the production of cards and stationery because, to be effective, they need to be professionally designed. Logos can also be too "busy" to read quickly, and riskier in terms of the type of impression they're likely to make. If they don't appeal to your clients' tastes, they may be a turnoff. Finally, it takes a lot of time and money for a logo to become a real identifier for a business. For a small company this may not be practical.

Instead, keep things simple. A clean layout and crisp type not only make your card easy to read, they show you to be a sophisticated and savvy businessperson.

Use a typeface, or font, that reflects your business. For example, stark block letters for a technologies company, or a simple script for a law or accounting firm.

In general, engraved stationery and cards are not worth the expense. Use quality paper that has some texture to it, too. A watermark is nice, but not essential.

Desktop publishing cards and stationery are efficient, but effective only if the print quality is high. Amateur printing will negatively impact your business.

If you farm out the printing, don't buy too much at once. You may save money by buying in bulk, but a new business usually changes cards and stationery within the first few years.

TIP #10: REMEMBER TO ENJOY YOUR (RETIREMENT) BUSINESS

Don't forget why you started on this quest. You're at or near the generally accepted and expected retirement age, but the thought of not working makes you ill. Or it makes you feel like you're a hundred and ten. And you're not alone. Americans now can expect to live about a third of their lives beyond the so-called retirement age. And they'll be healthier and more energetic during those years than any generation before them.

You picked up this book for one reason or another. Maybe you realized that you haven't planned well and you're not going to have enough retirement income to insure the lifestyle you'd like. Or maybe the thought of thirty years of shuffleboard, canasta, and an occasional tango competition sounds more like a nightmare than a dream.

Perhaps you just want to be productive. And at the same time, you have a real desire to realize a dream—the dream of starting and operating your very own business, especially designed to accommodate the needs and further the goals of an enterprising Gray Wave entrepreneur.

It's your dream. Only you can turn that dream into a reality—a reality that transforms the next third of your life into a profitable, fulfilling adventure. Now it's time to get out there and do it. And in the process, don't forget to cash in on some fun.

III.

RESOURCES FOR GRAY WAVE ENTREPRENEURS

❈Appendix A❈

SAMPLE BUSINESS PLAN FOR A GYPSY RETAIL BUSINESS

(Although this is a business plan for a gypsy retail business, it can be used as a model for a business plan for any type of Gray Wave business.)

GENERAL INFORMATION

The Art Cart
The Mall
Collegeville, NY 14435
(607) 512-5677
Fax (607) 513-5412
E-mail: jkp12@aol

MISSION STATEMENT

This plan will serve as an operations manual for the Art Cart, a proposed retail business dealing in low- and moderately-priced original art created by "unknown" (not-yet-famous) artists.

It will be owned and operated by Jacqueline K. Powers in Collegeville, N.Y., from a rented kiosk at The Mall. Rent is $500 a month, except during November and December, when it jumps to $1,000 a month.

Ms. Powers is seeking to borrow $20,000 and will use $10,000 of her own money to finance the start-up and first-year operation of the business.

The purpose of the business is to provide average consumers the opportunity to purchase and decorate their homes with origi-

nal, signed artwork at affordable prices. It also will provide
students, young and undiscovered artists the opportunity to sell
their work.

THE BUSINESS

The Art Cart will operate from a kiosk at The Mall, a 22-store
indoor mall in Collegeville, N.Y. It is the only mall in the
90,000-resident Milligan County area. It will cater to local residents, students from the two colleges, and tourists who come to
Collegeville and the surrounding area for recreation on the lake.

Prices for artwork for sale will range from as low as $10 for
a small drawing or watercolor to $500 for an exceptional oil
painting or sculpture. Ms. Powers will purchase her inventory
from art students at the colleges and from arts and craft shows
locally and regionally. In addition, she will both buy and sell
nationally by advertising on a home page on the World Wide
Web.

She will operate the kiosk from 3 to 7 P.M. weekdays and
all day Saturday and Sunday. A part-time salesperson will operate the business on weekends and when Ms. Powers is on buying trips or vacation.

THE MARKET

The primary market for the Art Cart will be local residents,
particularly residents of the new, upper-middle-class retirement
village being constructed on the north side of town, and the
condominium development for young professionals just completed near New Hope College.

A secondary market will be tourists who visit the mall for
vacation provisions and the students themselves, their parents,
and those reached on the Internet.

The Art Cart will pursue its markets with ads in local and
regional newspapers, in student newspapers, with notices at
health clubs and other recreation spots, and through special promotions including free ''decorating'' sessions for new home-
owners and area newcomers. It will reach tourists through
partnership agreements with hotels, inns, and restaurants, and
with notices at marinas.

The Competition

Currently, there is no establishment specializing in good quality, reasonably priced art within a 60-mile radius of Collegeville. There is one art gallery selling very pricey, very avant-garde work, with which the Art Cart will not compete.

There are two specialty import and gift shops that carry occasional artworks, but they, too, are priced at the high end. There is nothing comparable to the Art Cart within reasonable driving distance offering reasonable prices.

Financing

The $20,000 loan will be used as follows:

First-year Rent	$10,000
Equipment	5,000
Initial Inventory	5,000

The owner's $10,000 will be used for costs associated with the start-up such as a reception and initial advertising campaign, the part-time employee's salary, and cash reserve.

Financial Plan

	Jan	Feb	Mar	Apr	May	June	July	Aug	Sept	Oct	Nov	Dec	Total
Projected Sales	2,000	2,100	2,100	2,100	2,100	2,200	2,400	2,200	2,000	2,000	3,500	5,000	29,700
Operating Expenses/Rent	500	500	500	500	500	500	500	500	500	500	1,000	1,000	7,000
Debt Service	200	200	200	200	200	200	200	200	200	200	200	200	2,400
Inventory	300	300	300	300	300	300	300	300	300	300	300	300	3,600
Supplies	25	25	25	25	25	25	25	25	25	25	25	25	300
Telephone	100	100	100	100	100	100	100	100	100	100	100	100	1,200
Credit Card Commissions	81	90	55	50	60	105	100	135	125	85	175	200	1,261
Postage	30	30	30	30	30	30	30	30	30	30	30	30	360
Marketing and Advertising	125	125	125	125	125	125	125	125	125	125	125	125	1,500
Legal and Accounting Fees	100	100	100	100	100	100	100	100	100	100	100	100	1,200
Insurance	100	100	100	100	100	100	100	100	100	100	100	100	1,200
Miscellaneous	40	40	40	40	40	40	40	40	40	40	40	40	480
Total Operating Expenses	1,601	1,610	1,575	1,570	1,580	1,625	1,620	1,655	1,645	1,605	2,195	2,220	20,501
Net Profit (Loss)	399	490	525	530	520	575	780	545	355	395	1,301	2,780	9,195

SAMPLE MARKETING PLAN FOR A GYPSY RETAIL BUSINESS

(Although this plan is for a gypsy retail business it can be used as a basis for developing a marketing plan for any type of Gray Wave business.)

GOALS

- To launch the Art Cart with maximum attention September 31.

- To continue to attract new customers first year after launch through varied marketing, promotion, and advertising techniques.

SEPTEMBER

Direct Marketing

- Prepare and send invitations to opening reception.
- Plan and prepare party. $1,500

Advertising

- Two weeks of daily newspaper ads before launch. $300

Publicity

- Send press release and photos to local papers and magazines about new business. $110
- Follow with calls suggesting feature story.

OCTOBER

Direct Marketing

- Send letter to customer list and prospects for Christmas theme show on December 2. $260

Promotion

- Speak to downtown business group about supporting local artists and the business of art.

NOVEMBER

Direct Marketing

- Send reminder letter about December 2 open house along with list of inexpensive gift ideas. $260

Publicity

- Send holiday gift ideas column to editors $10

Advertising

- Two daily newspaper ads twice a week beginning two weeks before holiday art show opens. $120

DECEMBER

Advertising

- Weekly newspaper ad for holiday sales. $120

January

Advertising

- Three ads in spring regional tourism directories and magazines. $225

Promotion

- Send letter to retirement village developer and other area developers offering to decorate models with original art in exchange for acknowledgment and brochure distribution. $10
- Send similar letter to restaurateurs. $15

February

Direct Marketing

- Prepare and print brochure and price list. $100
- Mail brochure to prospective customer list. $32

Advertising

- Two ads in local newspapers. $60

March

Promotion

- Rent booth at Cabin Fever Frolic. $25
- Arrange four Saturday morning kids' face-painting sessions. $100

Advertising

- Two regular ads in local newspapers. $60
- Four ads for face-painting sessions. $120

Direct Marketing

- Mail notice of face-painting sessions. $128

APRIL

Direct Marketing

- Rent mailing list of tourists from Chamber of Commerce. $70
- Send welcoming letter and brochure to list. $224

MAY

Advertising

- Four weekly ads in newspapers. $120

JUNE

Advertising

- Two biweekly ads during SummerFest. $60

Direct Marketing

- Mailing notifying customer list of booth presence at SummerFest. $128

Promotion

- Booth rental at SummerFest. $75

JULY

Publicity

- Send press kit to regional magazines about Christmas open house with photos from last year's event. $150

August

Advertising

- Four weekly ads in newspapers. $120

Publicity

- Follow-up calls to regional magazines. $15

Total for Year   **$4,517**

⋘Appendix C⋙

NATIONAL AND REGIONAL SMALL BUSINESS RESOURCES

You're not on your own if you become a Gray Wave entrepreneur. There are lots of others out there who can give you help, advice, and support. Here are some national and regional resources you can tap into.

NATIONAL SMALL BUSINESS ASSOCIATIONS AND ORGANIZATIONS

Alliance for Fair Competition
3 Bethesda Metro Center, Suite 1100
Bethesda, MD 20814
(410) 235-7116
Fax (410) 235-7116
Combats anticompetitive and unfair trade practices by utilities.

American Association for Consumer Benefits
P.O. Box 100279
Fort Worth, TX 76185
(800) 872-8896
Fax (817) 735-1726
Promotes the availability of medical and other benefits to small business owners.

American Small Business Association
1800 North Kent Street, Suite 910
Arlington, VA 22209
(800) 235-3298
Supports legislation favorable to the small business enterprise.

American Woman's Economic Development Corporation
71 Vanderbilt Avenue, 3rd Floor
New York, NY 10169
(212) 692-9100
Fax (212) 692-9296

Sponsors training and technical assistance programs.

Association of Small Business Development Centers
1313 Farnam, Suite 132
Omaha, NE 68182
(402) 595-2387

Local centers providing advice for those planning to establish a small business.

BEST Employers Association
4201 Birch Street
Newport Beach, CA 92660
(800) 854-7417
(714) 756-1000
Fax (714) 553-0883

Provides small independent businesses with managerial, economic, financial, and sales information helpful for business improvement.

Business Coalition for Fair Competition
1101 King Street
Alexandria, VA 22314
(703) 739-2782
Seeks to eliminate unfair advantages of tax-exempt organizations that sell and lease products and services in the commercial marketplace.

Business Market Association
4131 North Central Expressway, Suite 720
Dallas, TX 75204
(214) 559-3900
Fax (214) 559-4143

Works to bring large corporate lobbying and benefits to companies who do not have the workforce to achieve those benefits.

Coalition of Americans to Save the Economy
1100 Connecticut Avenue NW, Suite 1200
Washington, DC 20036
(800) 752-4111

Works to protect the rights of small businesses by opposing the practice of national discount store chains demanding that suppliers discontinue the use of independent manufacturer's representatives.

Home Executives National Networking Association
P.O. Box 6223
Bloomingdale, IL 60108
(708) 307-7130

Aims to provide opportunities for personal and professional growth to home-based business owners.

Independent Small Business Employers of America
520 South Pierce, Suite 224
Mason City, IA 50401
(515) 424-3187
(800) 728-3187

Works to assist members in keeping their businesses profitable by maintaining good employee relations.

International Association for Business Organizations
P.O. Box 30149
Baltimore, MD 21270
(410) 581-1373

Establishes international business training institutions.

International Council for Small Business
c/o Jefferson Smurfit Center for Entrepreneurial Studies
St. Louis University
3674 Lindell Boulevard
St. Louis, MO 63108
(314) 658-3896
Fax (314) 658-3897

Fosters discussion of topics pertaining to small business management.

International Association of Business
701 Highlander Boulevard
Arlington, TX 76015
(817) 465-2922
Fax (817) 467-5920

Keeps members informed of trends in the business industry.

Mothers' Home Business Network
P.O. Box 423
East Meadow, NY 11554
(516) 997-7394

Offers advice and support services on how to begin a successful business at home; helps members communicate with others who have chosen the same career option.

Nation of Ishmael
2696 Ben Hill Road
East Point, GA 30344
(404) 349-1153

Nondenominational religious organization working to improve the economic, educational, spiritual, and social potential of black communities in the United States.

National Association for Business Organizations
P.O. Box 30149
Baltimore, MD 21270
(410) 581-1373

Represents the interests of small businesses to government and community organizations on small business affairs.

National Association for the Cottage Industry
P.O. Box 14850
Chicago, IL 60614
(312) 472-8116

Acts as an advocacy group for cottage workers.

National Association for the Self-Employed
P.O. Box 612067
Dallas, TX 75261-2067
(800) 551-4446

Acts as a forum for the exchange of ideas.

National Association of Home-Based Businesses
P.O. Box 30220
Baltimore, MD 21270
(410) 363-3698

Provides support and development services to home-based businesses.

National Association of Private Enterprise
P.O. Box 612147
Dallas, TX 75261-2147
(817) 428-4236
(800) 223-6273
Fax (817) 332-4525

Seeks to insure the continued growth of private enterprise through education, benefits programs, and legislation.

National Business Association
5025 Arapaho, Suite 515
Dallas, TX 75248
(214) 991-5381
(800) 456-0440
Fax (214) 960-9149

Promotes and assists the growth and development of small businesses.

National Business Owners Association
1200 18th Street NW, Suite 500
Washington, DC 20036

(202) 737-6501
Fax (202) 737-3909

Promotes the interests of small business.

National Federation of Independent Business
53 Century Boulevard, Suite 300
Nashville, TN 37214
(615) 872-5800

Presents opinions of small and independent business to state and national legislative bodies.

National Small Business Benefits Association
2244 North Grand Avenue E.
Springfield, IL 62702
(217) 753-2558
Fax (217) 753-2558

Offers discounts on group dental and life insurance, nationwide paging and travel programs, car rental, fax equipment, office supplies, and cellular phone services.

National Small Business United
1155 15th Street NW, Suite 710
Washington, DC 20005
(202) 293-8830
(800) 345-6728
Fax (202) 872-8543

Purposes are to promote free enterprise and to foster the birth and vigorous development of independent small businesses.

Service Corps of Retired Executives Association
409 3rd Street SW, Suite 5900
Washington, DC 20024
(202) 205-6762
Fax (202) 205-7636

Volunteer program sponsored by

U.S. Small Business Administration in which active and retired businessmen and businesswomen provide free management assistance to men and women who are considering starting a small business, encountering problems with their business, or expanding their business.

Small Business Assistance Center
554 Main Street
P.O. Box 1441
Worcester, MA 01601
(508) 756-3513
Fax (508) 791-4709

Offers planning and strategy programs to aid businesspersons in starting, improving, or expanding small businesses.

Small Business Exporters Association
4603 John Tyler Court, Suite 203
Annandale, VA 22003
(703) 642-2490
Fax (703) 750-9655

Promotes interests of small export companies.

Small Business Foundation of America
1155 15th Street
Washington, DC 20005
(202) 223-1103
Fax (202) 872-8543

Charitable organization that raises funds for educational and research on small businesses.

Small Business Legislative Council
1156 15th Street NW, Suite 510
Washington, DC 20005
(202) 639-8500

Permanent independent coalition of

trade and professional associations that share a common commitment to the future of small business.

Small Business Network
P.O. Box 30149
Baltimore, MD 21270
(410) 581-1373

Provides management and marketing services, business evaluations, and import and export management services.

Small Business Service Bureau
554 Main Street
P.O. Box 1441
Worcester, MA 01601-1441
(508) 756-3513
Fax (508) 791-4709

Provides national assistance concerning small business group insurance, cash flow, taxes, and management problems.

Support Services Alliance
P.O. Box 130
Schoharie, NY 12157-0130
(518) 295-7966
(800) 322-3920
Fax (518) 295-8556

Provides services and programs such as group purchasing discounts, health coverage, legislative advocacy, and business and financial support services.

REGIONAL SMALL BUSINESS ASSOCIATIONS AND ORGANIZATIONS

Alabama

Alabama Small Business Development Center Consortium

University of Alabama at Birmingham
Medical Towers Building 1
Birmingham, AL 35294
(205) 934-7260

Alaska

Alaska Small Business Development Center
University of Alaska at Anchorage
430 West 7th Avenue, Suite 110
Anchorage, AK 99501
(907) 274-7232

Arkansas

Arkansas Small Business Development Center
University of Arkansas at Little Rock
100 South Main, Suite 410
Little Rock, AR 72201
(501) 324-9043

California

SCORE Chapter 503
1700 East Florida Avenue
Hemet, CA 92344
(909) 652-4390

California Small Business Development Center Program
Department of Commerce
801 K Street, Suite 1700
Sacramento, CA 95814
(916) 324-5068

Colorado

Colorado Small Business Development Center
Colorado Office of Business Development
1625 Broadway, Suite 1710
Denver, CO 80202
(303) 892-3809

Connecticut

Connecticut Small Business Development Center
University of Connecticut
368 Fairfield Road, U-41, Room 422
Storrs, CT 06269-2041
(203) 486-4135

Delaware

Delaware Small Business Development Center
University of Delaware
Purnell Hall, Suite 5
Newark, DE 19716-2711
(302) 831-2747

Florida

Florida Small Business Development Association
P.O. Box 8871
Jacksonville, FL 32239
(904) 725-3980

Florida Small Business Development Center Network
University of W. Florida
Building 75, Room 231
Pensacola, FL 32514
(904) 474-3016

Georgia

Georgia Small Business Development Center
University of Georgia, Chicopee Complex
1180 East Broad Street
Athens, GA 30602-5412
(706) 542-5760

Hawaii

Hawaii Small Business Development Center Network
University of Hawaii at Hilo
523 West Lanikaula Street
Hilo, HI 96720
(808) 933-3515

Idaho

Idaho Small Business Development Center
Boise State University
1910 University Drive
Boise, ID 83725
(208) 385-1640

Illinois

Illinois Small Business Development Center
Department of Commerce and Community Affairs
620 East Adams Street, 6th Floor
Springfield, IL 62701
(217) 524-5856

Indiana

Indiana Small Business Development Center
Economic Development Council
1 North Capitol, Suite 420
Indianapolis, IN 46204
(317) 264-6871

Kokomo Small Business Development Center
106 North Washington
Kokomo, IN 46901
(317) 457-5301

SCORE Chapter 50
Federal Building, 0130
Ft. Wayne, IN 46802

SCORE Chapter 266
300 North Michigan Street
South Bend, IN 46601-1239
(219) 282-4350

SCORE Chapter 268
100 NW 2nd Street, Old Post
   Office, Suite 300
Evansville, IN 47708-1202
(812) 421-5879

Iowa

**Iowa Small Business Development
Center**
Iowa State University
137 Lynn Avenue
Ames, IA 50010
(515) 292-6351

Kansas

**Kansas Small Business
Development Center**
Wichita State University
1845 Fairmount
Wichita, KS 67260-0148
(316) 689-3193

Kentucky

**Kentucky Small Business
Development Center**
Center for Business Development
College of Business and Economics
Lexington, KY 40506-0034
(606) 257-7668

SCORE Chapter 75
800 Federal Place, Room 115
Louisville, KY 40201
(502) 582-5976

SCORE Chapter 128
501 Broadway, Room B-36
Paducah, KY 42001
(502) 442-5685

SCORE Chapter 276
1460 Newton Pike
Lexington, KY 40511-1231

Louisiana

**Louisiana Small Business
Development Center**
Northeast Louisiana University
College of Business Administration
700 University Avenue
Monroe, LA 71209-6435
(318) 342-5506

Maryland

**Maryland Small Business
Development Center**
Department of Economic and
Employment Development
217 East Redwood Street, 10th
   Floor
Baltimore, MD 21202
(410) 333-6995

SCORE Chapter 34
c/o Federal Information Center
P.O. Box 600
Cumberland, MD 21501-0600

Massachusetts

**Massachusetts Small Business
Development Center**
University of
   Massachusetts–Amherst
School of Management, Room 205
Amherst, MA 01003
(413) 545-6301

**Smaller Business Association of
New England**
204 2nd Avenue
P.O. Box 9117
Waltham, MA 02254-9117
(617) 890-9070

Michigan

**Michigan Association of Small
Businessmen**

394 West North Street
Ionia, MI 48846
(616) 527-0281

**Michigan Small Business
Development Center**
2727 2nd Avenue
Detroit, MI 48201
(313) 577-4848

SCORE Chapter 176
2581 I-75 Business Spur
Sault Ste. Marie, MI 49783
(906) 632-3301

**Small Business Association of
Michigan**
P.O. Box 16158
Lansing, MI 48901
(517) 482-8788

Minnesota

**Minnesota Small Business
Development Center**
500 Metro Square
121 7th Place
St. Paul, MN 55101-2146
(612) 297-5770

SCORE Rochester Chapter
220 South Broadway, Suite 100
Rochester, MN 55904
(507) 288-1122

Mississippi

**Mississippi Small Business
Development Center**
University of Mississippi
Old Chemistry Building, Suite 216
University, MS 38677
(601) 232-5001

Missouri

**Missouri Small Business
Development Center**

University of Missouri
300 University Place
Columbia, MO 65211
(314) 882-0344

Montana

**Montana Small Business
Development Center**
Montana Department of Commerce
1424 9th Avenue
Helena, MT 59620
(406) 444-4780

Nebraska

**Nebraska Small Business
Development Center**
University of Nebraska at Omaha
60th and Dodge Streets, CBA Room
   407
Omaha, NE 68182
(402) 554-2521

Nevada

**Nevada Small Business
Development Center**
University of Nevada–Reno
College of Business Administration-
032, Room 411
Reno, NV 89557-0100
(702) 784-1717

New Hampshire

**New Hampshire Small Business
Development Center**
University of New Hampshire
108 McConnell Hall
Durham, NH 03824
(603) 862-2200

New Jersey

**New Jersey Small Business
Development Center**

Rutgers University Graduate School
of Management
180 University Avenue
Newark, NJ 07102
(201) 648-5950

New Mexico

**New Mexico Small Business
Development Center**
Santa Fe Community College
P.O. Box 4187
Santa Fe, NM 87502-4187
(505) 438-1362

New York

**New York State Small Business
Development Center**
State University of New York
SUNY Central Place, S-523
Albany, NY 12246
(518) 443-5398

North Carolina

**National Federation of
Independent Business, North
Carolina Chapter**
225 Hillsborough Street, Suite 250
P.O. Box 710
Raleigh, NC 27602-0710
(919) 755-1166

**North Carolina Small Business
Development Center**
University of North Carolina
4509 Creedmoor Road, Suite 201
Raleigh, NC 27612
(919) 571-4154

North Dakota

**North Dakota Small Business
Development Center**
University of North Dakota
118 Gamble Hall
UND, Box 7308

Grand Forks, ND 58202
(701) 777-3700

Ohio

**Ohio Small Business Development
Center**
77 South High Street
P.O. Box 1001
Columbus, OH 43226
(614) 466-2711

SCORE Chapter 107
200 West 2nd Street, Room 505
Dayton, OH 45402-1430
(513) 225-2887

SCORE Chapter 383
Marietta College, Thomas Hall
Marietta, OH 45750
(614) 373-0260

Oklahoma

**Oklahoma Small Business
Development Center**
Southeastern Oklahoma State
University
P.O. Box 2584, Station A
Durant, OK 74701
(405) 924-0277

Oregon

**Oregon Small Business
Development Center**
Lane Community College
99 West 10th Avenue, Suite 216
Eugene, OR 97401
(503) 726-2250

Pennsylvania

**Pennsylvania Small Business
Development Center**
The Wharton School, University of
Pennsylvania
444 Vance Hall

3733 Spruce Street
Philadelphia, PA 19104-6374
(215) 898-1219

Puerto Rico

Puerto Rico Small Business Development Center
University of Puerto Rico
P.O. Box 5253 College Station
Mayaguez, PR 00681
(809) 834-3590

Rhode Island

Rhode Island Small Business Development Center
Bryant College
1150 Douglas Pike
Smithfield, RI 02917
(401) 232-6111

South Carolina

South Carolina Small Business Development Center
University of South Carolina
1710 College Street
Columbia, SC 29208
(803) 777-4907

South Dakota

South Dakota Small Business Development Center
University of South Dakota
414 East Clark
Vermillion, SD 57069
(605) 677-5272

Tennessee

SCORE Chapter 68
Federal Building, Room 148
167 North Main Street
Memphis, TN 38103-1816
(901) 544-3588

Tennessee Small Business Development Center
Memphis State University
Building 1, South Campus
Memphis, TN 38152
(901) 678-2500

Texas

North Texas–Dallas Small Business Development Center
Bill J. Priest Institute for Economic Development
1402 Corinth Street
Dallas, TX 75215
(214) 565-5833

Northwest Texas Small Business Development Center
Texas Tech University
2579 South Loop 289, Suite 114
Lubbock, TX 79423
(806) 745-3973

University of Houston Small Business Development Center
University of Houston
601 Jefferson, Suite 2330
Houston, TX 77002
(713) 752-8444

UTSA South Texas Border Small Business Development Center
UTSA Downtown Center
801 South Bowie Street
San Antonio, TX 78205
(210) 224-0791

Utah

Utah Small Business Development Center
102 West 500, Suite 315
Salt Lake City, UT 84101
(801) 581-7905

Vermont

**National Federation of
Independent Business/Vermont**
RR 1, Box 3517
Montpelier, VT 05602
(802) 229-9478

**Vermont Small Business
Development Center**
Vermont Technical College
P.O. Box 422
Randolph, VT 05060
(802) 728-9101

Virgin Islands

**Virgin Islands Small Business
Development Center**
University of the Virgin Islands
P.O. Box 1087
St. Thomas, VI 00804
(809) 776-3206

Virginia

**Virginia Small Business
Development Center**
1021 East Cary Street, 11th Floor
Richmond, VA 23219
(804) 371-8253

Washington

**Washington Small Business
Development Center**
Washington State University
245 Todd Hall
Pullman, WA 99164-4727
(509) 335-1576

Washington D.C.

**District of Columbia Small
Business Development Center**
Howard University
6th and Fairmont Street NW, Room
  128
Washington, DC 20059
(202) 806-1550

West Virginia

SCORE Chapter 377
1012 Main Street
Wheeling, WV 26003-2785

SCORE Chapter 488
522 9th Street
Huntington, WV 25701-2007

**West Virginia Small Business
Development Center**
1115 Virginia Street East
Charleston, WV 25301
(304) 558-2960

Wisconsin

**Wisconsin Small Business
Development Center**
University of Wisconsin
432 North Lake Street, Room 423
Madison, WI 53706
(608) 263-7794

Wyoming

**Wyoming Small Business
Development Center/State
Network Office**
951 North Poplar
Casper, WY 82601
(307) 235-4825

⋐⋟Appendix D⋐⋟

BOOKS FOR EVERY GRAY WAVE ENTREPRENEUR

Since I've already provided books as references in the individual chapters, this list focuses on books that look at elements of small business that apply to all the types of businesses discussed.

- *Accounting for the New Business: How to Do Your Own Accounting Simply, Easily, and Accurately,* by Christopher Malburg (Bob Adams, 1994).
- *Advertising Handbook: Make a Big Impact With a Small Business Budget,* by Dell Dennison and Linda Tobey (Self-Counsel Press, 1991).
- *All in One Business Planning Guide: How to Create Cohesive Plans for Marketing, Sales, Operations, Finance, and Cash Flow,* by Christopher Malburg (Bob Adams, 1994).
- *Anatomy of a Business Plan,* by Linda Pinson and Jerry Jinnett (Dearborn Financial, 1993).
- *Bottom Line Basics: Understand and Control Business Finances,* by Robert J. Low (Oasis Press, 1994).
- *Business Plans That Win: Lessons from the MIT Enterprise Forum,* by Stanley Rich and David Grumpert (Harper-Collins, 1987).
- *Collection Techniques for a Small Business,* by Gini Graham Scott and John J. Harrison (Oasis Press, 1994).
- *Complete Book of Small Business Legal Forms,* by Daniel Sitarz (Nova, 1991).

- *Crafting the Successful Business Plan,* by Erik Hyypia (Prentice-Hall, 1992).

- *Ernst and Young Business Plan Guide,* by Eric S. Siegel, Brian R. Ford, and Jay M. Burnstein (Wiley, 1993).

- *Finding Money for Your Small Business: The One-Stop Guide to Raising All the Money You Will Need,* by Max Fallek (Dearborn Financial, 1994).

- *Getting Paid in Full: Collect the Money You Are Owed and Develop A Successful Credit Policy,* by Kelsea W. Wilbur (Sourcebooks, 1993).

- *Guerrilla Advertising: Cost Effective Tactics for Small Business Success,* by Jay C. Levinson (Houghton Mifflin, 1984).

- *Guerrilla Financing: Alternative Techniques to Finance Any Small Business,* by Bruce Blechman and Jay C. Levinson (Houghton Mifflin, 1992).

- *Guerrilla Marketing Attack: New Strategies, Tactics, and Weapons for Winning Big Profits,* by Jay C. Levinson (Houghton Mifflin, 1989).

- *Guerrilla Selling: Unconventional Tactics for Increasing Your Sales,* by Bill Gallagher (Houghton Mifflin, 1992).

- *Hire the Best . . . and Avoid the Rest,* by Michael W. Mercer (AMACOM, 1993).

- *How to Promote, Publicize, and Advertise Your Growing Business: Getting the Word Out Without Spending a Fortune,* by Kim Baker and Sunny Baker (Wiley, 1992).

- *How to Start a Business Without Quitting Your Job: The Moonlight Entrepreneur's Guide,* by Philip Holland (Ten Speed Press, 1992).

- *Marketing Magic: Innovative and Proven Ideas for Finding Customers, Making Sales, and Growing Your Business,* by Don Debelak (Bob Adams, 1994).

- *Mid-Career Entrepreneur: How to Start a Business and Be Your Own Boss,* by Joseph R. Mancuso (Dearborn Financial, 1993).

- *Start Your Own Business: After Fifty—Sixty—or Seventy!,* by Lauraine Snelling (Bristol, 1990).

- *Starting Your Business: Tax Guide 203,* by Holmes F. Crouch (Allyear Tax, 1992).

- *Successful Business Plan: Secrets and Strategies,* by Rhonda M. Abrams (Oasis Press, 1993).

❧INDEX❧

BUILD YOUR OWN BUSINESS LIBRARY

with the

21ST CENTURY ENTREPRENEUR SERIES!

HOW TO OPEN A FRANCHISE BUSINESS
Mike Powers   77912-9/$12.50 US/$16.00 Can

HOW TO OPEN YOUR OWN STORE
Michael Antoniak   77076-8/$12.50 US/$15.00 Can

HOW TO START A HOME BUSINESS
Michael Antoniak   77911-0/$12.50 US/$16.00 Can

HOW TO START A SERVICE BUSINESS
Ben Chant and Melissa Morgan
                                 77077-6/$12.50 US/$15.00 Can

HOW TO START A MAIL ORDER BUSINESS
Mike Powers   78446-7/$12.50 US/$16.50 Can

HOW TO START A RETIREMENT BUSINESS
Jacqueline K. Powers   78447-5/$12.50 US/$16.50 Can